FOREIGN COOKING FOR BLOKES

Also by Duncan Anderson & Marian Walls:

COOKING FOR BLOKES
FLASH COOKING FOR BLOKES

FOREIGN
COOKING
FOR
BLOKES

Duncan Anderson & Marian Walls

TIME WARNER
BOOKS

First published in Great Britain in 1998 by Warner Books
Reprinted by Time Warner Books in 2006

A CIP catalogue record for this book
is available from the British Library.

ISBN-13: 978-0-7515-2078-1
ISBN-10: 0-7515-2078-0

Typeset by Solidus (Bristol) Limited
Printed and bound in Great Britain by
Clays Ltd, St Ives plc

Time Warner Books
An imprint of
Little, Brown Book Group
Brettenham House
Lancaster Place
London WC2E 7EN

A Member of the Hachette Livre Group of Companies

www.littlebrown.co.uk

CONTENTS

INTRODUCTION

OK. To deal with the cheap shot first, for a lot of blokes all cooking is foreign. You are more likely to see some blokes on a cycling holiday to Ulan Bator than doing something useful in the kitchen. Kitchens are the place where the plates live and the cold beers stay for their oh so brief lives. This is odd. I mean, a bloke can expend immeasurable money and effort on the pursuit of a football team which performs once or twice a week and then almost without exception disappointingly, or on sex which can happen more or less frequently and with better or worse results, but concentrate on something which happens at least three times a day? Naah. When it comes to food it is always the same. Which takeaway to go to? Is chicken tikka masala the best dish in the world or is it prawn dansak? Which whiz heat-processed, boil-in-a-bag, drop-in-the-oven, never-looks-vaguely-like-the-packet, gourmet delight for tonight?

Anyway, help is it at hand. You can choose any recipe in this book and you will be able to cook it even if you have never cooked anything else in your life before. Everything in this book is easy to cope with. We are not masterchefs, we are human beings. This book has food from Europe, India, China and the Far East, Mexico and America. It has information on what you might want to keep on hand if you want to cook from time to time. Things like herbs and spices which are the main difference between cooking from different places round the world. It has tips on knives and pans and other tools for cooking. The recipe chapters start with vegetables, eggs, then chicken, meat and desserts.

Although every recipe has everything you need to know from the ingredients to the tools to how long it takes, this book does not cover every basic. For instance, if you want to know how to boil an egg or make a shepherd's pie or about 200 other things you need *Cooking for Blokes*, the first run-away success in this series. In fact, if you haven't got it yet, now would be the time to go to the shop and order it. Or you could phone. I am sure they will keep you a copy.

If you already have a copy of *Cooking for Blokes*, you may notice some repetition in the first few chapters, but then some Rules of the Universe remain constant, including those about defrosting times for chicken.

HOW HOT IS YOUR OVEN?

OVENS AND TEMPERATURES

Although every recipe that needs an oven has got the correct cooking time and oven temperature in it, it has become somewhat of a tradition to start a cookbook with the equivalent temperatures for different kinds of oven. We hope you enjoy this piece of tradition, and that you find the rest of the book even more relevant to your life. Approximate equivalent temperatures are shown below for different ovens.

> 140°C, 275°F, Gas mark 1
> 150°C, 300°F, Gas mark 2
> 170°C, 325°F, Gas mark 3
> 180°C, 350°F, Gas mark 4
> 190°C, 375°F, Gas mark 5
> 200°C, 400°F, Gas mark 6
> 220°C, 425°F, Gas mark 7
> 230°C, 450°F, Gas mark 8
> 240°C, 475°F, Gas mark 9

Gas ovens and fan-assisted ovens get hotter quicker than standard electric ones.

In most ovens the top is hotter than the bottom. Most things are best cooked in the middle. Roast potatoes and vegetables are best cooked at the top if you like them crispy.

Fan-assisted ovens have less of a difference between top and bottom and need different cooking times. Please refer to your instruction book.

TOOLS

THE BASICS

In this book all the tools you need for a particular recipe are listed after the ingredients. The information in this chapter should help you decide which are the most suitable for you.

Sharp knives

Knives are the most important tools. They must be sharp. They do not need sharpening every day or even every week, but they will eventually get blunt. Just like some tools are better than others, and generally more expensive, so it is with knives. Within reason, more expensive knives last longer and keep a sharp edge longer.

If you only buy one knife choose a 'kitchen knife'. The blade should be about 16 to 20 cm (6½ to 8 inches) long with a comfortable handle. It should have a gently curved edge. It should have a smooth chopping blade rather than be serrated. This size and kind of knife can be used for chopping vegetables and meat as well as carving.

The next most important kind is a small knife for cutting up smaller things. This can double as a vegetable peeler. The blade should be about 10 cm (4 inches) long.

Knife sharpeners

Buy a cheap one and follow the instructions.

One kind looks like crossed fingers. You pull the knife through a few times and it puts an edge on both sides of the knife at the same time.

'Butcher's steels' (the long pointed sharpeners with a handle) need a lot of practice to use properly and can lead to injury in the overconfident starter.

Electric sharpeners, like a lot of time saving ideas are an expensive waste of space.

Chopping boards & hygiene

These should be made of plastic.

A plain round wooden board is all right for cutting bread on, but unhygienic for meat, fish or vegetables. Basic hygiene and the state of some food (remember salmonella in eggs and chickens) gives two rules for using chopping boards. First, keep them clean. Wash them every time you use them. Second, chop the vegetables, salad or cheese before chopping any meat or fish. This is because the salad may get infected with bugs from the meat. The bugs are killed by cooking. Two other obvious bits of hygiene advice. Wash your hands before doing any cooking. Don't let the juice from raw meat fall on either cooked meat or salad or cheese in the fridge. This means storing raw meat at the bottom of the fridge, and not letting it dribble.

Measuring spoons & cups

Recipes in this book use spoonfuls or cupfuls rather than weights for most things. If you look in any kitchen you will see that teaspoons and cups come in several sizes. This means the amounts and so the taste may be very different if you just use any cup or spoon. To get round this problem buy a set of spoons and cups in standard sizes. Look in the cooking section of your local supermarket. They come in plastic or stainless steel.

One teaspoonful is 5 ml.
One tablespoonful is 15 ml.

The cup set looks like a very large spoon set, and has four sizes:

1 cup	250 ml	approx. 9 fluid ounces
Half a cup	125 ml	4 fl oz
Third of a cup	80 ml	3 fl oz
Quarter cup	60 ml	2 fl oz

This makes for some easy conversions. A pint is 20 fl oz, and is approximately two and a quarter cups.

Some cups are based on 240 ml to the cup. Either sort will do. The difference between them is only about 5% and well within the tolerance of the recipes.

All of the recipes in this book are flexible and forgiving. You do not need to be obsessional about getting the exact amount of an ingredient to the nearest gram. Lots of the ingredients come in packs, tins or tubs in standard sizes. Recipes take advantage of this. Some use half a standard pack for instance for dried pasta. With meat and fish just ask for the amount you want, or look for a pack of about the same size.

Wooden spoons, spatulas and other spoons

Minimum requirements are a wooden spoon and a spatula (it gets into the corners better).

Next most important are a cooking spoon for getting stuff out of pans and on to plates, and a slotted spoon, which is the same but lets any fluid drain off.

Next is a fish slice which lets you lift out the flatter items.

If you must buy a set, make sure it is not going to melt if it gets warm or scratch your nice aluminium non-stick pans.

Bowls

You need bowls to mix things in. If the bowl looks OK you can use it to serve food in as well. Choose a plastic or heatproof glass one (e.g. Pyrex) and make sure it is big enough.

Colander or sieve

This is useful for draining vegetables after they have been washed, and again after they have been cooked or for draining cooked pasta.

Colanders come in metal and plastic, with and without bases. The ones with bases will stand up on their own so you can put them in the sink and keep your hands away from the boiling substances you pour in. Plastic ones are cheaper.

Sieves can do most of what a colander does, but they don't come with stands, but do have long handles. You can drain rice in them. You can also use a sieve as a fine strainer, to get the lumps out of gravy or sauce. You can push some cooked soups (such as Thick Vegetable Soup) through them to make them smooth.

Vegetable peeler

A small sharp knife will do, but there are some specially made vegetable peelers which are slightly safer and easier to use.

One is a bit like a knife and sometimes has an apple corer at the end furthest from the handle.

Another looks a bit like a letter D with the straight edge of the D being a slotted blade.

Apple corer

A sharp-ended tube on a handle. You push the corer through the apple from the top of the apple where the stalk would be. When you pull it out it takes the core and seeds out. Much easier and safer than trying to use a knife.

Garlic crusher

There's not a lot to say about these. You put the peeled garlic in and squeeze the handles together. The garlic gets pulped up. You poke the residue out and throw it away.

If you don't have a garlic crusher just squash it with something suitable or chop it up small. Prepared garlic is sold in tubes, jars and bottles. This makes the crusher an optional item.

Grater

These are made from metal or plastic and have a range of cutting surfaces for getting different sizes of gratings. Use these for grating breadcrumbs, cheese, carrot or whatever. Be careful when using them. The main problem is that you can end up with grated fingernail or finger if you loose your concentration.

You can buy pretty well everything we say needs to be grated already prepared, including cheese and even carrots.

Lemon zester

This is for getting the rind off lemons and oranges. It has four or five holes in a little scraper. There is no other tool which does it as quickly, or that makes such long strips of rind. If you use a knife and then slice it, the shreds come out a bit big. You can try using a grater, but it's not as easy.

Lemon juicer

There are various sorts of these. Some look like an upturned half lemon with ridges in the middle of a bowl to catch the juice, generally made of plastic. You can use them for oranges and limes as well. Another electrical gadget purchase failure was the motorised version which sits in the back of a cupboard smirking at our gullibility. You do not have to squeeze lemons to get lemon juice. Lemon juice comes in bottles. 1 lemon gives about 2 to 3 tablespoons of juice. Fresh juice does have the edge.

Pans – overall advice

Buy a cheap set and then buy one good quality pan a year. Many will have a ten-year guarantee. We recommend you start with a cast-iron enamelled casserole with a lid. A Le Creuset 18 cm (7 inches) is ideal. This is two pans in one. You will be able to use it as a saucepan on the hob and also in the oven. You can also try looking in street markets or car boot sales for second-hand cast-iron pans with enamelled insides. Who knows, you may be lucky.

The cheapest sets are aluminium. Only buy ones with a non-stick coating.

Saucepans

Buy pans with lids.

How many?
At least one and preferably two.

What size?
22 cm (8½ inches) across. 2 litres (3½ pints). This is big enough to cook pasta or rice or stew.

16 cm (6½ inches) across. 1 litre (1¾ pints). This is big enough for tomato sauce for pasta, custard or frozen peas.

Stick or non-stick?
Go for non-stick. Most aluminium pans have a non-stick coating. But remember, this is easy to remove with forks, metal implements and scouring pads. It can also make an interesting chemical burning smell if you heat it up too much with nothing in the pan, which may put you off eating for some time. If you scrape or burn it off you have to throw it away.

What metal?
Aluminium: The cheap ones will wear out in a couple of years. By this time you will have decided if you want to continue to cook and whether to keep buying cheap ones or go for something better.

Stainless steel: Very shiny. Quite expensive. Can last for as long as cast-iron. Thicker bases distribute the heat more evenly. This means that if you forget to stir, the food sticks evenly to the bottom of the pan rather than in the shape of the heating element. Thinner bases mean more stirring. Stainless steel saucepans can be soaked in hot soapy water and burnt on food will come away fairly easily.

Cast iron with enamel interior (e.g. Le Creuset): These are expensive, very durable and heavy. They cook very evenly. The enamel lining makes them practically non-stick. They do not like being heated up with nothing in them and the enamel may crack if you move them too quickly from heat to cold water. They can be soaked in water but the wooden handles don't like it. The handles can char if you cook on a too high gas. Handles and casserole lids can be bought separately and replaced. Steer clear of cast-iron that is not enamelled inside as it rusts if not treated properly.

Frying-pans

General advice as to sort of metal is as above.

Size should be about 25 to 28 cm (10 to 11 inches) across.

If you want to cook a lot of omelettes, buy a smaller one as well, say 20 cm (8 inches).

Wok

A wok is like a combination of a frying-pan and saucepan. There are a number of wok kits which include the wok itself (a sort of metal bowl with a handle), lid, chopsticks, spoon and whatever else is thought to be useful. They are the best thing to cook Chinese stir-fry in.

Authentic woks do not have a non-stick coating, but others do. Get one with a non-stick coating, but remember not to use metal tools on it. Buy one with a flat bottom (round ones can be unstable). Make sure it has a lid.

Larger woks are particularly useful. You can use them to cook larger quantities of food like chilli con carne or curries.

Casserole with lid

There are three sorts: pottery, ovenproof glass or cast iron. These are used for cooking in the oven. Cooking this way is an easy option because you can just put it in the oven and leave it to cook while you do something else.

If you go and look in a shop you will see some ovenproof glass (Pyrex type) casseroles. These and the pottery ones are both OK. Don't get them really hot and then put them in cold water or they may crack.

There are a bewildering number of sizes, but get one that holds at least 2 litres or 4 pints.

Our personal recommendation must be for a cast iron casserole. This is the 'flame-proof' kind. You can use it like a saucepan on the hob and then transfer it to the oven. This is very useful as it saves you having to use a frying-pan and then an ordinary casserole. The ideal size is a 25 cm oval casserole with straight sides. It holds 4 litres (7 pints) and can take a chicken, a small leg of lamb or most beef roasts, as well as being OK for all the casserole dishes in the book. It is fairly foolproof. It also means there is lots of juice for making gravy.

Large ovenproof dish

These come in all sizes. They can be made from pottery, glass or metal. If you get a big enough one it can be used as a roasting dish as well. The most useful one we use is 30 cm by 18 cm ($11\frac{1}{2}$ by $7\frac{1}{2}$

inches) and 6 cm (2 inches) deep and made of glass. It is big enough to roast a chicken in, or make lasagne or shepherd's pie.

Metal baking sheet about 25 cm (10 inches) across

This can be used for quickly warming things in the oven or cooking things that don't create a lot of liquid. It will also do as a tin to cook or heat pizzas and pizza bases.

Pie dish

A metal dish, coated with non-stick material. It should be about 22 cm (8½ inches) across, with sloping sides at least 3 cm (1 inch) deep.

The best have lots of holes in the bottom which help make the pastry base crisp. Pastry needs to get hot enough to evaporate the water from it and then cook. This cannot happen if it is full of something wet like pie filling and squashed against the bottom of a pottery dish, and so you have to cook the pastry shell empty first, which is a bit of a pain. The dish with the Aertex look lets the heat into the bottom and the steam out and so there is no need to pre-cook the case.

You can buy pottery pie dishes. Pies should have a pastry lid but tarts are topless. In this book the only 'pies' are from the USA where 'tarts' are called 'pies', so the 'pies' in this book have no lids.

Round ovenproof glass dish 25 cm (10 inches) diameter

This is used for cooking tarts, quiches and doubles as something you can roast chicken pieces on.

WHAT IS A SOY?

In this chapter you will find information about some of the ingredients used in the recipes in this book.

Anchovy

These salty brown fish fillets come in 50 g tins and are seen on the top of some pizza varieties. They are used in quite a few Italian dishes.

Basil

This herb is the basis of pesto, and typical of Italian food, though also used in Thai cooking. It can be used raw in a salad of sliced mozzarella cheese and tomatoes, or cut or torn up and added to pasta sauces. You can add a bit of it to salad. It comes in packets or bunches. Floppy leaves can be revived by putting them in cold water for 30 minutes.

Bouquet garni

These mixed herbs come in a pouch like a tea bag. It has a mixture of herbs in it, so you can substitute a teaspoon of mixed

Mediterranean herbs. It means you get little specks of herb in the dish, but so what. You should lift out the tea bag before serving the dish.

Cajun seasoning

This is another spice and herb mix, and it shares a lot of ingredients with curry powder. It is good sprinkled on chicken or salmon before cooking.

Calvados

This is a kind of apple brandy from France. You can buy Calvados for cooking in small bottles in supermarkets. You can use it in any dish where you have cooked apples to zip up the flavour.

Capers

They look like small green bullets and taste a bit like pickled gherkins but spicier. They are the edible flower buds of a spiny shrub, and are the flavouring in the fish and meat accompaniment, Sauce Tartare. They turn up in some French and Italian dishes. You can buy them preserved in brine in jars.

Cardamom

This beautiful spice can be bought already ground or as pods, which contain the seeds. It is used in curries but also in the sweet yoghurt dessert Shrikand.

Cheese

There are lots of different kinds of cheese. There are even lots of varieties of different strength of Cheddar from round the world. Many of the cheeses on sale have already been prepared by being sliced or grated.

Mozzarella is the one to put on top of pizza and in some Mexican recipes. It comes whole in a bag with some fluid (which helps to keep it fresh), which you drain off before using. Mozzarella also comes ready grated from some supermarkets.

The usual cheese sprinkled on pasta is Parmesan. It is a hard Italian cheese which needs to be grated before use. Fortunately it comes in tubs ready grated. If you buy it in a slab, grate with a normal grater or take long paper-thin curls off it with a vegetable peeler which some may say looks more flash. A slightly cheaper alternative is Pecorino, which also comes ready grated.

In recipes which need Cheddar you can use Red Leicester.

Lancashire, Cheshire and Caerphilly are almost interchangeable, all being crumbly mild cheese. The people of Lancashire, Cheshire and Caerphilly probably won't agree with this.

Edam, Gouda, Emmental and Gruyère are another group of similar cheeses, and they are often available ready sliced and grated.

Chilli

Some like it hot, but some don't. The cartoon image of someone sitting with steam coming out of their ears after the first mouthful of chilli or drinking the contents of the fire bucket, is not too inaccurate but it is only half of the story. Persistent hot chilli use will lead you to experience the ring of fire. The answer is be moderate.

Cooling it. You can add coconut milk or a carton of yoghurt to the dish. The heat of chillies develops with cooking, and the main source of heat is in the seeds, so you can scrape out the seeds before adding it to the dish.

If you like it simple you can buy tubes or jars of prepared chilli. They should be kept in the fridge after being opened and used within six weeks.

There are more than a dozen types of chilli, but you will only see a limited number in the shops. Check the pack to see how hot they are. The information should be on the label. Bird's eye chillies are small, about 3 cm (1 inch) long, thin and red and are very hot. These are favourites for Chinese, Thai and for our Universal Salsa recipe. Cayenne chillies are slightly bigger and marginally less hot. Jalapeño chillies are less hot again and you can buy them in jars for Mexican cooking. They make a good addition to pizza and even salads. Green or red chillies about 1 cm (half inch) across and 5 cm (2 inches) long are good for Indian food.

FRESH CHILLI — A WARNING! When you chop up the chillies be careful and avoid getting juice on your hands. It will sting. If you touch your eyes, mouth or other sensitive areas even an hour after chopping them they will smart and burn. So wash your hands or wear rubber gloves.

Chorizo

This is a spicy Spanish pork sausage. It is like a hotter and chunkier good quality version of salami. The flavouring comes from paprika and garlic. It is available at a lot of delicatessen counters. Ask for it sliced if you want it that way. Although you can eat it uncooked because it is 'cured' we use it in this book fried either with pasta or in some Mexican dishes. There are other spiced salami like sausages from Italy which you could use instead.

Cinnamon

This burnt-orange coloured spice comes from the bark of a tree. You can either buy it as a stick which looks like a dark orange cigarette, or ground up. If you use the stick version you should take it out of the dish you are cooking before serving. Although it gives up its flavour it never goes soft.

You can put a stick of it in a cup of hot chocolate, and in the USA they dust a bit on buttered toast to make cinnamon toast.

Cloves

This is another spice which comes in whole and ground form. The same thing applies. If you use the whole stuff take it out before serving. It is about 1 cm (half inch) long and has a stalk with a small bobble on the end. It looks a bit like a miniature of the mace that medieval knights used. We use them in risotto and some curries. You can also stick them in ham before roasting.

Coconut

Coconut has a subtle flavour, and can also take some of the heat out of a curry if you have added too much chilli.

You can buy coconut milk in 400 ml tins, or you can buy it powdered. If you use the powdered sort, you can keep the rest in the cupboard for next time you want it. Read the instructions on the packet, but in general they say mix it up beforehand with warm water, to make sure it dissolves. Two tablespoons of powder in 1 cup of warm water gives a reasonable thickness. Coconut powder is easy to make and measure in small quantities.

Desiccated coconut is dried grated coconut flesh. It comes in packs and may be in the cake ingredient section of the super-market.

Creamed coconut comes in a solid block and dissolves in warm water to make a thick creamy paste which is used in a lot of Thai and Indian food.

Coriander

Fresh coriander has a subtle but distinctive flavour which goes well in lots of oriental food and sauces. It is a major ingredient in our Universal Salsa and crops up in Chinese, Oriental, Indian and Mexican recipes. You can buy coriander leaves in packets or in bunches. If you buy a packet it will have been washed and prepared. If you buy a bunch you will need to check and wash it. For price the bunches win, with about three times as much usable coriander as a packet. You can use both the leaves and the stems. Some Chinese recipes even use the root, but not ours. Floppy leaves can be revived by putting them in cold water for 30 minutes.

Coriander powder is used in curries, and is ground from the seeds.

Couscous

Couscous is made from fine granules of semolina covered with wheat flour. It comes in packets, and is widely available. It is very easy to prepare using the recipe in this book. As well as making a fine accompaniment to any meat or fish dish, particularly if it has a little sauce, it makes a good salad. Dishes you might serve rice with you could experiment with couscous instead. We don't think that it'll be very good with Thai or Chinese dishes though.

Cream

Buy this in cartons. Single cream is fairly thin and the kind you pour on a piece of pie. Double cream is the one you can whip up so it becomes stiff, and is served in a dollop by the side of a slice of pie. By the way, when you are whipping up double cream don't overdo it. Butter is the end stage of whipping cream. Sour cream is a bit sharper and goes well with sweet things, as well as being a good accompaniment to baked potato and some Mexican dishes, particularly if you chop up a 15 g pack of chives and mix it in.

There are some cream alternatives that you might like to try. Fromage frais is like sour cream and crème fraîche is like thick cream. There is also wholemilk Greek yoghurt which is the creamiest and there are low fat alternatives. Smatana is a low-fat alternative to sour cream.

Cumin

This spice is used in curries and Mexican food. You can add it to tomato sauces to perk them up. It is not overpowering. It is called 'Jeera' in Punjabi, and you may find some better value packets of it if you go to the right shop.

Curry leaves

A whole leaf used in Indian cooking. Try to fish it out before eating. Sold dried.

Curry powder

Lots of different sorts are sold here. They range from the mild through medium to hot. There are even named specific ones like Madras, Rogan Josh or even Tikka or Tandoori. This variety lets you tailor any curry to the heat and degree of spiciness you want.

Dry sherry v rice wine or sake

Chinese and oriental food uses quite a lot of dry sherry. You can try to be more authentic by using rice wine, but it doesn't really make a lot of difference. There is one thing though, don't buy the cheapest sweet sherry. You must use a dry sherry (it may well have a number on the back to indicate sweetness). With sherry as with the rest of the products from the wine department, you generally get what you pay for. So buy a proper Spanish sherry.

Fish sauce

This is used in Thai cooking. It is made, though you probably don't want to know this, from some anchovy concoction. It comes in bottles and is the colour of whisky. It is used as a salt substitute, and you can get away with using soy sauce instead. There are often recipes on the bottle. The one on the bottle we have requires four different products to be bought from their range to make it. We think this is a record.

Five spice powder

A Chinese ground spice which you can experiment with adding to a lot of dishes. Use very sparingly. It is a pungent mixture of star anise, Szechuan pepper, fennel, cloves and cinnamon.

Galangal

See ginger

Garam masala

This is a mixture of a number of spices and saves the trouble of having some of each. Typically it may include turmeric, ground coriander, ground cumin, cinnamon, and ground cloves. It can make every meal taste the same if you use it as the only flavouring, as can using curry powder. It does not go off but it does lose some of its flavour if you keep it too long.

The flavours are enhanced if you warm them gently in a pan or on a baking tray for five minutes before cooking with them.

Ginger

Fresh ginger is a light brown irregular branched bulbous root. It is generally sold by weight, but most recipes say use a piece say 2 cm (1 inch) long. Buy firm, smooth ginger roots. Do not buy shrivelled up or mouldy stuff. It keeps for at least a month. You do not have to keep it in the fridge.

Fresh ginger is one of the tastes together with chilli and garlic which make freshly made curries and Chinese meals taste better than anything you can buy. It is very different from ground ginger,

WHAT IS A SOY?

which is the flavour of ginger biscuits.

Fresh galangal is similar to root ginger. It is also available dried in jars. If you can not find galangal use ginger instead.

Golden syrup and maple syrup

This is the stuff of steamed puddings. We use it in a recipe for Pecan Pie, but you could just as well used maple syrup which is a little thinner but has more flavour. Maple syrup is the stuff the Americans pour on their breakfast pancakes. When you buy it read the label carefully. There is proper Maple syrup and then a Maple-flavoured syrup which is just a flavoured sugar solution. The real stuff is much better.

Hoisin sauce

This is another soya bean based Chinese ingredient, with a slightly sweet and hot flavour. You can use it as a sauce in a small bowl with spare ribs or prawns, and also as part of stir fry sauces. You can paint it on grilled meat. It comes in bottles of about 300 g.

Another sauce worth keeping just to serve things with is plum sauce, which is particularly good with duck and chicken recipes. It has bits of chilli in and is quite sweet.

Honey

There are two kinds, set and runny. Set is cloudy and hard and the best for sandwiches. Runny is a light brown liquid and better for cooking with.

Lemon grass

OK. It looks like a kind of tough spring onion and it tastes of lemon. It is one of the central ingredients in Thai cookery. You can buy it freeze dried but fresh is best. Choose ones that look green and not brown.

To prepare it, cut the ends off and then crush the stalk. A Thai cook would put it on a flat surface and then lay his chopper flat on the lemon grass and then hit the knife with his hand. The idea is to flatten it to let the flavour out. Anyway, hit it lightly with a hammer or a rolling pin.

Lentils

There are lots of different kinds of lentils. One kind used in this book are Puy or Puy type which are small and dark green with the skins on. They hold together better than other sorts and are less likely to go to mush.

Red lentils are good for dahl, as are other split peas because they do go to mush quickly and that's what you want for a dahl.

Maple syrup

See golden syrup

Mushrooms

The most commonly available are button mushrooms. You can also buy bigger ones (flat field mushrooms) which you chop up or stuff. Oyster mushrooms are used in Chinese dishes and come with yellow or white tops. They are more solid and shrivel less.

Shitake mushrooms are available dried or fresh. They have longish stalks and dark brown tops. They can be a bit tough if dried and if not soaked or cooked or shredded properly. Chanterelle and Porcini mushrooms are European mushrooms and are worth looking out for. You can put them in with pasta sauces (the simpler the better, for instance, oil and garlic) for an unusual and authentic taste.

Mustard

English mustard is the bright yellow stuff, and hot. Dijon French mustard is a reasonable equivalent and Meaux wholegrain is excellent with meat. French and German mustards are darker, sweeter and less hot. American mustard comes in squeezy bottles, seems to be a bit too much like wallpaper paste for us, but is handy for squeezing on hot dogs.

Nutmeg

This spice which looks like a nut is available whole or ground. If you grate it yourself it tastes better. It is a good addition to cooked fruit and on top of rice pudding.

Oils

The best cooking oils are sunflower, corn oil and groundnut (which is made from peanuts). The cheapest are vegetable and rape seed oils. Olive oil is good for cooking Italian dishes. Make sure that you use an ordinary olive oil for this. 'Virgin' and 'Extra Virgin' are the best and most expensive but should be kept for making vinaigrette or adding to salads. If you heat them up, the subtle flavourings which separate them from the ordinary will just boil off. There are other oils which can add flavour to salad dressings, or to Chinese noodles, such as walnut or sesame oils.

Olive oil

There are books (many, big and long) about olive oils. For in depth knowledge consult one of them or see our oils paragraph above.

Olives

There are many kinds available. They come loose, in jars or tins; whole and pitted (with the stones out) or stuffed. We suggest using pitted olives, because olive stones are strong enough to break teeth. We can show you the teeth. If you ignore our advice and go for the ones with stones you can always cut the olive flesh from round the stone or use one of the tools sold to push the stone out.

Oregano

This herb is widely used in Italian dishes. You can substitute mixed Mediterranean herbs for it. You can add it to tomato sauces. It's great with lamb, pork, chicken, eggs or soups. It comes fresh, in which case pull off the leaves and discard the stalks, or put the whole lot in and lift it out at the end, and dried, in which case just add.

Oyster sauce

This is a thick brown sauce used in Chinese cooking. You can add it to a stir fry and it comes in bottles.

Parsley

This comes in two types. There is curly leafed parsley which is the standard kind, and flat leaf which looks similar to coriander. Both come prepared in packets or are available in bunches. The packets are supposedly ready to use and you should be able to use most of them. The bunches may need to be picked over. Floppy leaves can be revived by putting them in cold water for 30 minutes.

The easy way to tell the difference between coriander and flat leaf parsley at a market stall is that the coriander has the roots on and the parsley has the roots cut off. You can smell the difference by rubbing a leaf between your fingers, but this may not endear you to the stallholder.

Pasta

This is available dried or fresh from the chilled cabinet. Cooking times are on the packet. There are full instructions on cooking pasta in the 'How to' chapter (page 52–3).

There are the long thin ones such as spaghetti, linguine and fidelini (like spaghetti with a hole up the middle) and long flat ones like tagliatelle and tagliolini. There are dozens of shaped pastas, from tiny ones for putting in soup like stelline, through to tubes, twists and weird extruded shapes. Useful ones are the tubular penne, the twisted fusilli and the shell-shaped conchiglie. All of these pick up more of the sauce. Then, of course there are the flat (lasagne) and rolled tubes (cannelloni) ready for stuffing and then there are all the ready stuffed ones.

Pepper

Buy a grinder for black pepper. It is ten times better than ready ground. Paprika pepper is red and less hot, cayenne pepper is hotter, and chilli pepper the hottest. They all look similar. Make sure you use the right one.

Szechuan pepper is a black pepper used in Chinese cooking. If you cannot find any, just substitute the same amount of black pepper.

You can also buy peppercorns in brine in jars.

Pine nuts

Sometimes called pine kernels these little nuts come from pine cones, and are fried and added to couscous and some other dishes. They are also used in Italian recipes in pesto sauce and in other dishes, but not in this book.

Plum sauce

See hoisin sauce

Poppy seeds

Tiny black seeds, bought in packets and sometimes seen on the top of bread. Used in curry.

Prawns

These are available frozen or sometimes fresh. The cooked ones are pink. The raw ones are greyish-blue and come with the shells off or on. The bigger the prawn, the more expensive. Raw prawns should be kept in the fridge and cooked the same day.

Rice

There is information on some different kinds of rice and how to cook them in the 'How to' chapter (page 50).

Rosemary

This herb comes dry or fresh. It comes from a low shrub which you can grow on a windowsill and so have it free all the time. It is particularly good with meat, and you can throw in a couple of bits with any lamb you are cooking in the oven. We use it in Italian Oven Baked Beef. Don't add too much as it can be a bit overpowering.

Saffron

This fragrant yellow colouring is used in pilau rice and some other dishes. It is made from the dried stamens of a particular crocus, and the colour comes from the pollen. As it is hard to pick, it is very expensive, but you don't need very much. It needs to be soaked in a little milk for half an hour to get the colour out. If you have access to a Spanish shop, they may sell a number of different kinds at varying prices. It is used in paella.

Sesame oil

This is sold in little bottles and comes from sesame seeds. You can add it to Chinese noodles after cooking.

Sesame seeds

This comes in small packets. It has a subtle nutty flavour which is improved by putting them in the oven for 3 minutes to toast them. Throw them on top Chinese food.

Shitake mushrooms

See mushrooms

Smatana

See cream

Soy sauce

Well, here it is, the answer to the question posed at the start of this chapter, 'What is a soy?' Soy is a kind of sauce, made from fermented soya beans. The best stuff is naturally fermented and has a distinctive salty flavour. Take care when you are buying it. There is more than one kind. There is 'dark' soy sauce and 'light' soy sauce, Chinese and Japanese soy sauces and there are others as well but generally only available from specialist Chinese or Japanese shops. One brand which is reliably good is Kikkoman's which is Japanese but is good wherever you need soy sauce.

Squid

These are used in a lot of Asian dishes. They may be an acquired taste but they are worth getting into.

Cleaned and almost ready to use squid tubes are stocked in many supermarkets and some fishmongers. Don't buy unprepared squid unless you like slimy things and know how to take the quill out. But check the prepared ones, as you chop them, for a strip of clear plastic-like stuff. If you find it, throw it away. It is the quill.

Just make sure they are fresh. Once thawed, keep in the fridge and cook the same day. Wrap up any uncooked bits in paper and don't leave them in the bin in the kitchen. They start to smell really badly after about 24 hours.

Star anise

Spice with distinctive aniseed taste used in Chinese cooking. Comes whole as a star-shaped seed pod or ground. Take the pods out before serving. The powdered version is part of Chinese five spice.

Stock cubes

Stock cubes are concentrated extracts of beef, or chicken, lamb or fish or vegetables. They are a handy way of adding a bit of extra flavour but you can't be sure which part of the animal or vegetable has been used to make them.

You can buy ready-made stock in cartons from most supermarkets. You can also buy Swiss vegetable bouillon powder (vegetable stock), if you are worried·about the stuff that goes into meat or fish stock cubes.

Sunflower oil

See oils

Szechuan pepper

See pepper

Tabasco

A hot chilli sauce which should be used very sparingly. A couple of drops has quite a kick.

Tacos and Tortillas

You can buy packs of taco shells which you can fill with Mexican refried beans, chilli meat and shredded lettuce, tomato, cheese and avocado. You can buy packets of taco chips, nachos and similar for using in the recipes in the Mexican chapter.

You can buy small and large wheat tortillas in packets. They keep in the cupboard for quite a while. It is worth having a packet so you can put something together in an emergency. There are also corn tortillas which need to be quick fried to soften them up so that they are rollable or manageable; they become a hassle because once they cool down they won't be pliable anymore.

Tahini

This is ground-up sesame seeds which form a thick paste. Used in various dishes, you should stir it up to get the oil back into the paste before use.

You can add a teaspoon to bought hummus to make it more exciting. Spread the hummus on a plate, make a dimple in the middle and put the tahini in, and then dribble a tablespoon of olive oil round the edge. This is a fantastic snack or starter with warmed pitta bread and pitted black olives.

Tamarind

This is the brown pulp surrounding the seed from the Tamarind tree. It has a slightly acid taste like a cross between a date and apricot. It is used in Thai, Indian and other similar dishes. You either buy it in blocks in which case you soak it and squeeze the pulp to mush the flavour out, or you can buy an instant version in a plastic pot, where you add by the teaspoonful. Tamarind is one of the main components in HP Sauce.

Tarragon

This herb has a subtle aniseed flavour. It is good with chicken and meat. You can buy it dried, but fresh is better.

Tofu

This is a solid cake made from soya bean curds. It is a bit like a jelly in its ordinary state and tends to fall apart if stirred about too much. Sometimes it comes in cartons like small milk cartons. You can use it in Chinese food instead of meat. You can fry cubes of it and then warm them in the oven, and serve it as a side dish. Agé (pronounced agai) is a firmer textured form which you can buy in health food shops where you can also buy smoked tofu. Generally speaking the tofu from health shops seems more solid than that from supermarkets and it comes in clear vacuum packs. We prefer the health shop kind.

Tomato purée

This thick concentrated tomato sauce can be added to a tomato sauce for pasta, or meat to improve the flavour. It comes in tubes. It keeps for 4 weeks in the fridge. You can also buy little tins of it, but you have to throw away what you don't use.

Tortillas

See Tacos

Turmeric

This yellow powder spice is used to colour a lot of curries. It is called 'Haldi' in Punjabi, and you may find some better value packets and tins of it if you go to an Indian shop.

Vinegar

Vinegar is used in vinaigrette dressing and some recipes to give a sour taste (as in sweet and sour). A good all purpose one is white wine vinegar. Alternatives are red wine, sherry or even ones that have had herbs added. Don't use malt vinegar, it is cheap but only good for chip shops, or making pickles.

Worcestershire sauce

A mixture of flavours, it is a thin brown sauce and is sold in bottles. You can put it on steak when cooking as well as a number of other things. Incidentally, it contains both anchovies and tamarind. We just looked at the bottle.

GET A CUPBOARD

Having some ingredients that you keep in store will give you the basics to cook an unplanned-for meal or forgotten invitation. It will also be there for you when those unpredicted feelings of starving hunger overwhelm you and you are too weak to leave home without food. There is no need to go and get them all at once but if you buy one of them at a time you will have enough stuff to cook at least one meal. The recommended emergency meal is one of the simple pasta dishes.

There are some things which you don't use up every time you cook a recipe which includes it and if you treat them well they will be there in the short term future for further cooking adventures. With dried ingredients like pasta, flour and rice you must reseal the bags they are in by twisting or clipping or sticking. This keeps out the dust and the other creatures that would be happy to compete with you for the pleasure of eating them. Never keep the contents of an opened can like tomatoes or bamboo shoots in the can, even if you do put it in the fridge. You must always take things out of the can, store them in mugs or bowls or something similar.

Cans, jars, bottles and bags

Salt and pepper, preferably a pepper grinder
400 g tin of plum tomatoes

200 g tin of tuna
400 g tin of baked beans
400 g tin of red kidney beans
50 g tin of anchovies
Bottle of sunflower oil
Small bottle of olive oil
Bottle of soy sauce
Bottle of white wine vinegar
Tikka powder or your favourite curry powder
Packet of mixed Mediterranean herbs
Pack of Mexican chilli seasoning
500 g pack of pasta
500 g pack of long grain rice like Basmati
Carton of custard

Fridge

Tube of garlic paste
Mayonnaise
Small bottle of lemon juice
Butter or low fat spread
100 g tube tomato purée
Eggs
Cheese such as Cheddar
Small carton of grated Parmesan or Pecorino cheese

Frozen food

1 pack of chicken pieces (thighs, breasts or quarters)
1 pack of white fish (cod, hake or hoki)

Vegetables

Onions
Potatoes
Red pepper

These basics will provide the ingredients for more than one of the recipes in this book.

If you get really serious about the food from a particular region you will need a more exotic store cupboard than the one above. We have listed below what you may need to add to that list if you want to be able to whip up an Indian, Asian, Chinese or Mexican meal.

If Indian food is really for you and you want to cook a lot of it then you really must also have:

500 g packet of lentils or split peas (for dahls)
Turmeric
Garam masala
Chilli powder
Ground cumin
Yoghurt (in case your curry turns out too hot)
Jar or two of your favourite chutney, like mango.

If Chinese or Asian food is high on your list of favourites then you'll need to supplement you cupboard with:

Chinese egg noodles (medium)
Bottle of dry sherry
Small pack of cornflour
Ginger
Garlic

200 g tin of bamboo shoots
400 ml tin of coconut milk or a packet of dried coconut milk
Sesame oil

Mexican food lovers will need:

1 jar taco sauce
1 packet of wheat flour tortillas
400 g tin of refried beans, or kidney beans
1 jar of enchilada sauce
1 large bag of tortilla chips
Chilli powder

HOW TO ...

Here is the basic information on cooking vegetables, rice, pasta, noodles, pastry and dried beans. Also included is how to make breadcrumbs and the defrosting times for meat and chicken.

HOW TO COOK VEGETABLES

Frozen

For frozen peas, sweetcorn and other vegetables, follow the instructions on the bag. In general these will include adding the vegetables to boiling water with half a teaspoon of salt, and cooking for a few minutes. Cooking times are approximately 3 minutes for sweetcorn (off the cob) and 5 minutes for peas.

Fresh

Fresh vegetables take a bit more preparation than frozen and sometimes take longer than frozen vegetables to cook. There are times in the year when fresh vegetables will be much cheaper than frozen, and other times when they will be more expensive or simply unavailable.

Wash all fresh vegetables thoroughly. Throw away any leaves which are slimy and cut out any bits that look bad.

Organic vegetables are always better. They taste better and have not been treated with loads of pesticides, chemical fertilizers and preservatives. If you have the choice, buy organic.

Potatoes

Potatoes are probably the most widely used and versatile vegetable. They can be boiled, baked, roasted, mashed, deep fried as chips or pan fried in butter.

New potatoes have thin flaky skins which almost come off when the potatoes are scrubbed. They are smaller, often called 'Jersey' or 'Cyprus'. They are good for boiling or salads.

Old potatoes are larger, go under such names as Whites, King Edwards or Désirée Reds or Romanos. Good for mashing, roasting or baking.

Boiled potatoes

Potatoes can be cooked with their skins on or off. They are better for you with the skins on. If you are leaving their skins on be sure to give them a thorough wash or scrub and dig out any eyes or unpleasant looking bits. Old potatoes look better peeled.

Cook small to medium potatoes whole. Large ones should be cut in half or quarters, so that all the pieces of potatoes in the saucepan are about the same size. Generally speaking the smaller the potato piece the quicker it will cook. Put the potatoes in a saucepan of water with 1 teaspoon of salt, bring to the boil, turn the heat down and simmer for 20–25 minutes. Test them with a fork to see if they are done. When they are done the fork will easily pierce the potato. If they start to fall apart they are overdone. When they are done drain off the water and serve.

Mashed potatoes

Peel and cook as for boiled potatoes (above), and then drain off the water. Put them in a bowl or return them to the saucepan, then mash the potatoes up with a fork or a potato masher.

Add small blobs of butter or margarine and fresh ground pepper to taste. If you like them creamier add a little milk and mix well into the mashed potatoes.

Baked potatoes

Pick large old potatoes for this. Get about three potatoes to the kilogram. Do not peel, but give them a good scrub. Stick a metal skewer through each potato, it helps them to cook in the middle. If you like the skin very crispy then prick the skin with a fork and place on the top shelf of the oven on 230°C, 450°F, Gas mark 8 for about an hour.

To check if they are done, cover your hand preferably with an oven glove to protect it from the heat and squeeze the sides gently. If it gives easily it is done. If you like it less crispy cover in tin foil and remove ten minutes before taking from the oven. If not crispy at all leave the tin foil on.

Roast potatoes

Peel the potatoes, cutting away any nasty bits, and cutting out any eyes. Chop the potatoes in half if medium-sized or into quarters if large. Put the potato in an ovenproof dish with the some sunflower oil. Turn over the potatoes to coat them in oil.

Cook in the top of a preheated oven at 180°C, 350°F, Gas mark 4 for 60 minutes or so if you like them really well done. Turn over half-way through cooking.

You can heat the oil first by putting the dish with the oil in the oven for about 10 minutes before adding the vegetables. It helps to reduce sticking.

Pan fried potato in butter

This is a good way of using up cooked, left over potato. Just put a couple of spoons of butter in a frying-pan. Slice the potato and fry for about 10 minutes.

Chips

We are not going to cover chips in this book, there are so many kinds of oven chips and frozen chips available and so many chip shops that it is not worth the hassle and risk of cooking them. Chip pans are the most common cause of household fire in the country.

Carrots

This is a vegetable that is good eaten raw. Add grated carrot to salad, or cut them into large matchstick shapes to dip into things like guacamole.

They are good roasted, and can be peeled and cooked together in the same dish as a joint of meat.

To cook separately just peel and chop into quarters lengthways and put in an ovenproof dish with half a cup of water, a tablespoon of butter and a teaspoon of sugar. Cover with foil and cook in a preheated oven at 180°C, 350°F, Gas mark 4 for 30 minutes.

Cauliflower or broccoli

Break into 'florets' then cook in 5 cm (2 inches) of water with a teaspoon of salt for about 10 minutes. Test the florets with a fork to check if they are ready. Cauliflower and broccoli can be eaten raw, and the longer you cook them, the softer they get.

Cabbage

This comes in several colours: red, white and green. Treat them all the same. Throw away any nasty looking outer leaves. Cut out the central hard core and discard. Chop the cabbage roughly and cook in 2 cm (1 inch) of water with a teaspoon of salt for about 10 to 20 minutes.

Red and white cabbage are good shredded raw in salads particularly in the winter when lettuces are very expensive or hard to find.

Spinach

This is good raw as a salad leaf or lightly cooked. It shrinks when cooked so you will need at least 500 g (1 lb) of spinach for two people.

First, wash the spinach, shake out the excess water. Put the spinach into a saucepan with salt to taste and a blob (the size of small walnut) of butter. There is no need to add any more water. Cook the spinach in a medium-sized saucepan over a medium heat. As soon as the water on the leaves starts to hiss and bubble, and the butter to melt, stir the spinach gently. When it is floppy and transparent, two to three minutes later, it is cooked.

Strain off the liquid and serve.

Broad beans, runner beans, fine beans, sugar snaps and mangetout

All these small beans and peas are eaten in the pod. Cut off both ends, and pull any stringy bits from down the side. Cut them into pieces, except the sugar snaps and mangetout which should be cooked whole. Just cover with water, add salt to taste and boil rapidly for five to ten minutes until tender, testing them with a fork.

Corn on the cob

This is a cheap vegetable in the summer and is almost a meal in itself. There are several ways to cook corn: it can be boiled, baked or barbecued.

If boiling, pull all the leaves off and boil in salted water for 20 to 30 minutes. Check with a fork to see if the corn is soft enough to eat. The fork should pierce the corn easily. Serve with a blob of butter and freshly ground black pepper.

If barbecuing, keep the leaves on, and barbecue for 10 to 20 minutes turning a couple of times. If the leaves have been removed by the shop don't worry just turn the corn more often.

If baking the corn, pull the leaves of as for boiling, place on a baking tray, put a little oil or butter on the corn, sprinkle with salt and pepper and bake for about 45 minutes.

Courgettes

Courgettes are quick and easy to cook. Wash them and slice either across or lengthways. Put them in a pan with some oil or butter and some seasoning. Cook on a medium heat for about five minutes and serve. If you cook with 1 teaspoon cumin seed, it goes well with curries.

HOW TO MAKE SALAD

Salads are quick and easy, and are some of the simplest things to experiment with. There are some classic salads like Caesar Salad further on, but here are the basics.

Preparing salads

Make sure you have a clean chopping board or knife if you need them. You must not prepare salad on a board you have just used to cut raw meat or fish as you can transfer bugs which can give you food poisoning. As salad is raw, the bugs cannot be killed by cooking. Anyway, pick off any shrivelled, bad looking bits, wash the rest and shake dry or drain and chop if needed. Lettuce is better torn up than chopped.

Here is a bit of information on some salad ingredients.

Lettuces

The simplest salad is lettuce. There are a lot of different lettuces. Each has its own characteristics but they all make a good base for a green salad. Green salads are a lot less hassle than vegetables.

Go to your local street market or supermarket. Look at different lettuces, smell them and try them.

Iceberg lettuce is crisp and has a neutral taste. It can be sliced or cut into chunks. It keeps well in the fridge

Webb's wonder is a crispish round lettuce.

Cos lettuce has long, crisp leaves good for dipping in things.

Round lettuce has more floppy leaves.

Oak leaf has crisp bitterish, brown and green leaves.

Radicchio is small and slightly bitterish, the colour of red cabbage with white veins.

Frisée and lollo rosso have wobbly edges to the leaves. The lollo rosso has purple or red edges to the leaves. Both are very decorative 'designer' lettuce.

Mixing together lettuces of different colour and textures works well.

If lettuce is not available, try shredding white or red cabbage.

Put the washed and dried lettuce in a bowl and put vinaigrette on top. There is a recipe for vinaigrette on page 244.

Herbs

Fresh herbs can be used in salads, either as decoration or to give a more interesting flavour.

Basil is an aromatic herb, often used in Italian food.

Rocket has small leaves with a distinct taste like watercress.

Other herbs like parsley and coriander work well.

Tomatoes

Ordinary tomatoes can be a bit tasteless but are available all year.

Cherry tomatoes are small, sweet and expensive.

Beef tomatoes are large and good with steak.

Italian plum tomatoes are good for pasta sauces. They are the ones sold in tins, but are also available fresh in many shops.

Other ingredients

You can combine almost anything to make a salad. Other standard salad ingredients include: cucumber, green, red or yellow peppers, spring onions, olives, and shredded carrot.

If you want a more substantial salad try adding some of the following:

Hard-boiled eggs, tinned tuna, cheese or ham.
Fruit such as chopped apples, pears, oranges or bananas.
Walnuts, peanuts or even a few pecan nuts, cashew nuts or almonds.
Dried fruit like a couple of tablespoons of sultanas, raisins, apricot and dates.
Cooked vegetables like potato, green beans or French beans.

HOW TO COOK RICE

The most important thing to know about cooking rice is that you should use twice as much water as you do rice. Below is a recipe for plain boiled rice for two people.

Serves 2   ⊙ *Preparation 1 min, Cooking depends on sort of rice*
– Easy

INGREDIENTS
1 cup rice
2 cups water
1 teaspoon salt

EQUIPMENT

Saucepan with lid

Measuring cups and spoons

METHOD

Read the packet to get the correct cooking time. Put the rice, water and salt in the pan. Bring the water and rice to the boil, stirring once, to stop the rice sticking. Turn down the heat to low. Put the lid on the pan. Cook for the correct time until the fluid is absorbed (10–15 minutes for long grain or Basmati rice). Do not stir!

After the cooking time, take it off the heat and let it stand for a couple of minutes. Fluff it up with a fork to separate the grains and serve.

TIPS

The cup referred to is a standard measuring cup of 250 ml. It is approximately the same as a mug. For larger quantities use 1 cup of water and half a cup of rice per person.

Basmati is more fragrant than long grain, and also more forgiving, because it holds together during cooking.

Approximate cooking times (read the packet for more accurate timings):

Basmati	10 minutes
American long grain	15 minutes
Organic long grain brown rice	30–35 minutes
Brown quick cook	20–25 minutes

HOW TO COOK NOODLES

Serves 2   ℗ *Preparation 1 min, Cooking 4 min – Easy*

INGREDIENTS
2 sheets dried noodles
1 tablespoon sesame oil

EQUIPMENT
Saucepan
Sieve or colander to drain the noodles

METHOD
Check the cooking time on the packet. Boil at least a pint of water in a saucepan. Put the noodles in the water. Boil for about 4 minutes. Drain the noodles. Return to the pan. Add a tablespoon of sesame oil and stir round. Serve.

TIP
You get three sheets of noodles in a 250 g pack of Sharwoods medium noodles.

HOW TO COOK PASTA

Serves 2   ℗ *Preparation 1 min, Cooking 2–10 min – Easy*

INGREDIENTS
250 g dried pasta (generally half a pack or $2\frac{1}{2}$ cups)
1 teaspoon salt

EQUIPMENT
Saucepan
Wooden spoon
Sieve or colander

METHOD

Read the packet for the correct cooking time. Put at least a pint of water into the saucepan and bring to the boil. Put the pasta in the water. Stir the pasta once to stop it sticking to the bottom of the pan. Bring back to the boil and simmer for as long as the packet says. Add the salt.

The best way to judge if the pasta is cooked is to bite it. This is tricky, because if you fish out a bit and stick it in you mouth you may burn your mouth with the boiling water. Wait a bit and blow on it, then bite it.

You can trust the cooking time if you want to or put a bit on a plate and cut it with the edge of a fork. If it is hard it needs longer. If it is like mush it is overcooked.

HOW TO ROLL PASTRY

INGREDIENTS

Half a 500 g pack of pastry, chilled or frozen
2 tablespoons flour

EQUIPMENT

Rolling pin

METHOD

Make sure the pastry is well thawed, 4 hours in the fridge being typical. Keep the pastry in the fridge before rolling. Make sure that the surface that you are going to roll on is clean, dry and flat. Pastry can stick to the surface or rolling pin unless it is kept dry, so sprinkle the surface and the pastry with flour.

Roll and then turn the pastry through a quarter of a circle. Roll and turn, scattering more flour if needed.

It is remarkably easy.

HOW TO BAKE A PASTRY CASE

We have already said get a metal pie dish with holes in the bottom, but if you have already got another pie dish, or the dinner date is almost here and the shops are shut ... Anyway, don't panic. It's not so difficult.

METHOD

If you just put the filling in a raw pastry case it will not cook properly. If you just cook the case in the oven it will distort and shrink. So part cook it without the proper filling but lined with greaseproof paper and with some dried beans to keep the pastry in place.

Unroll the pastry (if ready-rolled), or roll out according to the instructions above. Line the dish. Pastry is fairly flexible so you can push it into place. If it tears patch it with a spare bit, moistening with a bit of water to make sure it sticks. Pastry shrinks when it cooks so if you trim it to the top of the rim it will shrink below that level. So cut it high.

Prick the bottom of the pastry with a fork at least five times to let steam out. Cut a piece of greaseproof paper and press gently on to the pastry. Fill the bottom with a layer of cheap dried beans, for instance butter beans.

Cook the pastry case at 200°C, 400°F, Gas mark 6 for 15 minutes until the top edges go golden.

Take the pastry case out of the oven.

HOW TO MAKE DRIED BEANS TURN OUT SOFT AND NOT LIKE BULLETS

① Preparation 5 min, Cooking time depends – Easy

INGREDIENTS
1½ cups dried beans or chickpeas is equivalent to 2 × 440 g tins.

EQUIPMENT
Saucepan with lid
Set measuring cups
Bowl

METHOD
Check over the dried beans. Throw away any stones or odd looking ones. Put the beans in a plastic bowl or one made from heatproof glass. Pour boiling water on top of them, and cover to a depth of about 5 cm (2 inches). This takes about a litre or two pints. (Don't add any salt until the beans are cooked or they won't soften). Leave the beans for 4 to 12 hours to swell up, preferably in a fridge. Drain and rinse the beans.

Put them in the saucepan with at least a pint of fresh water. Bring to the boil and boil vigorously for 10 minutes. Turn down the heat until the water is just simmering gently. Cook the beans till they are soft. This may take anything between 30 minutes and 2½ hours. Add more water if it gets low.

When the beans are done, take off the heat. Add salt to taste. Drain the beans and leave to cool down.

ADDITIONS & ALTERNATIVES
Approximate cooking times (read the packet for more accurate timings):

Red kidney beans	60–90 minutes
Chickpeas	150 minutes
Rose Coco (Borlotti) beans	150 minutes
Red split lentils	30 minutes
Green lentils with skin on	90 minutes

TIPS

Parsley is reputed to reduce the wind generating capacity of beans.

HOW TO MAKE BREADCRUMBS

You may have noticed how bread starts off really soft and moist and ends up rock hard as it dries out. Breadcrumbs are best made with bread that is not totally fresh or you end up with a kind of bread pellet which is very useful as bait when fishing but rubbish as a cooking ingredient.

1 slice of bread makes a cup of breadcrumbs.

Method 1: Rub two bits of bread together and you will get some breadcrumbs.

Method 2: Use a grater. Rub the bread against the grater. The main problem with this is that you can end up with grated finger nail or finger in the breadcrumbs if you loose your concentration. Scraped knuckles hurt.

Method 3: Cut the crust off the bread. Cut the bread into cubes and put in a food processor or liquidizer and process for about 15 seconds.

Method 4: Give up and buy some from your local baker or supermarket.

HOW TO DEFROST THINGS

Chicken Pieces

Overnight in the fridge or six hours at room temperature.

Chicken livers (225 g or 8 oz tub)

Four hours at room temperature or overnight in the fridge.

Lamb chops

Defrost in a single layer for four hours at room temperature or overnight in the fridge.

Half leg of lamb

Overnight in the fridge or 4 hours at room temperature.

Whole chicken (1.5 kg)

24 hours in fridge, 12 hours in a cool room.

Packet of extra large prawns

3 hours at room temperature.

Plaice, cod and haddock

Cook from frozen.

CHINESE

HOT SOUR VEGETABLES

Serves 4   ⏱ *Preparation 15 min, Cooking 8 min – Easy*

INGREDIENTS
1 small turnip
20 button mushrooms
227 g tin bamboo shoots
1 cm ($\frac{1}{2}$ inch) slice ginger
1 teaspoon cornflour
3 tablespoons sunflower oil
2 tablespoons soy sauce
1 tablespoon vinegar
1 teaspoon sugar
1 cup water
$\frac{1}{2}$ chicken stock cube
1 tablespoon chilli sauce

EQUIPMENT
Vegetable peeler
Sharp knife
Chopping board
Tin opener
Cup

Set of measuring spoons
Wooden spoon or spatula
Set of measuring cups
Frying-pan or wok

METHOD

Get everything washed, chopped and ready before starting to cook. Peel the turnip. Cut into $\frac{1}{2}$ cm ($\frac{1}{4}$ inch) slices. Wipe the mushrooms clean. Discard any nasty ones. Chop the end off the stalks. Cut into slices. Open the tin of bamboo shoots and drain. Peel the ginger and cut into tiny cubes. Mix the cornflour with a couple of tablespoons of water in a cup to make a thin paste.

Put the oil in the frying-pan on a moderate heat. Stir fry the ginger, turnip, mushrooms and bamboo shoots for 3 minutes. Add the soy sauce, vinegar, sugar, cornflour, water, stock cube and chilli sauce and cook for 3 minutes or until the sauce thickens.

ADDITIONS & ALTERNATIVES

Serve with rice or noodles.

Add a chopped spring onion before serving.
Use a $\frac{1}{4}$ teaspoon of chilli powder instead of the chilli sauce.
Try using sake instead of dry sherry.
Try oyster mushrooms instead of button mushrooms.
Add peeled sliced carrot or baby sweetcorn.

TIPS

You can buy prepared ginger in jars and bottles. It will keep for 6 weeks in the fridge or longer, just check on the pack.

There are full instructions on cooking rice and noodles in the 'How to' chapter.

PEKING SPECIAL VEGETABLES

Serves 2   ⓘ *Preparation 15 min, Cooking 15 min – Easy*

INGREDIENTS
10 cm (4 inch) piece cucumber
250 g packet bean sprouts
2 medium tomatoes
227 g tin sliced bamboo shoots
2 teaspoons cornflour
½ cup water
1 medium onion
1 cm (½ inch) fresh ginger
4 tablespoons sunflower oil
100g packet unsalted raw cashew nuts
1 tablespoon dry sherry
1 teaspoon sugar
2 tablespoons soy sauce

EQUIPMENT
Sharp knife
Chopping board
Sieve or colander
Tin opener
Cup
Set of measuring spoons
Set of measuring cups
Frying-pan or wok
Wooden spatula
Slotted spoon
Plate

METHOD

Get everything washed, chopped and ready before starting to cook. Cut the cucumber into 1 cm ($\frac{1}{2}$ inch) cubes. Wash and drain the bean sprouts. Cut the tomatoes into 1 cm ($\frac{1}{2}$ inch) slices. Open the tin of bamboo shoots and drain. Mix the cornflour and water together in the cup till smooth. Add the water slowly or it will go lumpy. Peel and chop the onion. Peel the ginger and cut into tiny cubes.

Put the oil in the frying-pan on a moderate heat. Fry the cashews for about three minutes till golden. Lift out with the slotted spoon and put on a plate. Stir fry the ginger and onion for 2 minutes. Add the cucumber, bean sprouts, tomatoes and bamboo shoots and stir fry for 3 minutes. Put the nuts back in, add the sherry, sugar, soy sauce and cornflour mixture. Stir and cook for about three minutes till it goes thick.

ADDITIONS & ALTERNATIVES

Serve with rice.

Try using sake instead of dry sherry.

Use a leek instead of the onion.

TIPS

There are full instructions on cooking rice in the 'How to' chapter.

You can buy prepared ginger in jars and bottles. It will keep for 6 weeks in the fridge or longer, just check on the pack.

Other combinations of vegetables can be used; simply keep in mind the balance of taste, texture and colour.

STIR FRY CHINESE CABBAGE

Serves 4   ⊙ *Preparation 10 min, Cooking 3 min – Easy*

INGREDIENTS
1 Chinese cabbage about 500 g (1 lb)
1 tablespoon water
1 teaspoon cornflour
2 garlic cloves
3 tablespoons oil
1 tablespoon dry sherry
1 teaspoon salt
1 teaspoon sugar

EQUIPMENT
Sharp knife
Chopping board
Set of measuring spoons
Cup
Garlic crusher
Saucepan with lid
Wooden spoon or spatula

METHOD
Wash and cut the Chinese cabbage into 2 cm (1 inch) slices. Mix the water and the cornflour in the cup. Peel and crush the garlic into the pan. Put the oil in the pan on a moderate heat. Fry the garlic for 2 minutes, stirring to stop it sticking. Add the cabbage and stir fry for 1 minute. Add the sherry, salt and sugar, put the lid on and cook for 1 minute. Add the cornflour mixture and cook for 1 minute until it thickens.

ADDITIONS & ALTERNATIVES
Serve with rice or noodles.
Try using sake instead of dry sherry.

TIPS

There are full instructions on cooking rice and noodles in the 'How to' chapter.

If you don't have a garlic crusher just squash it with something suitable or chop it up small. Prepared garlic is sold in tubes, jars and bottles. Just read the instructions for the suggested equivalent amount. Most keep for 6 weeks in the fridge, but the bottles keep longer.

MIXED VEGETABLES STIR FRY

Serves 2   ⏲ *Preparation 10 min, Cooking 8 min – Easy*

INGREDIENTS

250 g (8 oz) altogether of mixed vegetables such as carrot, mushroom, green beans, baby sweetcorn, broccoli, cauliflower
4 spring onions
1 cm ($\frac{1}{2}$ inch) fresh ginger
1 teaspoon cornflour
1 cup water
3 tablespoons sunflower oil
2 tablespoons soy sauce
1 teaspoon sugar
1 teaspoon chilli powder
$\frac{1}{4}$ teaspoon ground Szechuan pepper
$\frac{1}{4}$ teaspoon freshly ground black pepper
1 teaspoon salt
1 tablespoon sesame oil

EQUIPMENT

Sharp knife
Chopping board

Vegetable peeler (optional)
Set of measuring spoons
Frying-pan or wok
Wooden spoon or spatula
Slotted spoon
Plate
Set of measuring cups
Small bowls or plates
Cup

METHOD

Get everything washed, peeled, chopped and ready before starting to cook. Whatever vegetables you are using, cut them into thin slices. Cut any green beans into 2 cm (1 inch) lengths. Clean and prepare the spring onions. Cut the root end off, trim the leaves. Peel off and discard any dried up or slimy leaves. Chop into thin slices. Peel the ginger and cut into tiny cubes. Mix the cornflour and water together in the cup till smooth. Add the water slowly or it will go lumpy.

Put the 2 tablespoons of the oil in the frying-pan on a moderate heat. Stir fry the vegetable slices for 2 minutes. Lift out with the slotted spoon and put on a plate. Remove from the pan and allow to cool. Add a little more oil and fry the spring onion and ginger for 1 minute. Add the soy, sugar, chilli powder, Szechuan pepper, black pepper, salt and sesame oil and stir round. Put the vegetables back in and stir. Add the cornflour mixture from the cup and cook gently for 3 minutes, stirring all the time, until the sauce thickens.

ADDITIONS & ALTERNATIVES

This is a bit of a side dish though you can double the quantities easily.

Add $\frac{1}{4}$ teaspoon of five spice powder.

Serve with rice or noodles.

Try using sake instead of dry sherry.

CHINESE CHILLI AUBERGINES

Serves 2   ⏲ *Preparation 5 min, Cooking 5 min – Easy*

INGREDIENTS
1 large aubergine
1 cm ($\frac{1}{2}$ inch) fresh ginger
$\frac{1}{2}$ cup boiling water
$\frac{1}{2}$ chicken stock cube
4 spring onions
3 tablespoons sunflower oil
2 tablespoons soy sauce
1 teaspoon sugar
1 teaspoon chilli sauce

EQUIPMENT
Bowl
Sharp knife
Chopping board
Set of measuring spoons
Frying-pan or wok
Wooden spoon or spatula
Set of measuring cups

METHOD
Dutch aubergines don't need soaking. Just wash, cut the ends off,
and cut into 1 cm ($\frac{1}{2}$ inch) strips. Peel the ginger and cut into tiny
cubes. Mix the aubergines and ginger in the bowl.

Crumble the stock cube into the water and stir till dissolved.

Clean and prepare the spring onions. Cut the root end off, trim the leaves. Peel off and discard any dried up or slimy leaves. Chop into thin slices.

Put the oil in the frying-pan on a moderate heat. Fry the aubergine and ginger for about 3 minutes, stirring to stop them sticking. Add the soy, water and stock cube, sugar and chilli sauce. Bring to the boil, then turn down the heat till it is just boiling (simmering). Cook for 3 minutes. Just before serving, stir in the spring onions.

ADDITIONS & ALTERNATIVES

Serve with rice or noodles.

Try using sake instead of dry sherry.

TIPS

You can buy prepared ginger in jars and bottles. It will keep for 6 weeks in the fridge or longer, just check on the pack.

There are full instructions on cooking rice and noodles in the 'How to' chapter.

STIR FRY SPINACH

Serves 2 ① *Preparation 3 min, Cooking 10 min – Easy*

INGREDIENTS

500 g (1lb) spinach
2 cloves garlic
3 tablespoons sunflower oil
2 tablespoons soy sauce
1 teaspoon sugar
1 teaspoon sesame oil
1 teaspoon salt

EQUIPMENT
Sharp knife
Chopping board
Garlic crusher
Set of measuring spoons
Frying-pan or wok
Wooden spoon or spatula

METHOD
Wash the spinach and chop into 1 cm ($\frac{1}{2}$ inch) strips. Peel and crush the garlic into the pan. Put the oil in the frying-pan on a moderate heat. Fry the garlic for 2 minutes, stirring to stop it sticking. Add the spinach and stir fry for 2 minutes. Add the soy, sugar, sesame oil and salt. Stir round and cook for 3 minutes.

ADDITIONS & ALTERNATIVES
This is a vegetable side dish but with rice or noodles it could make a frugal vegetarian meal.

Sprinkle with 1 tablespoon of sesame seeds roasted in the oven for 3 minutes before serving.

Try young, tender cabbage or spring greens instead of the spinach. If you do, shred it before cooking.

TIPS
If you don't have a garlic crusher just squash it with something suitable or chop it up small. Prepared garlic is sold in tubes, jars and bottles. Just read the instructions for the suggested equivalent amount. Most keep for 6 weeks in the fridge, but the bottles keep longer.

CHINESE PUMPKIN & LEEK

Serves 4   ① *Preparation 10 min, Cooking 15 min – Easy*

INGREDIENTS
3 medium leeks
500 g (1 lb) piece pumpkin
4 tablespoons sunflower oil
1 tablespoon soy sauce
$\frac{1}{2}$ chicken stock cube
$\frac{1}{2}$ cup water
1 teaspoon sugar
1 teaspoon salt
$\frac{1}{4}$ teaspoon freshly ground pepper

EQUIPMENT
Sharp knife
Chopping board
Vegetable peeler
Set of measuring spoons
Wooden spoon or spatula
Frying-pan or wok
Set of measuring cups

METHOD
Clean the leeks. First take off the outer leaves, cut the roots off and trim the top. Split the leeks in half lengthways. Hold the leeks under running water and wash any grit out. Shake them dry. Cut into 2 cm (1 inch) slices. Peel the pumpkin. Throw away the seeds. Chop into 1 cm ($\frac{1}{2}$ inch) cubes.

Put the oil in the frying-pan on a moderate heat. Fry the pumpkin for about three minutes, stirring to stop it sticking. Add the leek and stir fry for 1 minute. Add the soy, stock cube and water, sugar, salt and pepper. Bring to the boil, then turn down the heat till it is just boiling (simmering). Cook for 5 minutes or until the pumpkin is tender. (Stick a fork in to see if it is done, some pumpkin is tougher than others.)

ADDITIONS & ALTERNATIVES
Use courgettes or marrow instead of the pumpkin.

SPICY FISH IN SAUCE

Serves 2 to 3   ① *Preparation 15 min, Cooking 7 min – Easy*

INGREDIENTS
500 g (1 lb) pack white fish fillets (cod, hake, hoki, halibut fillets)
2 tablespoons dry sherry
1 teaspoon salt
$\frac{1}{2}$ teaspoon ground pepper
2 spring onion
2 cloves garlic
1 cm ($\frac{1}{2}$ inch) piece fresh ginger
4 tablespoons tomato ketchup
1 tablespoon Worcestershire sauce
$\frac{1}{4}$ teaspoon Tabasco
1 teaspoon sugar
1 teaspoon cornflour
1 tablespoon water
3 tablespoons sunflower oil

EQUIPMENT
Sharp knife
Chopping board
Bowl
Set of measuring spoons
2 cups

Frying-pan or wok
Wooden spoon or spatula

METHOD

You can cook the fish from frozen. Cut the fish into 2 cm (1 inch) chunks. Put the fish in the bowl with the sherry, salt and pepper. Leave to stand for 10 minutes.

Meanwhile, clean and prepare the spring onions. Cut the root end off, trim the leaves. Peel off and discard any dried up or slimy leaves. Chop into thin slices. Peel the garlic then chop it into tiny pieces. Peel the ginger and cut into tiny cubes. Mix the ketchup, Worcestershire sauce, Tabasco and sugar in a cup. Dissolve the cornflour in the water in the other cup.

Put the oil in the frying-pan on a moderate heat. Fry the fish mixture for 3 minutes, stirring to stop it sticking. Put the garlic, ginger and spring onion in the pan and stir fry for 30 seconds. Add the ketchup mixture and stir fry for 1 minute. Add the cornflour mixture, stirring until thick, for about 1 minute.

ADDITIONS & ALTERNATIVES

Serve with rice or noodles
Try using rice wine instead of dry sherry.

TIPS

Prepared garlic is sold in tubes, jars and bottles. Just read the instructions for the suggested equivalent amount. Most keep for 6 weeks in the fridge, but the bottles keep longer.

You can buy prepared ginger in jars and bottles. It will keep for 6 weeks in the fridge or longer, just check on the pack.

There are full instructions on cooking rice and noodles in the 'How to' chapter (pages 50–2).

FISH IN SOY

Serves 4   ① *Preparation 5 min, Cooking 15 min* — *Easy*

INGREDIENTS
600 g ($1\frac{1}{4}$ lb) pack white fish fillets (cod, hake, hoki or halibut)
4 spring onions
2 cm (1 inch) slice fresh ginger
4 tablespoons sunflower oil
2 tablespoons sherry
2 tablespoons soy sauce
1 tablespoon sugar
$\frac{1}{2}$ cup water
1 teaspoon sesame seed oil

EQUIPMENT
Sharp knife
Chopping board
Frying-pan or wok
Wooden spoon or spatula
Set of measuring spoons
Set of measuring cups

METHOD
You can cook the fish from frozen. Cut the fish into 4 cm (2 inch) squares. Clean and prepare the spring onions. Cut the root end off, trim the leaves. Peel off and discard any dried up or slimy leaves. Chop into thin slices. Peel the ginger and cut into tiny cubes.

Put the oil in the frying-pan on a moderate heat. Fry the spring onions and ginger for about 30 seconds, stirring to stop it sticking. Add the fish and stir round gently to separate. Add the sherry and stir fry for another 30 seconds. Add the soy sauce, sugar and water. Bring to the boil, then turn down the heat till it is just boiling

71

(simmering) and cook for 10 minutes. Add the sesame seed oil and stir.

ADDITIONS & ALTERNATIVES
Serve with rice or noodles

Try using sake instead of dry sherry.

You can buy prepared ginger in jars and bottles. It will keep for 6 weeks in the fridge or longer, just check on the pack.

TIPS
There are full instructions on cooking rice and noodles in the 'How to' chapter.

CHINESE SQUID & BROCCOLI

Serves 2 to 3 ① *Preparation 15 min, Cooking 8 min — Easy*

INGREDIENTS
500 g (1 lb) prepared squid tubes
1 tablespoon dry sherry
1 tablespoon cornflour
2 teaspoons salt
5 spring onions
1 medium head broccoli, about 250 g (8 oz)
4 tablespoons sunflower oil
1 teaspoon sesame seed oil

EQUIPMENT
Sharp knife
Chopping board
Saucepan
Slotted spoon
Bowl
Set of measuring spoons

Frying-pan or wok
Wooden spoon or spatula
Plate

METHOD

Throw the squid tentacles away. Cut the squid open and wash. Now would be a good time to check for the clear plastic-like quill. If it is there take it out and throw away. Cut into ½ cm (¼ inch) slices.

Put some water in the saucepan, bring to the boil, then drop in the squid slices. Cook for 2 minutes. Lift out with the slotted spoon and put in the bowl. Add the sherry, cornflour and 1 teaspoon of the salt to the bowl. Stir and leave for 10 minutes.

Meanwhile, clean and prepare the spring onions. Cut the root end off, trim the leaves. Peel off and discard any dried up or slimy leaves. Chop into 2 cm (1 inch) pieces. Wash the broccoli then break or cut into pieces each about 2 cm (1 inch) across.

Put 2 tablespoons of sunflower oil in the pan and put over a moderate heat. Add the broccoli, 1 teaspoon of salt and stir fry for 2 minutes. Add 2 tablespoons of water and cook until just tender, about three minutes. Add a bit more water if it gets too dry. Lift out with the slotted spoon and put on a plate.

Put 2 tablespoons of the oil in the frying-pan on a high heat. Fry the squid and onion for 2 minutes, stirring to stop it sticking. Put the squid in the middle of the broccoli, dribble the sesame oil on top and serve.

TIPS

Squid tubes are stocked by supermarkets and some fishmongers. Don't buy unprepared squid unless you like slimy things and know how to take the quill out. But check the prepared ones, as you chop them for a strip of clear plastic-like stuff. If you find it, throw it away. It is the quill.

CHINESE PRAWN OMELETTE

Serves 4   ① *Preparation 5 min, Cooking 10 min — Easy*

INGREDIENTS
225 g (8 oz) pack frozen prawns
5 tablespoons sunflower oil
6 eggs
$\frac{1}{2}$ teaspoon salt

EQUIPMENT
Set of measuring spoons
Frying-pan or wok
Wooden spoon or spatula
Slotted spoon
Plate
Bowl
Fork

METHOD
Make sure the prawns are thawed.

Put 2 tablespoons of the oil in the frying-pan on a moderate heat. Fry the prawns for about 30 seconds, stirring to stop them sticking. Lift out with the slotted spoon and put on a plate.

Break the eggs into a bowl and pick out any bits of shell. Add the prawns and salt and mix the eggs up with a fork.

Heat 3 tablespoons of oil in the pan for at least a minute till it gets hot. Add the egg and prawn mixture. Cut the omelette into quarters with the spatula and flip each piece over and cook until golden brown. Lift out the bits on to a plate.

ADDITIONS & ALTERNATIVES
Try adding half a 15 g pack of coriander, washed, dried and chopped.

CHINESE CHICKEN & BROCCOLI

Serves 2 to 4   ⏲ *Preparation 15 min, Cooking 24 min — Easy*

INGREDIENTS

2 chicken breasts, about 500 g (1 lb)
1 tablespoon soy sauce
2 teaspoons sugar
2 tablespoons dry sherry
500g (1 lb) sprouting broccoli
$\frac{1}{2}$ cup water
3 spring onions
$\frac{1}{2}$ teaspoon salt
1 cm ($\frac{1}{2}$ inch) fresh ginger
3 cloves garlic
4 tablespoons sunflower oil
1 cup water
$\frac{1}{2}$ chicken stock cube
$\frac{1}{2}$ teaspoon salt

EQUIPMENT

Sharp knife
Chopping board
Bowl
Set of measuring spoons
Wooden spatula
Saucepan with lid
Set of measuring cups
Slotted spoon
Plate
Frying-pan or wok

75

DEFROSTING

Make sure frozen chicken is completely thawed before use. This means leaving it in the fridge overnight, or out of the fridge, covered, for 6 hours.

METHOD

Cut the chicken into $\frac{1}{2}$ cm ($\frac{1}{4}$ inch) slices. Put the soy sauce, sugar and sherry in the bowl with the chicken. Stir round and leave for 10 minutes.

Meanwhile, wash the broccoli and put it in the saucepan with $\frac{1}{2}$ cup of water and $\frac{1}{2}$ teaspoon salt. Put the lid on and cook for 5 minutes. Take the lid off. Lift out with the slotted spoon and put on a plate.

Clean and prepare the spring onions. Cut the root end off, trim the leaves. Peel off and discard any dried up or slimy leaves. Chop into 2 cm (1 inch) pieces. Peel the ginger and cut into tiny cubes. Peel the garlic then chop it into thin slices.

Put the oil in the frying-pan on a moderate heat. Fry the garlic and ginger for 3 minutes, stirring to stop it sticking. Add the chicken and spring onions and stir fry for 2 minutes. Add the broccoli, water, stock cube and 1 teaspoon salt. Bring to the boil, then turn down the heat till it is just boiling (simmering). Cook for 5 minutes.

ADDITIONS & ALTERNATIVES

Serve with rice or noodles.
Try using sake instead of dry sherry.

TIPS

Use a head of broccoli or a cauliflower instead of the sprouting broccoli. Just cut into florets and throw the stems away.

Prepared garlic is sold in tubes, jars and bottles. Just read the instructions for the suggested equivalent amount. Most keep for 6 weeks in the fridge, but the bottles keep longer.

You can buy prepared ginger in jars and bottles. It will keep for

6 weeks in the fridge or longer, just check on the pack.

There are full instructions on cooking rice and noodles in the 'How to' chapter.

CHINESE CHICKEN & VEGETABLES

Serves 4   ① *Preparation 15 min, Cooking 12 min — Easy*

INGREDIENTS
1 medium aubergine, about 250 g ($\frac{1}{2}$ lb)
2 green peppers
20 button mushrooms, about 250 g ($\frac{1}{2}$ lb)
2 boneless chicken breasts, about 500 g (1 lb)
1 tablespoon dry sherry
2 tablespoons soy sauce
$\frac{1}{2}$ teaspoon sugar
1 cm ($\frac{1}{2}$ inch) piece fresh ginger
4 tablespoons sunflower oil
1 cup water
$\frac{1}{2}$ chicken stock cube
1 cm ($\frac{1}{2}$ inch) piece fresh ginger

EQUIPMENT
Sharp knife
Chopping board
Bowl
Set of measuring spoons
Wooden spatula
Set of measuring cups
Frying-pan or wok

DEFROSTING

Make sure frozen chicken is completely thawed before use. This means leaving it in the fridge overnight, or out of the fridge, covered, for 6 hours.

METHOD

Dutch aubergines don't need soaking. Just wash, cut the ends off, and cut into 1 cm ($\frac{1}{2}$ inch) strips. Chop the end off the peppers, split in half, and scrape out the seeds. Cut the pepper into strips. Wipe the mushrooms clean. Discard any nasty ones. Chop the end off the stalks. Slice. Cut the chicken into 1 cm ($\frac{1}{2}$ inch) strips. Put the chicken in the bowl with the sherry, soy sauce and sugar. Stir round then leave for 10 minutes. Peel the ginger and cut into tiny cubes.

Put the oil in the frying-pan on a moderate heat. Fry the ginger for 1 minute, stirring to stop it sticking. Add the chicken and stir fry for 2 minutes. Add mushrooms and pepper to pan and stir fry for 2 minutes. Add aubergine, water and stock cube. Bring to the boil, stirring. Cook for 5 minutes.

ADDITIONS & ALTERNATIVES

Serve with rice or noodles.

Try using some Shitake mushrooms instead of the button mushrooms.

TIPS

You can buy prepared ginger in jars and bottles. It will keep for 6 weeks in the fridge or longer, just check on the pack.

There are full instructions on cooking rice and noodles in the 'How to' chapter.

CHINESE CURRIED CHICKEN

Serves 4　　　　　　　　⏲ *Preparation 20 min, Cooking 1 hr — Easy*

INGREDIENTS
8–12 boneless chicken thighs, about 1 kg (2 lb)
2 medium onions
2 cloves garlic
4 tablespoons sunflower oil
1 tablespoon medium curry powder
2 tablespoons tomato ketchup
1 teaspoon salt
$\frac{1}{2}$ teaspoon fresh ground pepper
2 cups water
1 chicken stock cube
4 medium-sized potatoes about 400 g (3/4 lb)
1 cup milk
1 green pepper

EQUIPMENT
Sharp knife
Chopping board
Garlic crusher
Saucepan with lid
Set of measuring cups
Set of measuring spoons
Wooden spoon

DEFROSTING
Make sure frozen chicken is completely thawed before use. This means leaving it in the fridge overnight, or out of the fridge, covered, for 6 hours.

METHOD

Chop chicken into 5 cm (2 inch) chunks. Peel and chop the onions into 1 cm ($\frac{1}{2}$ inch) slices. Peel and crush the garlic into the pan. Put the oil in the pan on a moderate heat. Fry the chicken, onion and garlic for about three minutes, stirring to stop it sticking. Add the curry powder, tomato ketchup, salt and pepper, water and stock cube. Bring to the boil, then turn down the heat till it is just boiling (simmering). Put a lid on and cook for 20 minutes. Check the water level from time to time and top it up if needed.

Meanwhile, peel the potatoes, cutting away any nasty bits, and cutting out any eyes. Chop the potatoes into quarters. Add to the pan with the milk. Cover again and simmer for 30 minutes. Chop the end off the pepper and cut out the seeds. Cut the pepper into quarters. Add the pepper and cook for 5 minutes.

ADDITIONS & ALTERNATIVES

Serve with rice.

Try using sake instead of dry sherry.

Try other boneless chicken pieces or boneless turkey instead.

TIPS

If you don't have a garlic crusher just squash it with something suitable or chop it up small. Prepared garlic is sold in tubes, jars and bottles. Just read the instructions for the suggested equivalent amount. Most keep for 6 weeks in the fridge, but the bottles keep longer.

You can buy prepared ginger in jars and bottles. It will keep for 6 weeks in the fridge or longer, just check on the pack.

There are full instructions on cooking rice in the 'How to' chapter.

CHICKEN & CHESTNUT STIR FRY

Serves 2   ⏱ *Preparation 10 min, Cooking 5 min — Easy*

INGREDIENTS

2 boneless chicken breasts, about 500 g (1 lb)
1 teaspoon salt
1 teaspoon cornflour
4 spring onions
3 tablespoons soy sauce
2 tablespoons dry sherry
1 tablespoon sugar
1 tablespoon cornflour
$\frac{1}{2}$ cup hot water
$\frac{1}{2}$ chicken stock cube
240 g tin whole chestnuts
4 tablespoons sunflower oil

EQUIPMENT

Sharp knife
Chopping board
Bowl
Set of measuring spoons
Wooden spoon or spatula
2 small bowls
Tin opener
Frying-pan or wok
Set of measuring cups

DEFROSTING

Make sure frozen chicken is completely thawed before use. This means leaving it in the fridge overnight, or out of the fridge, covered, for 6 hours.

METHOD

Get everything ready before starting to cook. Cut the chicken into 2 cm (1 inch) cubes. Put the chicken in the bowl and add the salt and cornflour. Stir round. Clean and prepare the spring onions. Cut the root end off, trim the leaves. Peel off and discard any dried up or slimy leaves. Chop into 2 cm (1 inch) pieces. Put the soy, sherry, sugar and cornflour in a small bowl and stir round. Dissolve the stock cube in the hot water. Open the tin of chestnuts and drain.

Put the oil in the frying-pan on a moderate heat. Fry the chicken, spring onions and chestnuts for 2 minutes, stirring to stop it sticking. Put the water and stock cube and soy and sherry mixture in the pan. Bring to the boil, stirring all the time, for 3 minutes till the sauce thickens.

ADDITIONS & ALTERNATIVES

Serve with rice or noodles.

Try using sake instead of dry sherry.

TIPS

There are full instructions on cooking rice and noodles in the 'How to' chapter.

BRAISED CHICKEN & LEEK

Serves 2   ⏲ *Preparation 30 min, Cooking 12 min — Easy*

INGREDIENTS
4-6 boneless chicken thighs, about 500 g (1 lb)
3 tablespoons soy sauce
2 tablespoons dry sherry
½ cup hot water
½ chicken stock cube
3 medium leeks, about 250 g (8 oz)
4 spring onions
2 cm (1 inch) piece fresh ginger
4 tablespoons sunflower oil
1 tablespoon sugar
2 teaspoons salt
1 teaspoon sesame seed oil

EQUIPMENT
Bowl
Wooden spoon or spatula
Set of measuring spoons
Sharp knife
Chopping board
Set of measuring cups
Frying-pan or wok
Slotted spoon
Plate

DEFROSTING
Make sure frozen chicken is completely thawed before use. This means leaving it in the fridge overnight, or out of the fridge, covered, for 6 hours.

METHOD

Put the chicken in the bowl with the soy sauce and sherry. Stir round and put in the fridge for 30 minutes. Dissolve the stock cube in the hot water.

Clean the leeks. First take off the outer leaves, cut the roots off and trim the top. Split the leeks in half lengthways. Hold the leeks under running water and wash any grit out. Shake them dry. Cut into 2 cm (1 inch) slices.

Clean and prepare the spring onions. Cut the root end off, trim the leaves. Peel off and discard any dried up or slimy leaves. Chop into thin slices. Peel the ginger and cut into tiny cubes.

Put the oil in the frying-pan on a moderate heat. Fry the chicken for 1 minute, stirring to stop it sticking. Lift out with the slotted spoon and put on a plate. Put the spring onions and ginger in the pan and stir fry for 1 minute. Add the chicken, leeks, water and stock, sugar and salt. If there is any soy and sherry mixture left in the bowl you left the chicken in, add that as well. Bring to the boil and cook for 7 minutes. Stir in the sesame oil.

ADDITIONS & ALTERNATIVES

Serve with rice or noodles.

Try using sake instead of dry sherry.

TIPS

You can buy prepared ginger in jars and bottles. It will keep for 6 weeks in the fridge or longer, just check on the pack.

There are full instructions on cooking rice and noodles in the 'How to' chapter.

STIR FRY CHICKEN & PEPPERS

Serves 2   ① *Preparation 10 min, Cooking 8 min — Easy*

INGREDIENTS
3 red peppers
2 cm (1 inch) fresh ginger
2 chicken breasts, about 500 g (1 lb)
1 teaspoon cornflour
2 teaspoons soy sauce
3 tablespoons oil
1 tablespoon sugar
2 tablespoons water
2 teaspoons dry sherry

EQUIPMENT
Sharp knife
Chopping board
Set of measuring spoons
Cup
Frying-pan or wok
Wooden spoon or spatula
Slotted spoon
Plate

DEFROSTING
Make sure frozen chicken is completely thawed before use. This means leaving it in the fridge overnight, or out of the fridge, covered, for 6 hours.

METHOD
Chop the end off the peppers and cut out the core and seeds. Cut the pepper into rings. Peel the ginger and cut into tiny cubes. Cut the chicken into 2 cm (1 inch) cubes. Mix the cornflour and the soy sauce in the cup.

Put 1 tablespoon of the oil in the frying-pan on a moderate heat. Fry the peppers for about 1 minute. Add the water and fry for 2 minutes. Lift out with the slotted spoon and put on a plate.

Put the remaining oil in the pan and heat on a moderate heat. Add the chicken and ginger and stir-fry for 2 minutes. Add the sugar, sherry and soy and cornflour and stir. Bring to the boil, then turn down the heat till it is just boiling (simmering), stirring all the time. Add the peppers again and simmer for 1 minute.

ADDITIONS & ALTERNATIVES
Try using other boneless chicken pieces.

TIPS
You can buy prepared ginger in jars and bottles. It will keep for 6 weeks in the fridge or longer, just check on the pack.

CHINESE CHICKEN OMELETTE

Serves 2   ⓘ *Preparation 15 min, Cooking 15 min — Easy*

INGREDIENTS
1 boneless chicken breast
1 teaspoon dry sherry
$\frac{1}{2}$ teaspoon sugar
3 spring onions
2 tablespoons sunflower oil
$\frac{1}{2}$ cm ($\frac{1}{4}$ inch) slice fresh ginger
6 medium eggs
Salt and pepper

For the sauce
$\frac{1}{2}$ chicken stock cube
$\frac{1}{4}$ cup hot water

2 tablespoons oyster sauce
$\frac{1}{2}$ teaspoon sugar
$\frac{1}{2}$ teaspoon cornflour

EQUIPMENT
Sharp knife
Chopping board
2 bowls
Set of measuring spoons
Wok or frying-pan
Plate
Set of measuring cups
Wooden spatula
Spoon

DEFROSTING
Make sure frozen chicken is completely thawed before use. This means leaving it in the fridge overnight, or out of the fridge, for 6 hours.

METHOD
Cut the chicken into small cubes and put into the bowl with the sherry and sugar. Stir round and leave for 10 minutes.

Meanwhile, clean and prepare the spring onions. Cut the root end off, trim the leaves. Peel off and discard any dried up or slimy leaves. Chop into thin slices. Peel the ginger and cut into tiny cubes.

Put 1 tablespoon of oil in the wok and stir fry the chicken, ginger and spring onions till the chicken is cooked, which should take 2 or 3 minutes. Pour it out of the wok on to a plate.

Break the eggs into a bowl and pick out any bits of shell. Add a little salt and pepper and mix the eggs up with a fork.

Wipe the wok to clean off any bits of the previous mixture. Add the other tablespoon of oil. Heat the pan, then pour in the eggs and fry until the underside begins to firm up, then spread the chicken mixture on top. Lift up a corner of the omelette to allow the uncooked egg to run underneath. Cut the omelette into quarters with the spatula and flip each piece over and cook until golden brown. Lift out the bits on to a plate.

Mix all the sauce ingredients in the wok then heat until boiling, stirring all the time. Pour over the omelette.

ADDITIONS & ALTERNATIVES
Try using sake instead of dry sherry.
Use other boneless chicken pieces.

TIPS
You can buy prepared chopped ginger root in jars. It will keep for 6 weeks in the fridge.

SWEET CHICKEN WINGS

Serves 2   ① *Preparation 5 min, Cooking 40 min — Easy*

INGREDIENTS
500 g (1 lb) chicken wings
3 tablespoons oyster sauce
1 tablespoon soy sauce
1 teaspoon brown sugar
1 ½ cups water
1 chicken stock cube
2 cm (1 inch) piece fresh ginger
1 teaspoon sea salt
¼ teaspoon black pepper

EQUIPMENT
Saucepan with lid
Slotted spoon
Plate

Set of measuring spoons
Set of measuring cups
Wooden spoon or spatula
Sharp knife
Chopping board

METHOD

Put the chicken wings into a pan with enough cold water to cover them. Bring to the boil, then turn down the heat till it is just boiling (simmering). Put a lid on and cook for 10 minutes. Lift out with the slotted spoon and put on to a plate. Pour the hot water away.

Put the oyster sauce, soy sauce, sugar, water and stock cube in the pan and stir round. Put the chicken wings back into the pan. Bring to the boil, then turn down the heat till it is just boiling (simmering). Put a lid on and cook for 20 minutes.

Meanwhile, peel the ginger and cut into tiny cubes. Put the chicken on a serving plate and sprinkle the salt, pepper and ginger over the wings.

ADDITIONS & ALTERNATIVES

Serve with rice or noodles.
Try using sake instead of dry sherry.

TIPS

There are full instructions on cooking rice and noodles in the 'How to' chapter.

CHINESE CHICKEN & CASHEW NUTS

Serves 2 to 3 ① *Preparation 10 min, Cooking 15 min — Easy*

INGREDIENTS

2 boneless, skinless chicken breasts
2 teaspoons cornflour
1 teaspoon salt
$\frac{1}{2}$ teaspoon black pepper
2 tablespoons dry sherry
100 g can bamboo shoots
2 spring onions
1 green pepper
1 tablespoon water
9 tablespoons oil
100 g packet of cashew nuts
1 tablespoon soy sauce
1 teaspoon sugar

EQUIPMENT

Sharp knife
Chopping board
Bowl
Set of measuring spoons
Wooden spoon or spatula
Tin opener
Cup
Frying-pan or wok
Slotted spoon
2 plates
Paper kitchen towel

DEFROSTING

Make sure frozen chicken is completely thawed before use. This means leaving it in the fridge overnight, or out of the fridge, covered, for 6 hours.

METHOD

Get everything washed, chopped and ready before starting to cook.

Cut the chicken into 2 cm (1 inch) slices. Put 1 teaspoon of cornflour, salt, pepper and 1 tablespoon of sherry in the bowl. Add the chicken and stir round. Open the tin of bamboo shoots and drain.

Clean and prepare the spring onions. Cut the root end off, trim the leaves. Peel off and discard any dried up or slimy leaves. Chop into thin slices.

Chop the end off the green peppers and cut out the core and seeds. Cut the pepper into 1 cm ($\frac{1}{2}$ inch) strips. Mix 1 teaspoon of cornflour with the water in a cup.

Put 3 tablespoons of oil in the frying-pan on a moderate heat. Fry the chicken for about three minutes till it is golden, stirring to stop it sticking. Lift out with the slotted spoon and put on a plate.

Put 5 tablespoons of the oil in the pan and put in the cashew nuts. Stir fry for 1 minute. Lift out with the slotted spoon and put on paper kitchen towel on a plate.

Put 1 tablespoon of oil in the pan. Heat, then add the bamboo shoots, spring onion and green pepper and stir fry for 1 minute. Add the cornflour mixture, sherry, soy sauce and sugar. Stir fry for 1 minute till thick. Put the chicken back in the pan and stir round to cover with the sauce. Put on a serving plate and put the cashew nuts on top.

ADDITIONS & ALTERNATIVES

Serve with rice or noodles.
Use other boneless chicken pieces.
Try using rice wine instead of dry sherry.

TIPS

There are full instructions on cooking rice and noodles in the 'How to' chapter.

SPECIAL ROAST DUCK

Serves 6   ① *Preparation 20 min, Cooking 2 hrs 30 min — Easy*

INGREDIENTS
1.75 kg (4 lb) duck
4 tablespoons soy sauce
2 tablespoons honey
3 tablespoons dry sherry
1 tablespoon yellow bean paste
$\frac{1}{2}$ teaspoon ground ginger
$\frac{1}{2}$ teaspoon salt
6 spring onions
3 cloves garlic

EQUIPMENT
Paper kitchen towel
Set of measuring spoons
Bowl
Sharp knife
Chopping board
Wire rack
Ovenproof dish or roasting dish
Aluminium foil
Spoon

METHOD

Wash and clean duck and leave to drain. Throw away any bags of giblets you may find inside. Do check it is empty. Dry the duck with paper kitchen towel.

Mix the soy sauce, honey, dry sherry, yellow bean paste, ground ginger and salt in the bowl. Paint the outside of the duck with half the mixture. Dollop it on with a spoon and spread it over the duck with the back or the spoon. Leave for 15 minutes.

Clean and prepare the spring onions. Cut the root end off, trim the leaves. Peel off and discard any dried up or slimy leaves. Chop into thin slices. Peel the garlic, then chop it into tiny pieces. Mix the spring onions and garlic with the other half of the mixture. Put all of this inside the duck.

Put the duck on a wire rack on the roasting dish. Cover the top with aluminium foil and roast at 170°C, 325°F, Gas mark 3 for 2 hours. Take off the foil. Roast for a final 30 minutes, spooning the juices over the top every ten minutes. Serve sliced or in chunks.

ADDITIONS & ALTERNATIVES

Put out small bowls of hoisin sauce and plum sauce to dip the duck in.

Serve on a special occasion with Chinese pancakes, chopped spring onion and chopped cucumber. First, remove the crispy skin, and cut into 1 cm ($\frac{1}{2}$ inch) strips. Next, cut the meat off the bone and shred it with two forks. Serve the skin and meat on separate plates. Put a little hoisin sauce on a pancake, then duck, spring onions, cucumber and crispy skin. Roll up and eat.

TIPS

Prepared garlic is sold in tubes, jars and bottles. Just read the instructions for the suggested equivalent amount. Most keep for 6 weeks in the fridge, but the bottles keep longer.

There are full instructions on cooking rice and noodles in the 'How to' chapter.

CHINESE PORK & PEPPERS

Serves 2 ⊕ *Preparation 15 min, Cooking 5 min — Easy*

INGREDIENTS
2 green peppers
100 g (4 oz) pork fillet
6 tablespoons sunflower oil
1 teaspoon salt
3 tablespoons water
1 tablespoon soy sauce
1 teaspoon sugar
1 tablespoon dry sherry

EQUIPMENT
Sharp knife
Chopping board
Set of measuring spoons
Frying-pan or wok
Wooden spoon or spatula
Slotted spoon
Plate

METHOD
Chop the end off the peppers, split in half, and scrape out the seeds. Cut into ½ cm (¼ inch) strips.

Cut the pork into wafer thin slices. Put 2 tablespoons of the oil in the frying-pan on a moderate heat. Stir fry the pork for 2 minutes. Lift out with the slotted spoon and put on a plate.

Put the rest of the oil in the pan. Heat. Add the green peppers, salt and 3 tablespoons of water. Stir fry for 2 minute. Add the pork, soy sauce, sugar and sherry. Bring to the boil and cook for 30 seconds.

ADDITIONS & ALTERNATIVES

Serve with rice or noodles.

Try using sake instead of dry sherry.

Try adding $\frac{1}{2}$ teaspoon five spice powder with the pork.

TIPS

There are full instructions on cooking rice and noodles in the 'How to' chapter.

Don't overcook the pepper. It should be crisp.

STIR FRY PORK & BEANS

Serves 2   ① *Preparation 10 min, Cooking 10 min — Easy*

INGREDIENTS

250 g (8 oz) runner beans
250 g (8 oz) pork fillet
1 cm ($\frac{1}{2}$ inch) piece fresh ginger
4 tablespoons sunflower oil
1 teaspoon salt
3 tablespoons water
1 tablespoon soy sauce
1 teaspoon sugar
1 tablespoon dry sherry

EQUIPMENT

Sharp knife
Chopping board
Set of measuring spoons
Frying-pan or wok
Wooden spoon or spatula
Slotted spoon
Plate

METHOD

Wash the beans, chop the end off the beans. Cut into 2 cm (1 inch) strips.

Cut the pork into wafer thin slices. Peel the ginger and cut into tiny cubes.

Put 2 tablespoons of the oil in the frying-pan on a moderate heat. Stir fry the pork and ginger for 2 minutes. Lift out with the slotted spoon and put on a plate.

Put the rest of the oil in the pan. Heat. Add the green beans, salt and 3 tablespoons of water. Stir fry for 4 minutes. Add the pork, soy sauce, sugar and sherry. Bring to the boil and cook for 30 seconds.

ADDITIONS & ALTERNATIVES

Serve with rice or noodles.

Try using sake instead of dry sherry.

Use stick beans or mangetout instead of the runner beans.

TIPS

There are full instructions on cooking rice and noodles in the 'How to' chapter.

You can buy prepared ginger in jars and bottles. It will keep for 6 weeks in the fridge or longer, just check on the pack.

HOT CHINESE PORK & CUCUMBER

Serves 2   ⏱ *Preparation 10 min, Cooking 6 min — Easy*

INGREDIENTS
250 g (8 oz) pork fillet
2 tablespoons soy sauce
1 teaspoon cornflour
2 green peppers
$\frac{1}{2}$ cucumber
4 tablespoons oil
2 fresh chillies
2 teaspoons wine vinegar
1 teaspoon salt
1 teaspoon sugar
1 tablespoon sesame seed oil

EQUIPMENT
Sharp knife
Chopping board
Bowl
Set of measuring spoons
Wooden spoon or spatula
Frying-pan or wok
Slotted spoon

METHOD
Cut the pork into 1 cm ($\frac{1}{2}$ inch) chunks. Put in the bowl with the soy and cornflour. Mix around. Leave to stand for 10 minutes.

Chop the end off the green peppers and cut out the core and seeds. Cut the peppers into rings. Wash the cucumber and cut into 1 cm ($\frac{1}{2}$ inch) cubes.

Put the oil in the frying-pan on a moderate heat. Fry the whole chillies for 1 minute. Lift out with the slotted spoon and throw away. Put the pork in the pan and stir fry for 3 minutes. Add the vinegar, salt and sugar and stir fry for 30 seconds. Add the cucumber and green pepper. Stir fry for 1 minute. Stir in the sesame oil.

ADDITIONS & ALTERNATIVES
Serve with rice or noodles.

Try using sake instead of dry sherry.

TIPS
There are full instructions on cooking rice and noodles in the 'How to' chapter.

RED PORK ROAST

Serves 4 to 6 ① Preparation 10 min, Cooking 2 hrs 15 min — Easy

INGREDIENTS
1 kg (2 lb) belly pork
Water for boiling
2 teaspoons sugar
$\frac{1}{2}$ cup water
6 tablespoons soy sauce
240 g tin whole chestnuts
5 tablespoons dry sherry

EQUIPMENT
Sharp knife
Chopping board
Saucepan with lid
Kettle
Bowl
Set of measuring cups
Set of measuring spoons

Slotted spoon
Wooden spoon or spatula
Casserole with lid
Oven glove
Tin opener
Spoon

METHOD

Cut the pork into 4 cm (2 inch) pieces. Put in the saucepan. Cover with boiling water. Bring to the boil, then turn down the heat till it is just boiling (simmering). Put a lid on and cook for 15 minutes.

Mix the sugar, water and 4 tablespoons of the soy sauce in the bowl. Lift out the pork with the slotted spoon and put it in the bowl. Stir round. Put the pork pieces into the casserole and cook with the lid on for 1 hour in the oven at 150° C, 300° F, Gas mark 2. Stir it a couple of times.

Meanwhile, open the tin of chestnuts and drain. Add the chestnuts, sherry and soy sauce and put back in the oven for another hour. It should come out tender and red. Slice it and serve.

ADDITIONS & ALTERNATIVES

Serve with rice or noodles.
Try using rice wine instead of dry sherry.
Serve with a vegetable stir fry.

TIPS

There are full instructions on cooking rice and noodles in the 'How to' chapter.

Belly pork is like streaky bacon in a lump.

Most tinned chestnuts are vacuum packed and not only have no fluid to drain but have ring pull tops.

STIR FRY PORK & BEAN SPROUTS

Serves 2 to 3   ① *Preparation 10 min, Cooking 6 min — Easy*

INGREDIENTS
500 g (1 lb) pork fillet
1 teaspoon salt
½ teaspoon black pepper
2 tablespoons soy sauce
4 tablespoons sunflower oil
4 spring onions
250 g pack bean sprouts
1 teaspoon sugar
2 tablespoons dry sherry
2 tablespoons water

EQUIPMENT
Sharp knife
Chopping board
Set of measuring spoons
Bowl
Wooden spoon or spatula
Frying-pan or wok
Slotted spoon
Plate

METHOD
Cut the pork into ½ cm (¼ inch) slices. Cut the slices into 2 cm (1 inch) squares. Put the salt, pepper, 1 tablespoon of soy and 1 tablespoon of the oil in a bowl. Stir round. Add the pork and leave for 10 minutes.

Clean and prepare the spring onions. Cut the root end off, trim the leaves. Peel off and discard any dried up or slimy leaves. Chop into 2 cm (1 inch) pieces.

Wash the bean sprouts and drain.

Put the oil in the frying-pan on a high heat. Fry the pork for 2 minutes, stirring to stop it sticking. Lift out with the slotted spoon and put it on a plate. Put the bean sprouts and spring onions in the pan and stir fry for 1 minute. Add the remaining soy sauce and the sugar, sherry and water. Stir fry for 30 seconds. Put the pork back in the pan and stir fry for 1 minute.

ADDITIONS & ALTERNATIVES
Serve with rice or noodles.

Try using sake instead of dry sherry.

Use shredded white cabbage instead of the bean sprouts.

TIPS
There are full instructions on cooking rice and noodles in the 'How to' chapter.

PORK & BABY SWEETCORN

Serves 4   ℗ *Preparation 10 min, Cooking 6 min — Easy*

INGREDIENTS
500 g (1 lb) pork fillet
1 tablespoon dry sherry
1 tablespoon soy sauce
1 teaspoon cornflour
1 tablespoon sunflower oil
50 g (2 oz) mangetout peas
1 pack baby sweetcorn, about 400 g
200 g (8 oz) button mushrooms, about 20
1 teaspoon salt
2 teaspoons sugar

EQUIPMENT
Sharp knife
Chopping board
Set of measuring spoons
Bowl
Wooden spoon or spatula
Set of measuring cups
Frying-pan or wok

METHOD
Cut the pork into very thin slices. Put the sherry, soy sauce and the cornflour in the bowl. Add the pork and stir.

Wipe the mushrooms clean. Discard any nasty ones. Chop the end off the stalks.

Put the oil in the frying-pan on a moderate heat. Fry the pork for about three minutes, stirring to stop it sticking. Add the mangetout, baby corn, mushrooms and salt and stir fry for 2 minutes. Add the sugar and stir fry for 1 minute.

ADDITIONS & ALTERNATIVES
Serve with rice or noodles.

Try using rice wine instead of dry sherry.

Try fine or Kenyan beans instead of mangetout.

Use oyster mushrooms or Shitake mushrooms.

TIPS
There are full instructions on cooking rice and noodles in the 'How to' chapter.

STEWED PORK & BAMBOO SHOOTS

Serves 4   ⊕ *Preparation 15 min, Cooking 25 min — Easy*

INGREDIENTS
750 g (1½ lb) pork shoulder
4 spring onions
225 g can bamboo shoots
2 cm (1 inch) piece fresh ginger
2 cloves garlic
2 tablespoons sunflower oil
2 tablespoons soy sauce
2 tablespoons dry sherry
8 Shitake mushrooms
1 teaspoon salt
1 teaspoon sugar
1 cup water

EQUIPMENT
Sharp knife
Chopping board
Tin opener
Garlic crusher
Plate
Set of measuring spoons
Wooden spoon or spatula
Frying-pan with a lid or wok

METHOD
Cut the pork into 2 cm (1 inch) pieces. Clean and prepare the spring onions. Cut the root end off, trim the leaves. Peel off and discard any dried up or slimy leaves. Chop into thin slices. Peel the ginger and cut into tiny cubes. Open the tin of bamboo shoots and

drain. Peel and crush the garlic on to a plate. Wipe the mushrooms clean. Discard any nasty ones. Chop the end off the stalks.

Put the oil in the frying-pan on a moderate heat. Fry the ginger, garlic and spring onions for about 1 minute, stirring to stop it sticking. Add the pork and stir fry for 2 minutes. Add the soy and sherry and stir for 1 minute. Add the bamboo shoots and mushrooms. Stir fry for 30 seconds. Add the salt, sugar and water. Bring to the boil, then turn down the heat till it is just boiling (simmering). Put a lid on and cook for 20 minutes.

ADDITIONS & ALTERNATIVES

Serve with rice or noodles.

Try using sake instead of dry sherry.

Use button mushrooms or oyster mushrooms instead of Shitake.

TIPS

Prepared garlic is sold in tubes, jars and bottles. Just read the instructions for the suggested equivalent amount. Most keep for 6 weeks in the fridge, but the bottles keep longer.

You can buy prepared ginger in jars and bottles. It will keep for 6 weeks in the fridge or longer, just check on the pack.

There are full instructions on cooking rice and noodles in the 'How to' chapter.

CHINESE BEEF & BROCCOLI

Serves 4   ① *Preparation 5 min, Cooking 10 min — Easy*

INGREDIENTS
500 g (1 lb) rump steak
1 tablespoon soy sauce
1 tablespoon dry sherry
4 tablespoons sunflower oil
1 tablespoon cornflour
2 cloves garlic
2 cm (1 inch) piece fresh ginger
1 large head broccoli, about 500 g (1 lb)
2 teaspoons sugar
2 tablespoons oyster sauce

EQUIPMENT
Sharp knife
Chopping board
Set of measuring spoons
Bowl
Set of measuring cups
Plate
Frying-pan or wok
Wooden spoon or spatula

METHOD
Cut the beef into very thin slices across the grain, and then into strips about 4 cm (2 inch) long. Mix the soy sauce, sherry, 1 tablespoon of the oil and cornflour in the bowl. Put the beef in and stir round and leave for 10 minutes.

Peel the garlic then chop it into tiny pieces. Peel the ginger and cut into tiny cubes. Wash the broccoli and break into florets.

Put the oil in the frying-pan on a moderate heat. Fry the garlic and ginger for about two minutes, stirring to stop it sticking. Put the broccoli in the frying-pan with the sugar and oyster sauce. Stir fry for 3 minutes. Add the beef and stir fry until the colour changes for about 3 minutes.

ADDITIONS & ALTERNATIVES

Serve with rice or noodles.

Use a cauliflower or a pack of sprouting broccoli instead of the broccoli.

You can use soy sauce instead of the oyster sauce.

TIPS

Prepared garlic is sold in tubes, jars and bottles. Just read the instructions for the suggested equivalent amount. Most keep for 6 weeks in the fridge, but the bottles keep longer.

You can buy prepared ginger in jars and bottles. It will keep for 6 weeks in the fridge or longer, just check on the pack.

There are full instructions on cooking rice and noodles in the 'How to' chapter.

STIR FRY BEEF & ASPARAGUS

Serves 2 ⏲ *Preparation 10 min, Cooking 8 min — Easy*

INGREDIENTS
250 g ($\frac{1}{2}$ lb) sirloin steak
2 cloves garlic
1 tablespoon dry sherry
1 tablespoon soy sauce
$\frac{1}{2}$ teaspoon sugar
1 tablespoon black bean sauce
1 bunch fresh asparagus
1 teaspoon salt
4 tablespoons sunflower oil
1 cup water
1 stock cube
1 tablespoon cornflour

EQUIPMENT
Sharp knife
Chopping board
Garlic crusher
Bowl
Set of measuring spoons
Wooden spoon or spatula
Set of measuring cups
Saucepan
Slotted spoon
Plate
Frying-pan or wok
Cup

METHOD

Cut the steak into very thin slices. Peel and crush the garlic into the bowl. Add the sherry, soy sauce, sugar and black bean sauce. Mix round and put in the fridge for 15 minutes. Wash the asparagus. Cut about 2 cm (1 inch) off the white (non-pointed) end and discard. Chop the rest into 2 cm (1 inch) lengths.

Put at least three cups of water in the saucepan with 1 teaspoon of salt. Bring to the boil, then add the asparagus. Cook for 3 minutes. Lift out with the slotted spoon and put on a plate.

Put the oil in the frying-pan on a moderate heat. Add beef slices and marinade and stir fry for 2 minutes. Add cooked asparagus, 1 cup of water and stock cube. Stir for 1 minute.

Mix the cornflour with a little water in a cup and add to the pan, stir for 2 minutes till the sauce thickens.

ADDITIONS & ALTERNATIVES

Serve with rice or noodles.

Try using sake instead of dry sherry.

TIPS

If you don't have a garlic crusher just squash it with something suitable or chop it up small. Prepared garlic is sold in tubes, jars and bottles. Just read the instructions for the suggested equivalent amount. Most keep for 6 weeks in the fridge, but the bottles keep longer.

There are full instructions on cooking rice and noodles in the 'How to' chapter.

BEEF & CHINESE LEAVES

Serves 2   ⏱ *Preparation 20 min, Cooking 10 min — Easy*

INGREDIENTS

250 g ($\frac{1}{2}$ lb) sirloin steak
6 tablespoons sunflower oil
1 tablespoon dry sherry
2 tablespoons soy sauce
1 teaspoon sugar
1 clove garlic
$\frac{1}{2}$ cm ($\frac{1}{4}$ inch) fresh ginger
500 g (1 lb) Chinese cabbage leaves
$\frac{1}{4}$ cup water
$\frac{1}{2}$ chicken stock cube
Salt to taste

EQUIPMENT

Sharp knife
Chopping board
Set of measuring spoons
Bowl
Garlic crusher
Small bowl
Wooden spoon or spatula
Slotted spoon
Plate
Set of measuring cups
Frying-pan or wok

METHOD

Get everything washed, chopped and ready before starting to cook. Cut the steak into very thin slices and put into the bowl. Add 1 tablespoon of the oil and the sherry, soy sauce and sugar.

109

Mix round and put in the fridge for 15 minutes.

Peel and crush the garlic into the small bowl. Peel the ginger and cut into tiny cubes. Wash the Chinese cabbage and cut into 1 cm ($\frac{1}{2}$ inch) slices.

Put the remaining 5 tablespoons of oil in the frying-pan on a moderate heat. Stir fry the beef for one minute. Lift out with the slotted spoon and put on a plate.

Put the garlic and ginger in the pan. Stir fry for a minute. Add the shredded cabbage, water and stock cube. Bring to the boil, then turn down the heat till it is just boiling (simmering). Cook for 5 minutes. Add the beef. Stir together for 2 minutes.

ADDITIONS & ALTERNATIVES

Serve with rice or noodles. If Chinese leaves are not available use white cabbage or Savoy cabbage instead.

TIPS

There are full instructions on cooking rice and noodles in the 'How to' chapter.

If you don't have a garlic crusher just squash it with something suitable or chop it up small. Prepared garlic is sold in tubes, jars and bottles. Just read the instructions for the suggested equivalent amount. Most keep for 6 weeks in the fridge, but the bottles keep longer.

You can buy prepared ginger in jars and bottles. It will keep for 6 weeks in the fridge or longer, just check on the pack.

BEEF & ONION STIR FRY

Serves 2   ⏲ *Preparation 20 min, Cooking 15 min — Easy*

INGREDIENTS
250 g ($\frac{1}{2}$ lb) rump steak
1 tablespoon dry sherry
2 tablespoons soy sauce
$\frac{1}{2}$ teaspoon sugar
$\frac{1}{4}$ teaspoon ground ginger
2 onions
1 tablespoon cornflour
$\frac{1}{2}$ cup water
4 tablespoons sunflower oil
Salt to taste

EQUIPMENT
Sharp knife
Chopping board
Bowl
Set of measuring spoons
Wooden spoon or spatula
Cup
Frying-pan or wok
Slotted spoon
Plate
Set of measuring cups

METHOD
Cut the steak into very thin slices and put into the bowl. Add the sherry, soy sauce, sugar and ground ginger. Mix round and put in the fridge for 15 minutes.

Peel and cut the onions into 1 cm ($\frac{1}{2}$ inch) slices. Mix the cornflour and water together in the cup till smooth. Add the water slowly or it will go lumpy.

Put I tablespoon of the oil in the frying-pan on a moderate heat. Fry the onion for about two minutes, stirring to stop it sticking. Lift out with the slotted spoon and put on a plate. Add the rest of the oil. Stir fry the beef for three minutes. Add onion. Add the cornflour and water mixture. Cook for two minutes till sauce thickens.

ADDITIONS & ALTERNATIVES
Serve with rice or noodles.

Try sirloin steak instead of rump.

TIPS
There are full instructions on cooking rice and noodles in the 'How to' chapter.

Prepared garlic is sold in tubes and jars. Just read the tube or jar for the suggested equivalent amount. It keeps for 6 weeks in the fridge.

FRIED BANANA

Serves 6   ① *Preparation 8 min, Cooking 8 min — Easy*

INGREDIENTS
3 tablespoons yellow bean paste
3 tablespoons honey
3 tablespoons sesame seeds
6 ripe bananas
3 tablespoons sunflower oil

EQUIPMENT
Set of measuring spoons
Bowl

Baking sheet or ovenproof dish
Frying-pan or wok
Knife for spreading bean paste
Wooden spoon or spatula
Slotted spoon
Plate

METHOD

Mix the bean paste and the honey in a bowl. Put the sesame seeds on the baking sheet and put in an oven at 150°C, 300°F, Gas mark 2 for 5 minutes. Take out and let cool.

Peel the bananas. Put the oil in the frying-pan on a moderate heat. Fry the banana for about 4 minutes till it is golden. Spread the banana with bean paste and then turn over in the oil. Lift out with the slotted spoon and put on a plate. Sprinkle with sesame seeds.

ADDITIONS & ALTERNATIVES

Serve with cream, ice cream or yoghurt.

Try golden syrup instead of honey.

Try sprinkling with 1 tablespoon toasted flaked almonds.

ASIAN

TOFU WITH SHITAKE MUSHROOMS

Serves 4   ⏱ *Preparation 35 min, Cooking 10 min — Easy*

INGREDIENTS
400 g (12 oz) pack of tofu
1 cup water
16 Shitake mushrooms
2 teaspoons dry sherry
1 teaspoon sugar
2 teaspoons soy sauce
2 spring onions
2 tablespoons sunflower oil
1 cm ($\frac{1}{2}$ inch) piece fresh ginger
2 tablespoons oyster sauce
2 teaspoons cornflour

EQUIPMENT
Sharp knife
Chopping board
Bowl
Set of measuring cups
Set of measuring spoons
Slotted spoon

Saucepan
Frying-pan or wok
Cup or small bowl

METHOD

Tofu is quite fragile and will fall apart if handled too roughly. Cut the tofu into 2.5 cm (1 in) cubes. Put the tofu in a bowl and cover with boiling water. Leave for 30 minutes then lift it out with a slotted spoon.

Meanwhile, put 1 cup of water in the saucepan. Bring to the boil, then turn down the heat till it is just boiling (simmering). Put the mushrooms in and cook for 5 minutes. Take off the heat. Lift the mushrooms out and keep the liquid in the pan. Add the sherry, sugar and soy to the pan.

Clean and prepare the spring onions. Cut the root end off, trim the leaves. Peel off and discard any dried up or slimy leaves. Split them in half and chop into 2.5 cm (1 inch) pieces. Peel the ginger and cut into tiny cubes.

Put the oil in the frying-pan over a moderate heat. Stir fry the spring onion and ginger for 30 seconds, then add the mushrooms and stir fry for another minute. Pour the mushroom liquid, sherry and soy mixture from the pan into the wok. Bring to the boil, then slide in the tofu and simmer gently for 4 minutes. Mix the oyster sauce and cornflour and a little cold water till any lumps of flour have gone. Pour into the wok and gently stir it round. Simmer gently until the sauce goes thick which takes about a minute.

ADDITIONS & ALTERNATIVES

Serve with rice.

Try using sake instead of dry sherry. Try smoked tofu or agé instead of ordinary tofu. It's more tasty and falls apart less easily. Try buying tofu from a wholefood shop, you will be surprised at the difference.

Use sliced oyster mushrooms or button mushrooms instead.

TIPS

You can buy prepared chopped ginger root in jars. It will keep for 6 weeks in the fridge.

There are full instructions on cooking rice in the 'How to' chapter.

CHILLI OMELETTE

Serves 4   ① *Preparation 10 min, Cooking 10 min — Easy*

INGREDIENTS

6 medium eggs
1 teaspoon salt
$\frac{1}{2}$ teaspoon fresh ground black pepper
$\frac{1}{2}$ fresh red chilli
4 spring onions
2 tablespoons sunflower oil
1 clove garlic

EQUIPMENT

Bowl
Fork or whisk
Sharp knife
Chopping board
Set of measuring spoons
Frying-pan
Garlic crusher
Spoon
Slotted spoon
Spatula
Plate

METHOD

Break the eggs into a bowl and pick out any bits of shell. Mix the eggs, salt and pepper up with a fork or a whisk.

Chop the end off the chilli, split in half, and scrape out the seeds. Cut the chilli into tiny bits.

Clean and prepare the spring onions. Cut the root end off, trim the leaves. Peel off and discard any dried up or slimy leaves. Chop into thin slices.

Put the oil in the frying-pan on a moderate heat. Peel and crush the garlic into the frying-pan. Fry the onion, garlic and chilli for about three minutes till it is golden, stirring to stop it sticking. Lift them out with the slotted spoon and put them on a plate.

Heat the pan then pour in the eggs and fry until the underside begins to firm up, then spread the onion, chilli, and garlic on top. Lift up a corner of the omelette to allow the uncooked egg to run underneath. Cut the omelette into quarters with the spatula and flip each piece over and cook until golden brown. Lift out with the spatula and put on to a plate.

ADDITIONS & ALTERNATIVES

Serve as a starter or with salad.

Add a few chopped coriander leaves to the mixture before cooking.

TIPS

FRESH CHILLI — A WARNING! When you chop up the chillies be careful and avoid getting juice on your hands. If you touch your eyes, mouth or other sensitive areas, even an hour after chopping them they will smart and burn. So wash your hands or wear rubber gloves.

Prepared chilli is sold in tubes and jars. Just read the label for the suggested equivalent amount. It keeps for 6 weeks in the fridge.

If you don't have a garlic crusher just squash it with something suitable or chop it up small. Prepared garlic is sold in tubes, jars and bottles. Just read the instructions for the suggested equivalent amount. Most keep for 6 weeks in the fridge.

CORIANDER FISH

Serves 4   ① *Preparation 20 min, Cooking 15 min — Easy*

INGREDIENTS
750 g (1 $\frac{1}{2}$ lb) white fish (hake, cod, haddock)
2 medium onions
2 cloves garlic
2$\frac{1}{2}$ cm (1 in) piece fresh ginger
1 green chilli
1 bunch coriander
1 teaspoon ground cumin
Salt to taste
2 tablespoons sunflower oil
$\frac{3}{4}$ cup water

EQUIPMENT
Food processor or liquidizer (optional)
Sharp knife
Chopping board
Bowl
Garlic crusher
Set of measuring spoons
Frying-pan or wok
Wooden spoon
Set of measuring cups
Spoon

METHOD

Get everything washed, chopped and ready before starting to cook.

Cut the fish into 2 cm (1 inch) cubes. Peel the onions and slice one thinly. Chop the other into quarters and put in the bowl. Peel and crush the garlic into the bowl. Peel the ginger and cut into thin slices and put in the bowl. Chop the end off the chillies, split in half, and scrape out the seeds. Cut the chilli into thin strips. Wash, shake dry and chop the coriander. Add the cumin and salt. Either put the contents of the bowl in a food processor or liquidizer and grind till smooth, or chop up till very small.

Put the oil in the frying-pan on a moderate heat. Fry the sliced onion for about three minutes till it is golden, stirring to stop it sticking. Add the paste/chopped bits and stir fry for about 5 minutes. Add the water. Bring to the boil, then turn down the heat till it is just boiling (simmering). Add the fish and cook for 5 minutes.

ADDITIONS & ALTERNATIVES

Serve with rice.

TIPS

FRESH CHILLI — A WARNING! When you chop up the chillies be careful and avoid getting juice on your hands. If you touch your eyes, mouth or other sensitive areas, even an hour after chopping them they will smart and burn. So wash your hands or wear rubber gloves.

Prepared chilli is sold in tubes and jars. Just read the tube or jar for the suggested equivalent amount. It keeps for 6 weeks in the fridge.

If you don't have a garlic crusher just squash it with something suitable or chop it up small. Prepared garlic is sold in tubes, jars and bottles. Just read the instructions for the suggested equivalent amount. Most keep for 6 weeks in the fridge.

You can buy prepared chopped ginger root in jars. It will keep for 6 weeks in the fridge.

There are full instructions on cooking rice in the 'How to' chapter.

THAI FISH CURRY

Serves 4   ① *Preparation 10 min, Cooking 25 min — Easy*

INGREDIENTS
600 g pack white fish fillets (cod, hake, hoki or halibut)
2 tablespoons tamarind water
3 medium onions
6 cloves garlic
1 cm (½ inch) piece fresh ginger
1 red chilli
10 unsalted raw cashew nuts
1 tablespoon dried lemon grass
2 tablespoons sunflower oil
1 teaspoon turmeric
1 teaspoon salt
400 ml tin coconut milk

EQUIPMENT
Sharp knife
Chopping board
Set of measuring cups
Set of measuring spoons
Fork for mashing
Plastic bag
Slotted spoon
Garlic crusher

Frying-pan
Saucepan

METHOD

Sprinkle the fish with the tamarind water and set aside.

Peel and slice the onions and garlic very thinly. Peel the ginger and cut into tiny cubes. Chop the end off the chilli, split in half, and scrape out the seeds. Cut the chilli into tiny bits. Put the cashew nuts in the plastic bag and crush into tiny bits with something suitable. Put the ginger, chilli, cashew nuts and dried lemon grass into a bowl and mash up with the fork.

Put the oil in the saucepan on a moderate heat. Fry the onion and garlic for about two minutes till it is soft, stirring to stop it sticking. Add the mashed paste from the bowl and fry for 2 minutes. Add the turmeric, salt and coconut milk. Bring to the boil, stirring all the time, then turn down the heat till it is just boiling (simmering). Add the fish and simmer very gently for about 20 minutes, until the fish is tender.

ADDITIONS & ALTERNATIVES

Serve with rice.

TIPS

You can buy pots of tamarind extract, just add water. You can also buy blocks of it which need to be soaked for 10 minutes and then squeezed to get the juice out.

Prepared garlic is sold in tubes, jars and bottles. Just read the instructions for the suggested equivalent amount. Most keep for 6 weeks in the fridge, but the bottles keep longer.

You can buy prepared ginger in jars and bottles. It will keep for 6 weeks in the fridge or longer, just check on the pack.

There are full instructions on cooking rice in the 'How to' chapter.

MILD MALAY PRAWN CURRY

Serves 4   ⏲ *Preparation 10 min, Cooking 20 min — Easy*

INGREDIENTS
2 cm (1 inch) piece galangal (or ginger)
375 g (12 oz) white cabbage
2 medium onions
1 clove garlic
2 tablespoons sunflower oil
$\frac{1}{2}$ teaspoon powdered turmeric
2 teaspoons dried lemon grass
400 ml tin coconut milk
500 g (1 lb) medium cooked prawns

EQUIPMENT
Grater
Sharp knife
Chopping board
Garlic crusher
Deep frying-pan or wok
Large saucepan
Set of measuring spoons
Set of measuring cups
Wooden spoon

METHOD
Wash and grate the galangal. Rinse the cabbage and chop into 1 cm ($\frac{1}{2}$ inch) strips. Peel and chop the onions. Peel and crush the garlic into the pan.

Put the oil in the frying-pan on a moderate heat. Fry the onion and garlic for about three minutes till it is golden, stirring to stop it sticking. Add the turmeric, galangal and lemon grass and fry for about 3 minutes, stirring constantly. Add the coconut milk and

122

bring to the boil, then turn down the heat till it is just boiling (simmering). Put in the cabbage and prawns and simmer gently for about 6 minutes.

ADDITIONS & ALTERNATIVES

Serve with rice or noodles

Try serving with Universal Salsa (p. 333).

TIPS

If you don't have a garlic crusher just squash it with something suitable or chop it up small. Prepared garlic is sold in tubes, jars and bottles. Just read the instructions for the suggested equivalent amount. Most keep for 6 weeks in the fridge, but the bottles keep longer.

You can buy prepared ginger in jars and bottles. It will keep for 6 weeks in the fridge or longer, just check on the pack.

SQUID WITH SESAME SEEDS

Serves 4 ① *Preparation 40 min, Cooking 5 min* — *Moderate*

INGREDIENTS

16 small or 4 medium prepared squid

2 cm (1 inch) piece fresh ginger

½ cup dry sherry

1 tablespoon sugar

¼ cup soy sauce

1 teaspoon salt

2 tablespoons sunflower oil

Half cucumber

1 lime

1 tablespoon sesame seeds

EQUIPMENT
Sharp knife
Chopping board
Ovenproof dish or heatproof bowl
Set of measuring cups
Set of measuring spoons
Small saucepan
Frying-pan

METHOD
Throw the squid tentacles away. Cut the squid open and wash. Now would be a good time to check for the clear plastic-like quill. If it is there, take it out and throw away. Lay the squid flat and cut some diamond shapes on it without cutting right through. Put the squid in a heatproof bowl.

Peel the ginger and cut into tiny cubes. Put the ginger, sherry, sugar, soy sauce and salt in a pan and heat till it is about to boil. Pour over the squid and stir round. Leave the squid in the marinade for 30 minutes to get the flavour.

Meanwhile, cut the cucumber into thin sticks, and cut the lime into quarters.

Put the oil in a frying-pan over a moderate heat. Fish out the squid from the bowl and fry for about two minutes a side. Pour the marinade into the frying-pan and cook for another minute till it boils. Sprinkle the sesame seeds over the squid before serving.

ADDITIONS & ALTERNATIVES
Serve with the cucumber sticks and the lime, and rice or noodles.

Try serving with Universal Salsa (p. 333).

Use mirin or sweet rice wine instead of the sherry and sugar.

TIPS
There are full instructions on cooking rice and noodles in the 'How to' chapter.

Squid tubes are stocked by supermarkets and some fishmongers. Don't buy unprepared squid unless you like slimy things and know how to take the quill out. But check the prepared ones, as you chop them, for a strip of clear plastic-like stuff. If you find it, throw it away. It is the quill.

THAI SQUID

Serves 4 ⏲ *Preparation 15 min, Cooking 4 min — Moderate*

INGREDIENTS
16 prepared small squid about 500g (1 lb)
15 g pack or small bunch coriander
1 fresh red chilli
$\frac{1}{2}$ cm ($\frac{1}{4}$ inch) slice fresh ginger
2 cloves garlic
6 spring onions
2 tablespoons sunflower oil
1 tablespoon fish sauce
1 tablespoon dry sherry
1 tablespoon oyster sauce
Salt and pepper

EQUIPMENT
Sharp knife
Chopping board
Set of measuring spoons
Frying-pan or wok
Wooden spatula
Bowl or plate

METHOD
Pull the squid tentacles out (if there are any). Trim the tentacles off and throw the rest of the head away. Cut the squid open and

wash. Now would be a good time to check for the clear plastic-like quill. If it is there take it out and throw away. Cut into rings.

Wash and chop the coriander. Chop the end off the chilli, split in half, and scrape out the seeds. Cut the chilli into thin strips, then into tiny bits. Peel the ginger and cut into matchsticks. Cut the other way so you end up with tiny cubes. Peel the garlic then chop it into tiny pieces.

Clean and prepare the spring onions. Cut the root end off, trim the leaves. Peel off and discard any dried up or slimy leaves. Chop into thin slices.

Put the oil in the wok or frying-pan on a moderate heat. Stir fry the onion and garlic for about two minutes. Add the ginger and squid and stir fry over high heat for 90 seconds, until the squid go white. Add the fish sauce and sherry and stir. Add the chillies, oyster sauce, salt and pepper and spring onions. Stir fry for 1 minute. Put on a plate with the coriander.

ADDITIONS & ALTERNATIVES
Serve with rice or noodles.

Try serving with Universal Salsa (p. 333).

Try using sake instead of dry sherry.

Try using soy sauce instead of fish sauce.

TIPS
FRESH CHILLI — A WARNING! When you chop up the chillies be careful and avoid getting juice on your hands. If you touch your eyes, mouth or other sensitive areas, even an hour after chopping them, they will smart and burn. So wash your hands or wear rubber gloves.

Prepared chilli is sold in tubes and jars. Just read the label for the suggested equivalent amount. It keeps for 6 weeks in the fridge.

Prepared garlic is sold in tubes, jars and bottles. Just read the instructions for the suggested equivalent amount. Most keep for 6 weeks in the fridge, but the bottles keep longer.

You can buy prepared ginger in jars and bottles. It will keep for 6 weeks in the fridge or longer, just check on the pack.

Squid tubes are stocked by supermarkets and some fish-mongers. Don't buy unprepared squid unless you like slimy things and know how to take the quill out. But check the prepared ones, as you chop them for a strip of clear plastic-like stuff. If you find it, throw it away. It is the quill.

STIR FRY CHICKEN WITH BEAN SPROUTS

Serves 2 ⏲ *Preparation 25 min, Cooking 5 min — Easy*

INGREDIENTS
2 boneless chicken breasts, about 250 g (8 oz)
1 tablespoon dry sherry
1 teaspoon sugar
3 tablespoons sunflower oil
Salt to taste
4 spring onions
1 cm ($\frac{1}{2}$ inch) fresh ginger
150 g (5 oz) pack fresh bean sprouts
1 small carrot
2 tablespoons soy sauce

EQUIPMENT
Sharp knife
Chopping board
Set of measuring spoons
Bowl
Wooden spoon
Sieve or colander

Vegetable peeler
Frying-pan or wok
Slotted spoon
Plate

DEFROSTING

Make sure frozen chicken is completely thawed before use. This means leaving it in the fridge overnight, or out of the fridge, covered, for 6 hours.

METHOD

Cut the chicken into very thin slices. Put the sherry, sugar and 1 tablespoon of the sunflower oil and salt in the bowl. Stir round, add the chicken and leave in the fridge for 15 minutes.

Meanwhile, clean and prepare the spring onions. Cut the root end off, trim the leaves. Peel off and discard any dried up or slimy leaves. Chop into 2 cm (1 inch) lengths. Peel the ginger and cut into tiny cubes. Wash the bean sprouts and then drain in a sieve or colander. Peel and chop the carrot into matchsticks (like the ginger), cutting off both ends.

Put the other 2 tablespoons of oil in the wok. Add the chicken and stir-fry for 2 minutes. Fish out the chicken with the slotted spoon and put on the plate. Add the carrot and stir fry for 2 minutes. Add the spring onions, ginger and bean sprouts and stir round. Add the soy sauce and the chicken. Stir fry for 30 seconds, then serve.

ADDITIONS & ALTERNATIVES

Serve with rice or noodles.

Try using sake instead of dry sherry.

Use other boneless chicken pieces.

TIPS

You can buy prepared chopped ginger root in jars. It will keep for 6 weeks in the fridge.

There are full instructions on cooking rice and noodles in the 'How to' chapter.

JAPANESE CHICKEN & RICE

Serves 6 ⏱ *Preparation 40 min, Cooking about 15 to 20 min — Easy*

INGREDIENTS
500 g (1 lb) chicken boneless thighs
$\frac{1}{2}$ cup soy sauce
2 tablespoons dry sherry
$\frac{1}{4}$ cup sugar
8 Shitake mushrooms (fresh or dried)
2 $\frac{1}{2}$ cups rice
5 cups water
1 teaspoon salt
1 cup frozen peas

EQUIPMENT
Sharp knife
Chopping board
Wooden spoon
Set of measuring cups
Set of measuring spoons
Bowl
Saucepan with lid

DEFROSTING
Make sure frozen chicken is completely thawed before use. This means leaving it in the fridge overnight, or out of the fridge, covered, for 6 hours.

METHOD

Skin the chicken and cut it into thin strips. Put the chicken, soy sauce, sherry and sugar in a bowl. Stir round and leave for 30 minutes.

If you use dried mushrooms, they need to be soaked for 15 minutes in water, then drained. Cut the mushroom tops into fine slivers and throw away the stalks (they are tough).

Check the cooking time for the rice on the packet. Put the rice, water and salt in the saucepan. Stir once. Put the chicken, mushrooms and soy mixture on the rice, then scatter the frozen peas on top. Put the lid on the saucepan, then put it on a high heat till it boils, then reduce heat to very low until the rice and chicken are tender and the liquid has been absorbed which will be at least the cooking time given for the rice on the packet.

ADDITIONS & ALTERNATIVES

Serve with shredded spring onions. Clean and prepare the spring onions. Cut the root end off, trim the leaves. Peel off and discard any dried up or slimy leaves. Chop into thin slices.

TIPS

Make sure the saucepan lid fits well.

Don't keep looking at the rice as it cooks.

If you use Basmati rice the cooking time will be about 12–15 minutes. The best rice to use is Japanese short grained rice, but it is hard to find, and any white rice is good enough. The rice is meant to be a bit sticky.

COLD CHICKEN WITH TAHINI

Serves 4   ① *Preparation 15 min plus an hour to cool,*
Cooking 20 min — Moderate

INGREDIENTS
4 boneless chicken breasts (about 650 g or $1\frac{1}{4}$ lb)
$\frac{1}{2}$ cup dry sherry
$\frac{1}{2}$ teaspoon salt
3 tablespoons tahini
3 tablespoons soy sauce
1 teaspoon sugar
1 teaspoon wine vinegar

EQUIPMENT
Sharp knife
Chopping board
Plate with lip
Bamboo steamer
Saucepan
Set of measuring cups
Set of measuring spoons
Bowl

DEFROSTING
Make sure frozen chicken is completely thawed before use. This means leaving it in the fridge overnight, or out of the fridge, covered, for 6 hours.

METHOD
Make three or four cuts 1 cm ($\frac{1}{2}$ in) deep into the chicken through the skin. Put the chicken on the plate and the plate in the steamer. Put some water in the saucepan. Put the steamer on top of the saucepan. Pour the sherry and salt over the chicken. Bring the water to the boil, turn down the heat till it is just boiling

(simmering). Put the lid on the steamer and cook for 20 minutes.

Mix the tahini, soy, sugar and vinegar in the bowl.

Take the chicken from the steamer and leave for 15 minutes, then put in the fridge for 45 minutes.

Cut the chicken into thin slices. Serve with the sauce.

ADDITIONS & ALTERNATIVES

Serve with salad or rice.

Use peanut butter instead of tahini.

Use sake (rice wine) instead of the dry sherry.

TIPS

There are full instructions on cooking rice in the 'How to' chapter.

THAI CHICKEN WITH BASIL

Serves 4 ⏱ *Preparation 20 min, Cooking 10 min — Easy*

INGREDIENTS

500 g (1 lb) skinless and boneless chicken breasts
1 small bunch basil
4 spring onions
2 small red (bird's eye) chillies
3 tablespoons sunflower oil
2 tablespoons fish sauce
1 teaspoon sugar
$\frac{1}{2}$ teaspoon ground coriander

EQUIPMENT

Sharp knife
Chopping board
Set of measuring spoons
Frying-pan or wok
Slotted spoon or fish slice

Bowl
Wooden spatula

DEFROSTING

Make sure frozen chicken is completely thawed before use. This means leaving it in the fridge overnight, or out of the fridge, covered, for 6 hours.

METHOD

Get everything washed, chopped and ready before starting to cook. Cut the chicken into $\frac{1}{2}$ cm ($\frac{1}{4}$ inch cubes). Wash and chop the basil. Clean and prepare the spring onions. Cut the root end off, trim the leaves. Peel off and discard any dried up or slimy leaves. Chop into thin slices. Chop the end off the chillies, split in half, and scrape out the seeds. Cut the chilli into thin strips, then into tiny bits.

Heat the oil in the frying-pan and stir fry the chicken for 3 minutes. Lift the chicken out and put in a bowl. Put the chillies, spring onion and half the basil in the pan and stir fry for 1 minute, then add the fish sauce, sugar, coriander and chicken. Stir fry for another 2 minutes. Put on a plate and cover with the rest of the basil.

ADDITIONS & ALTERNATIVES

Serve with rice or noodles.

If you can't get the fish sauce, use 2 tablespoons of soy sauce.

TIPS

FRESH CHILLI — A WARNING! When you chop up the chillies be careful and avoid getting juice on your hands. If you touch your eyes, mouth or other sensitive areas, even an hour after chopping them, they will smart and burn. So wash your hands or wear rubber gloves.

Prepared chilli is sold in tubes and jars. Just read the label for the suggested equivalent amount. It keeps for 6 weeks in the fridge.

THAI PEANUT CHICKEN

Serves 4   ⏲ *Preparation 5 min, Cooking 1 hr 45 min — Easy*

INGREDIENTS
2 cloves garlic
2 teaspoons salt
$\frac{1}{2}$ teaspoon ground black pepper
1 kg ($2\frac{1}{4}$ lb) chicken pieces
400 ml tin coconut milk
1 tablespoon soy sauce
2 teaspoons sugar
$\frac{1}{4}$ cup peanut butter
1 tablespoon ground cumin
1 tablespoon ground coriander
$\frac{1}{2}$ teaspoon chilli powder
1 lime or 3 tablespoons lime juice

EQUIPMENT
Sharp knife
Chopping board
Garlic crusher
Bowl
Large saucepan with lid
Slotted spoon
Plate
Set of measuring spoons
Juicer (if using fresh lime)
Set of measuring cups

DEFROSTING
Make sure frozen chicken is completely thawed before use. This means leaving it in the fridge overnight, or out of the fridge, covered, for 6 hours.

134

METHOD

Peel and crush the garlic into the bowl. Add the salt, pepper and chicken and stir round.

Put the chicken in the saucepan and add the coconut milk. Bring to the boil, then turn down the heat till it is just boiling (simmering). Put a lid on and cook gently for 1 hour, stirring from time to time. Lift out the chicken with the slotted spoon and put on a plate.

Add the soy sauce, sugar, peanut butter, cumin, coriander and chilli to the pan. Bring to the boil, then turn down the heat till it is just boiling (simmering) for 10 minutes. Put the chicken in again and simmer for 15 minutes. Meanwhile, juice the lime. Add the juice to the pan and serve.

ADDITIONS & ALTERNATIVES

Serve with rice or noodles.

Use the rest of the coriander to make Universal Salsa (p. 333).

TIPS

Lime juice comes in bottles like lemon juice.

FRESH CHILLI — A WARNING! When you chop up the chillies be careful and avoid getting juice on your hands. If you touch your eyes, mouth or other sensitive areas, even an hour after chopping them, they will smart and burn. So wash your hands or wear rubber gloves.

Prepared chilli is sold in tubes and jars. Just read the label for the suggested equivalent amount. It keeps for 6 weeks in the fridge.

If you don't have a garlic crusher just squash it with something suitable or chop it up small. Prepared garlic is sold in tubes, jars and bottles. Just read the instructions for the suggested equivalent amount. Most keep for 6 weeks in the fridge, but the bottles keep longer.

There are full instructions on cooking rice and noodles in the 'How to' chapter.

THAI BARBECUE CHICKEN

Serves 4   ⏲ *Preparation 15 min, Cooking 10 min — Easy*
Think ahead. This needs to stand in the fridge for
2 hours before cooking.

INGREDIENTS
2 cloves garlic
1 cm (½ inch) fresh root ginger
2 teaspoons ground black pepper
1 small bunch fresh coriander
8 chicken thighs

For the sauce
1 tablespoon sugar
2 tablespoons soy sauce
2 tablespoons sunflower oil

EQUIPMENT
Sharp knife
Chopping board
Garlic crusher
Bowl
Set of measuring spoons
Wooden spoon
Cup
Brush or teaspoon
Barbecue

DEFROSTING
Make sure frozen chicken is completely thawed before use. This means leaving it in the fridge overnight, or out of the fridge, covered, for 6 hours.

METHOD

Peel and crush the garlic into the bowl. Peel the ginger and cut into tiny cubes. Wash, shake dry and chop the coriander into little bits. Put the ginger, coriander and pepper in the bowl. Stir round. Slash the chicken thighs. Put in the bowl, stir until coated, and put in the fridge for 2 hours. Mix the sugar, soy sauce and oil in the cup.

Cook the chicken on a barbecue. Brush the sauce on to the chicken as it cooks (or spoon it on). Turn the chicken over to cook evenly. It should take about 10 minutes.

ADDITIONS & ALTERNATIVES

Try grilling it if you don't have a barbecue.

Serve with salad or with other barbecue food.

Try other chicken pieces.

TIPS

It is easy to double up the amount and makes a change from sausages or burgers.

If you don't have a garlic crusher just squash it with something suitable or chop it up small. Prepared garlic is sold in tubes, jars and bottles. Just read the instructions for the suggested equivalent amount. Most keep for 6 weeks in the fridge, but the bottles keep longer.

You can buy prepared chopped ginger root in jars. It will keep for 6 weeks in the fridge.

FRIED VINEGAR CHICKEN

Serves 4   ① *Preparation 10 min, Cooking 40 min — Moderate*
Think ahead. This needs to stand in the fridge for
2 hours before cooking.

INGREDIENTS
2 cloves garlic
1 kg (2 lb) chicken pieces
2 teaspoons salt
1 teaspoon ground black pepper
2 bay leaves
¾ cup white wine vinegar
1 cup sunflower oil

EQUIPMENT
Sharp knife
Chopping board
Garlic crusher
Bowl
Wooden spoon or spatula
Set of measuring spoons
Saucepan with lid
Set of measuring cups
Frying-pan
Slotted spoon

METHOD
Peel and crush the garlic into the bowl. Stir the chicken with the
salt, pepper and garlic in the bowl. Put the bay leaves between the
chicken pieces and dribble the vinegar over the top. Leave for 2
hours in the fridge.

Put the chicken and vinegar in the saucepan. Bring to the boil,
then turn down the heat till it is just boiling (simmering). Put a lid

on and cook for 30 minutes or so until the chicken is tender; turning the chicken from time to time. Keep the chicken moist with a bit of water if the vinegar evaporates. This stops it sticking to the pan. Drain the chicken.

Put the oil into the frying-pan and heat until very hot. Carefully put the chicken pieces in the oil (it may spit if still wet) and fry until crispy. Lift out with a slotted spoon and drain.

ADDITIONS & ALTERNATIVES
Serve with salad and rice or noodles.

TIPS
There are full instructions on cooking rice and noodles in the 'How to' chapter.

If you don't have a garlic crusher just squash it with something suitable or chop it up small. Prepared garlic is sold in tubes, jars and bottles. Just read the instructions for the suggested equivalent amount. Most keep for 6 weeks in the fridge, but the bottles keep longer.

INDONESIAN LAMB

Serves 4   ① *Preparation 20 min, Cooking 2 hr — Easy*

INGREDIENTS

750 g (1½ lb) lean lamb steak
1 teaspoon pepper
4 tablespoons sunflower oil
1 fresh red chilli
2 large onions
4 cm (1½ inch) piece fresh ginger
6 cloves garlic
1 teaspoon salt
1 teaspoon powdered turmeric
2 teaspoons brown sugar
400 ml tin coconut milk
¼ bunch fresh coriander

EQUIPMENT

Sharp knife
Chopping board
Set of measuring spoons
Bowl
Wooden spatula
Saucepan with lid
Slotted spoon
Plate
Garlic crusher
Set of measuring cups

METHOD

Get everything washed, chopped and ready before starting to cook.
Cut the lamb into 1 cm (½ inch) cubes. Put the lamb and pepper in
the bowl and stir round. Put 2 tablespoons of oil in a large pan over a

moderate heat and stir fry the meat for about 5 minutes, until light brown. Lift out with the slotted spoon and put on a plate.

Chop the end off the chilli, split in half, and scrape out the seeds. Keep in large bits so you can fish them out at the end of the cooking. Peel and slice the onions thinly. Peel the ginger and cut into tiny cubes.

Peel and crush the garlic into the pan. Put 2 tablespoons of oil in the pan on a moderate heat. Fry the onion, ginger and garlic for about five minutes till it is golden, stirring to stop it sticking.

Add the salt, turmeric, sugar and stir fry for another minute. Add the chilli, lamb and the coconut milk. Bring to the boil, then turn down the heat till it is just boiling (simmering). Put a lid on and cook for $1\frac{1}{2}$ hours. Check the fluid level from time to time and top it up if needed with a little water.

Meanwhile, wash, shake dry and chop the coriander. Just before serving, stir in the coriander.

ADDITIONS & ALTERNATIVES
Serve with rice.

TIPS
FRESH CHILLI — A WARNING! When you chop up the chillies be careful and avoid getting juice on your hands. If you touch your eyes, mouth or other sensitive areas, even an hour after chopping them, they will smart and burn. So wash your hands or wear rubber gloves.

If you don't have a garlic crusher just squash it with something suitable or chop it up small. Prepared chilli and garlic are sold in tubes and jars. Just read the label for the suggested equivalent amount. It keeps for 6 weeks in the fridge.

You can buy prepared ginger in jars and bottles. It will keep for 6 weeks in the fridge or longer, just check on the pack.

There are full instructions on cooking rice and noodles in the 'How to' chapter.

AFGHAN SPICY LAMB CAKES

Serves 4 (3 each) ① *Preparation 15 min, Cooking 30 min — Easy*

INGREDIENTS
350 g (12 oz) lean minced lamb
3 medium potatoes
1 onion
15 g packet fresh parsley
15 g packet fresh coriander
6 eggs
$\frac{1}{2}$ teaspoon ground cumin
3 tablespoons plain flour
$\frac{1}{2}$ teaspoon salt
1 teaspoon freshly ground black pepper
2 tablespoons sunflower oil

EQUIPMENT
Vegetable peeler
Sharp knife
Chopping board
Grater
Bowl
Small bowl or cup
Fork
Set of measuring spoons
Frying-pan
Wooden spoon or spatula
Ovenproof dish

DEFROSTING
Make sure frozen lamb is completely thawed before use.

METHOD

Peel the potatoes, cutting away any nasty bits, and cutting out any eyes. Chop the potatoes into quarters. Peel the onion. Wash, shake dry and finely chop the parsley and coriander. Grate the potato and onion into the bowl. Break the eggs one at a time into the cup and pick out any bits of shell. Add the eggs to the potato and onion and mix with a fork. Add the lamb, parsley, coriander, cumin powder, flour, salt and pepper and stir round.

Put the oil in the frying-pan and heat over a moderate heat. Divide the mixture up into 12 mini burgers, of about three tablespoons each. They will be too runny to squash in your hands. Just drop the mixture in the pan using the back of the spoon to shape them. Fry them for about 5 minutes each side till golden brown, shaking the pan to stop them sticking. Cook a few at a time. Keep the cooked ones warm in the oven at 140°C, 275°F, Gas mark 1 in an ovenproof dish.

ADDITIONS & ALTERNATIVES

Serve with rice or salad.

TIPS

There are full instructions on cooking rice in the 'How to' chapter.

KOREAN CHILLI BEEF SOUP

Serves 4   ① *Preparation 10 min, Cooking 2 hrs 10 min — Easy*

INGREDIENTS

500 g (1 lb) braising beef
8 cups (2 litres) water
12 spring onions
2 teaspoons chilli powder
2 tablespoons sesame oil
2 cloves garlic
1 tablespoon tahini
1 teaspoon sugar
$\frac{1}{2}$ teaspoon white pepper
2 tablespoons dark soy sauce

EQUIPMENT

Sharp knife
Chopping board
Set of measuring cups
Saucepan with lid
Slotted spoon
Bowl
Set of measuring spoons
Frying-pan
Wooden spoon
Garlic crusher

METHOD

Cut the beef into 1 cm ($\frac{1}{2}$ inch) cubes. Put the beef and water in the saucepan. Bring to the boil, then turn down the heat till it is just boiling (simmering). Put a lid on and cook for 2 hours until the meat is falling apart. Check that it doesn't boil dry. When the beef is cooked, lift it out of the pan with a slotted spoon and put

144

in a bowl. Do not throw away the fluid from the saucepan.

Meanwhile, clean and prepare the spring onions. Cut the root end off, trim the leaves. Peel off and discard any dried up or slimy leaves. Chop into thin slices.

Put the chilli powder and the sesame oil in the frying-pan over a moderate heat. Peel and crush the garlic into the pan. Add the spring onions and fry for 2 minutes. Add the tahini, sugar, pepper and soy sauce and fry for another 2 minutes. Add the meat and stir in the pan for 2 minutes. Put the contents of the frying-pan back in the saucepan, bring to the boil, then turn down the heat till it is just boiling (simmering). Stir and cook for 5 minutes.

ADDITIONS & ALTERNATIVES

Use peanut butter instead of tahini.

Use fresh chilli instead of chilli powder.

TIPS

If you don't have a garlic crusher just squash it with something suitable or chop it up small. Prepared garlic is sold in tubes, jars and bottles. Just read the instructions for the suggested equivalent amount. Most keep for 6 weeks in the fridge, but the bottles keep longer.

This is a good winter soup. It gets very cold in Korea (you must have seen MASH).

Prepared chilli is sold in tubes and jars. Just read the label for the suggested equivalent amount. It keeps for 6 weeks in the fridge.

SHREDDED STEAK WITH TAHINI

Serves 4   ① *Preparation 20 min, Cooking 3 min — Easy*
Think ahead. This needs to stand in the fridge for
3 hours before cooking.

INGREDIENTS
750 g (1½ lb) rump steak
2 cloves garlic
3 spring onions
1 cm (½ inch) fresh root ginger
1 tablespoon sugar
2 tablespoons tahini
1 tablespoon sesame oil
½ cup soy sauce
½ cup water
½ teaspoon fresh ground black pepper

For the sauce
1 spring onion
1 clove garlic
1 tablespoon dry sherry
¼ cup soy sauce
1 teaspoon chilli sauce

EQUIPMENT
Sharp knife
Chopping board
Garlic crusher
Bowl
Set of measuring spoons
Set of measuring cups
Small bowl

146

Wooden spoon
Griddle pan or frying-pan

METHOD

You want to cut the beef into very thin strips about 1 cm ($\frac{1}{2}$ inch) wide.

Peel and crush the garlic into the bowl. Clean and prepare the spring onions. Cut the root end off, trim the leaves. Peel off and discard any dried up or slimy leaves. Chop into thin slices. Peel the ginger and cut into tiny cubes. Put the spring onions and ginger in the bowl. Add the sugar, tahini, sesame oil, soy sauce, water and pepper. Add the steak, cover and put in the fridge for at least 3 hours.

Make the sauce. Clean and finely slice the spring onions. Peel and crush the garlic. Put these in a bowl with the sherry, soy sauce and chilli sauce. Put in the fridge.

Cook the steak for a very short time on either a hot griddle or a hot, heavy frying-pan. Dip the cooked steak in the sauce.

ADDITIONS & ALTERNATIVES

Serve with rice.

Try lamb or pork fillet instead of the beef.

Try cooking this for a barbecue. Put some foil on the grill, and everyone cook their own bits.

TIPS

The meat needs to be good quality because you are cooking it for such a short time.

If you don't have a garlic crusher just squash it with something suitable or chop it up small. Prepared garlic is sold in tubes, jars and bottles. Just read the instructions for the suggested equivalent amount. Most keep for 6 weeks in the fridge.

You can buy prepared chopped ginger root in jars. It will keep for 6 weeks in the fridge.

There are full instructions on cooking rice in the 'How to' chapter.

CRISPY BEEF & VEGETABLES

Serves 4   ⏱ *Preparation 20 min, Cooking 10 min — Easy*
Think ahead. Needs to stand for 2 hours.

INGREDIENTS
500 g (1 lb) rump steak
2 cloves garlic
1 cm ($\frac{1}{2}$ inch) fresh ginger
1 tablespoon dry sherry
1 teaspoon sugar
$\frac{1}{4}$ cup soy sauce
4 spring onions
1 medium carrot
1 fresh red chilli
1 medium green pepper
4–6 sticks young celery, about 250 g (8 oz)
4 tablespoons vegetable oil
2 teaspoons sesame oil

EQUIPMENT
Sharp knife
Chopping board
Bowl
Wooden spoon
Garlic crusher
Set of measuring cups
Set of measuring spoons
Frying-pan or wok

148

METHOD

There's quite a lot of chopping in this so take your time, and make sure your knife is sharp.

Cut the beef into very thin slices, then cut across the slices into matchsticks. Put in a bowl. Peel and crush the garlic into the bowl. Peel the ginger and cut into tiny cubes. Add the ginger to the bowl with the sherry, sugar and soy sauce. Mix together then put in the fridge for 2 hours.

Meanwhile, clean the vegetables and cut into fine strips. Clean and prepare the spring onions. Cut the root end off, trim the leaves. Peel off and discard any dried up or slimy leaves. Chop into thin slices lengthways, then into 2 cm (1 inch) lengths. Peel and chop the carrot, cutting off both ends. Cut the tops off the chilli and the green pepper and throw away the seeds. Trim the celery and cut into thick matchsticks.

Heat 2 tablespoons of the oil in the frying-pan over a medium heat. Stir fry the chilli for 1 minute. Add the other vegetables and stir fry for 2 minutes. Fish them all out and put on a plate. Add the rest of the oil to the pan and turn the heat up. Stir fry the meat until it is crispy at the edges, about 3 to 5 minutes. Add the cooked vegetables and stir fry for 30 seconds.

ADDITIONS & ALTERNATIVES

Serve with rice or noodles.

Try using sake instead of dry sherry.

TIPS

FRESH CHILLI — A WARNING! When you chop up the chillies be careful and avoid getting juice on your hands. If you touch your eyes, mouth or other sensitive areas, even an hour after chopping them, they will smart and burn. So wash your hands or wear rubber gloves.

Prepared chilli and prepared garlic are sold in tubes and jars.

Just read the label for the suggested equivalent amount. It keeps for 6 weeks in the fridge.

You can buy prepared chopped ginger root in jars. It will keep for 6 weeks in the fridge.

ORIENTAL BEEF STEW

Serves 4   ① *Preparation 20 min, Cooking 3 hours — Easy*

INGREDIENTS
1 kg (2 lb) shin beef, or other cheap cut
About 8 cups water
2 medium onions
10 cloves garlic
5 cm (2 inch) piece fresh ginger
3 whole star anise
2 tablespoons sunflower oil
2 teaspoons Szechuan peppercorns
2 teaspoons fresh ground black pepper
$\frac{3}{4}$ cup soy sauce
$\frac{1}{4}$ cup dry sherry
3 tablespoons hoisin sauce

EQUIPMENT
Sharp knife
Chopping board
Saucepan with lid
Set of measuring spoons
Set of measuring cups
Frying-pan or wok
Wooden spoon

150

METHOD

Cut the meat into 5 cm (2 in) cubes. Put them in a pan with enough water to cover them. Peel and chop the onions into quarters. Peel 4 cloves of garlic. Peel the ginger and cut into thin slices. Add them to the pan with the star anise and bring to the boil. Skim the brown froth off. Turn down the heat till it is just boiling (simmering). Put a lid on and cook for 2 hours.

Peel and chop the other 6 cloves of garlic. Put the oil in the frying-pan with the Szechuan peppercorns, the black pepper and the garlic and stir fry for 1 minute over a medium heat. Add the soy sauce, the dry sherry and the hoisin sauce and stir fry for a minute. Add this lot to the beef then simmer for another hour.

Take out the star anise.

ADDITIONS & ALTERNATIVES

Serve with rice.

Try using sake instead of dry sherry.

Try using braising or stewing steak.

Use black peppercorns instead of Szechuan.

TIPS

This beef stew needs to cook for an age because the meat is a cheap cut and would be tough otherwise.

You can find Szechuan peppercorns and star anise with other herbs and spices and hoisin sauce will be with the rice, noodles or stir fry things in the supermarket.

Prepared garlic is sold in tubes, jars and bottles. Just read the instructions for the suggested equivalent amount. Most keep for 6 weeks in the fridge.

You can buy prepared chopped ginger root in jars. It will keep for 6 weeks in the fridge.

There are full instructions on cooking rice in the 'How to' chapter.

PACIFIC BEEF & TOMATOES

Serves 4   ⏲ *Preparation 15 min, Cooking 50 min — Easy*

INGREDIENTS
750 g (1½ lb) braising beef
2 large onions
5 cloves garlic
½ cm (¼ inch) fresh ginger
400 g tin tomatoes
2 tablespoons butter
3 cups water
2 tablespoons soy sauce
Salt and ground black pepper

EQUIPMENT
Sharp knife
Chopping board
Tin opener
Set of measuring spoons
Saucepan with lid
Slotted spoon
Wooden spoon
Bowl
Set of measuring cups

METHOD
Cut the beef into 1 cm (½ inch) cubes. Peel and slice the onion. Peel and slice the garlic. Peel the ginger and cut into thin slices. Stack the slices up then cut into matchsticks.

Put the butter in the saucepan on a moderate heat. Fry the onion, garlic and ginger for about three minutes till it is golden, stirring to stop it sticking. Take the onions, garlic and ginger out with a slotted spoon. Fry the beef to seal it, until it turns brown.

152

Open the tin of tomatoes. Pour the juice into the frying-pan with the meat. Use the wooden spoon to mash the tomatoes while they are still in the can. Pour the mashed tomatoes into the pan. Add the onions, garlic and ginger. Bring to the boil, then turn down the heat till it is just boiling (simmering). Cook until the tomato begins to soften. Add the water, soy sauce, salt and pepper and bring to the boil, then reduce the heat till it is just boiling (simmering) for about 40 minutes until the meat is very tender. Check the water level from time to time and top it up if needed.

ADDITIONS & ALTERNATIVES
Serve with rice or noodles.

Add $\frac{1}{2}$ teaspoon chilli powder.

TIPS
There are full instructions on cooking rice and noodles in the 'How to' chapter.

If you don't have a garlic crusher just squash it with something suitable or chop it up small. Prepared garlic is sold in tubes, jars and bottles. Just read the instructions for the suggested equivalent amount. Most keep for 6 weeks in the fridge, but the bottles keep longer.

You can buy prepared ginger in jars and bottles. It will keep for 6 weeks in the fridge or longer, just check on the pack.

BEEF SATAY

Serves 4 ⏲ *Preparation 20 min, Cooking 10 min — Easy*
Think ahead. This needs to stand in the fridge for
3 hours before cooking.

INGREDIENTS

1 medium onion
1 clove garlic
1 cm (½ inch) fresh root ginger
2 teaspoons ground coriander
1 teaspoon ground cumin
1 teaspoon chilli powder
1 teaspoon powdered lemon grass
3 tablespoons soy sauce
1 tablespoon sugar
2 tablespoons sunflower oil
500 g (1 lb) rump steak
200 g jar satay sauce

EQUIPMENT

Food processor or liquidizer (optional)
Sharp knife
Chopping board
Garlic crusher
Set of measuring spoons
Bowl
16 bamboo skewers
Saucepan
Wooden spoon

METHOD

You can use a food processor or liquidizer to prepare the onion,
garlic and ginger, or just chop it up small.

Peel and chop the onion very fine. Peel and crush the garlic into the bowl. Peel the ginger and cut into tiny cubes. Put the onion, garlic, ginger, coriander, cumin, chilli powder, lemon grass, soy sauce, sugar and oil into the bowl and stir round.

Cut the beef into 1 cm ($\frac{1}{2}$ inch) cubes. Put these in the bowl, stir round and put in the fridge for 3 hours.

Put the bamboo skewers in a sink full of water for at least half an hour. It helps them go through the meat without splintering. Push several cubes of meat on to each skewer and grill for about 10 minutes.

Heat the satay sauce in the saucepan, following the instructions on the jar.

Serve hot with the sauce as a dip, and with a plate of cubed cucumber.

ADDITIONS & ALTERNATIVES

Serve with rice or noodles and 1 cm ($\frac{1}{2}$ inch) cucumber cubes and chopped spring onions.

TIPS

Satay sauce also comes in packets. If you don't have a garlic crusher just squash it with something suitable or chop it up small. Prepared garlic is sold in tubes, jars and bottles. Just read the instructions for the suggested equivalent amount. Most keep for 6 weeks in the fridge.

You can buy prepared chopped ginger root in jars. It will keep for 6 weeks in the fridge.

There are full instructions on cooking rice and noodles in the 'How to' chapter.

INDONESIAN BEEF

Serves 4 ⓘ *Preparation 20 min, Cooking 2 hr — Moderate*

INGREDIENTS
8 small new potatoes
3 large onions
6 cloves garlic
2 cm (1 inch) piece fresh ginger
1 tablespoon dried lemon grass
2 fresh red chillies
15 unsalted raw cashew nuts
750 g (1 ½ lb) braising steak
3 tablespoons sunflower oil
½ teaspoon powdered turmeric
2 teaspoons ground coriander
2 teaspoons ground cumin
400 ml tin coconut milk
1 teaspoon salt

EQUIPMENT
Food processor or liquidizer (optional)
Sharp knife
Chopping board
Bowl
Plastic bag
Set of measuring spoons
Saucepan with lid
Slotted spoon
Wooden spoon
Plate
Set of measuring cups

METHOD

Get everything except the potatoes washed, chopped and ready before starting to cook. You can use a food processor or liquidizer to prepare the onion, garlic and ginger, or just chop it up small. So either peel and roughly chop the onion, garlic and ginger and put in the food processor with the dried lemon grass or chop till really tiny and mash up together in the bowl.

Chop the end off the chillies, split in half, and scrape out the seeds. Put the cashew nuts in the plastic bag and crush into tiny bits with something suitable. Cut the beef into 2 cm (1 inch) slices.

Put the oil in the saucepan and fry the meat for about 5 minutes until evenly coloured. Lift out with the slotted spoon and put on a plate.

Fry the onion mush for 5 minutes, stirring. Add the turmeric, coriander and cumin and fry for 1 minute. Add the coconut milk. Bring to the boil, stirring from time to time, then turn down the heat till it is just boiling (simmering). Put the lid on and cook for 5 minutes. Add the meat, the crushed cashews and salt and cook for 1 hour. Check the fluid level from time to time and top it up with water if needed.

Meanwhile, scrub or peel the potatoes. Add to the pan and cook for another half hour.

ADDITIONS & ALTERNATIVES
Serve with rice.

TIPS
FRESH CHILLI — A WARNING! When you chop up the chillies be careful and avoid getting juice on your hands. If you touch your eyes, mouth or other sensitive areas, even an hour after chopping them, they will smart and burn. So wash your hands or wear rubber gloves.

If you don't have a garlic crusher just squash it with something suitable or chop it up small. Prepared chilli and garlic is sold in tubes and jars. Just read the label for the suggested equivalent amount. It keeps for 6 weeks in the fridge.

You can buy prepared ginger in jars and bottles. It will keep for 6 weeks in the fridge or longer, just check on the pack.

There are full instructions on cooking rice and noodles in the 'How to' chapter.

INDIAN

HOT BOMBAY POTATO

Serves 4　　　　ⓘ *Preparation 20 min, Cooking 40 min — Easy*

INGREDIENTS
12 medium potatoes, about 750 g ($1\frac{1}{2}$ lb)
1 teaspoon salt
2 green chillies
3 large onions
2 teaspoons cumin seed
$\frac{1}{2}$ × 250 g packet butter

EQUIPMENT
Vegetable peeler
Saucepan
Sharp knife
Chopping board
Set of measuring spoons
Frying-pan
Wooden spoon

METHOD
Peel the potatoes, cutting away any nasty bits, and cutting out any eyes. Chop the potatoes into quarters. Boil the potatoes in the saucepan with a teaspoon of salt for about 20 minutes. Take out

when done and cut into 1 cm ($\frac{1}{2}$ inch) cubes.

Meanwhile, chop the end off the chillies, split in half, and scrape out the seeds. Cut the chilli into tiny bits. Peel and chop the onion into $\frac{1}{2}$ cm ($\frac{1}{4}$ inch) slices.

Put the butter in the frying-pan and heat over a moderate heat. Fry the onion and cumin seed for about 3 minutes till it is golden, stirring to stop it sticking. Add the potatoes, salt and chillies. Stir gently for 3 minutes and serve.

ADDITIONS & ALTERNATIVES
Serve with rice and other curries.

TIPS
Potatoes are cooked when a fork will go into them without pushing hard. If you push too hard they will fall apart.

FRESH CHILLI — A WARNING! When you chop up the chillies be careful and avoid getting juice on your hands. If you touch your eyes, mouth or other sensitive areas, even an hour after chopping them, they will smart and burn. So wash your hands or wear rubber gloves.

Prepared chilli is sold in tubes and jars. Just read the label for the suggested equivalent amount. It keeps for 6 weeks in the fridge.

Prepared garlic is sold in tubes and jars. Just read the label for the suggested equivalent amount. It keeps for 6 weeks in the fridge.

You can buy prepared chopped ginger root in jars. It will keep for 6 weeks in the fridge.

MUNG DAHL

Serves 4 　　　*① Preparation 5 min, Cooking 40 min — Easy*

INGREDIENTS
250 g pack yellow split peas
1 teaspoon salt
$\frac{1}{2}$ teaspoon turmeric
$\frac{1}{2}$ teaspoon chilli powder
2 cups water
2 medium onions
2 cm (1 inch) root ginger
2 tablespoons sunflower oil
1 teaspoon garam masala

EQUIPMENT
Sieve
Saucepan
Set of measuring spoons
Set of measuring cups
Sharp knife
Chopping board
Frying-pan
Wooden spoon or spatula

METHOD
Put the split peas in the sieve and wash thoroughly. Pick over them to see there are no small stones. Put the split peas in the saucepan with the salt, turmeric, chilli powder and water. Bring to the boil, then turn down the heat till it is just boiling (simmering). Cook for 30 minutes. Add a little more water if it gets dry. It should end up smooth not watery.

Meanwhile, peel and chop the onion into thin slices. Peel the ginger and cut into tiny cubes.

Put the oil in the frying-pan and heat over a moderate heat. Fry the onion for about 5 minutes till it is brown, stirring to stop it sticking.

Add the onion to the split peas and stir round for 2 minutes. Stir in the garam masala.

ADDITIONS & ALTERNATIVES

Serve with rice and pickle on its own or with other curries.

Keep half the cooked onion to put on top before serving.

Peel and finely slice 3 or 4 cloves of garlic and cook them with the onions.

INDIAN POTATO & PEAS

Serves 4   ① *Preparation 20 min, Cooking 45 min — Easy*

INGREDIENTS
8 medium potatoes, about 500 g (1 lb)
6 large onions
3 cloves garlic
4 cm (2 inch) piece fresh ginger
½ cup sunflower oil
400 g tin tomatoes
1 teaspoon salt
1 teaspoon chilli powder
2 tablespoons garam masala
1 teaspoon turmeric
2 cups of water
250 g pack frozen peas

EQUIPMENT
Sharp knife
Chopping board

Bowl
Large saucepan with lid
Wooden spoon or spatula
Tin opener
Set of measuring spoons
Set of measuring cups

METHOD

Peel the potatoes, cutting away any nasty bits, and cutting out any eyes. Chop the potatoes into 1 cm ($\frac{1}{2}$ inch) cubes. Peel and chop the onion into small bits. Put in the bowl. Peel the garlic then chop it into tiny pieces. Put it in the bowl. Peel the ginger and cut into tiny cubes.

Put the oil in the saucepan over a moderate heat. Fry the onion, garlic and ginger for about 5 minutes till brown, stirring to stop it sticking.

Open the tin of tomatoes. Pour the juice into the pan. Use the wooden spoon to mash the tomatoes while they are still in the can. Pour the mashed tomatoes into the pan. Continue to cook, stirring as the mixture boils. Add the salt, chilli powder, garam masala and turmeric and stir round. Add the potatoes and stir over a medium heat for 5 minutes. Add the water. Bring to the boil, then turn down the heat till it is just boiling (simmering). Put a lid on and cook for 10 minutes. Add the frozen peas and simmer for another 10 minutes.

ADDITIONS & ALTERNATIVES

Serve with rice and pickles.

TIPS

There are full instructions on cooking rice in the 'How to' chapter.

COCONUT RICE

Serves 4   ① *Preparation 5 min, Cooking 22 min — Easy*

INGREDIENTS
3 cups long grain rice
2 × 400 ml tins coconut milk
3 cups water
1 teaspoon salt
1 large onion
3 tablespoons sunflower oil
$\frac{1}{2}$ cup raisins
100 g packet flaked almonds

EQUIPMENT
Set of measuring cups
Tin opener
Saucepan with lid
Sharp knife
Chopping board
Set of measuring spoons
Frying-pan
Wooden spoon or spatula
Slotted spoon
Plate

METHOD
Read the packet to get the correct cooking time for the rice. Open the tins of coconut milk. Put the rice, coconut milk, water and salt in the saucepan. Bring to the boil, stirring once, to stop the rice sticking. Turn the heat down to low. Put the lid on the pan and simmer for the time given on the packet, until the fluid is absorbed (10–15 minutes for long grain or Basmati rice). Do not stir and do not keep looking ... have faith! After the cooking time,

164

take it off the heat and let it stand for a couple of minutes. Fluff it up with a fork to separate the grains and serve.

Meanwhile, peel and chop the onion into thin slices. Put the oil in the frying-pan and heat over a moderate heat. Fry the onion for about 3 minutes till it is golden, stirring to stop it sticking. Lift out with the slotted spoon and put on a plate. Stir fry the raisins for 1 minute till they plump up. Lift out with the slotted spoon. Stir fry the almonds for 2 minutes till lightly brown. Put the rice in the bowl and then put the onion, raisins and almonds on top. Stir in just before serving.

ADDITIONS & ALTERNATIVES
Serve with curries or dahl and naan bread.

TIPS
This is an ideal accompaniment to any of the vegetarian curries.

Naan bread is sold in the bread section of many supermarkets.

SESAME POTATO CURRY

Serves 4   ① *Preparation 20 min, Cooking 25 min — Easy*

INGREDIENTS
12 medium potatoes, about 750 g (1½ lb)
3 carrots
1 large onion
4 cloves garlic
5 tablespoons sunflower oil
2 tablespoons sesame seeds
½ teaspoon chilli powder
1 teaspoon turmeric
1 teaspoon salt

EQUIPMENT
Vegetable peeler
Sharp knife
Chopping board
Set of measuring spoons
Saucepan with lid or wok with lid
Wooden spoon or spatula
Slotted spoon
Plate

METHOD
Peel the potatoes, cutting away any nasty bits, and cutting out any eyes. Chop the potatoes into 1 cm (½ inch) cubes. Peel and chop the carrots, cutting off both ends. Peel and chop the onion into thin slices. Peel the garlic then chop it into tiny pieces.

Put the oil in the pan and heat over a moderate heat. Fry the potato and carrot for about 7 minutes, stirring to stop it sticking. Add the onion and fry for 3 minutes. Lift out with the slotted spoon and put on a plate.

Put the sesame seeds and garlic in the pan. Stir fry for 3 minutes. Add the chilli, turmeric and salt. Stir round, then add the potatoes, carrots and onion. Give them a stir to coat with the mixture then turn the heat down. Put the lid on and cook on a low heat for 10 minutes, stirring from time to time.

QUICK CHICKPEA CURRY

Serves 4   ① *Preparation 15 min, Cooking 15 min — Easy*

INGREDIENTS
2 large onions
4 cloves garlic
$\frac{1}{2}$ × 50 g pack parsley
5 tablespoons sunflower oil
420 g tin chickpeas
400 g tin tomatoes
2 tablespoon medium curry powder

EQUIPMENT
Sharp knife
Chopping board
Set of measuring spoons
Saucepan with lid or wok with lid
Wooden spoon or spatula
Tin opener
Set of measuring cups

METHOD
Peel and chop the onion into tiny bits. Peel the garlic then chop it into tiny pieces. Wash, shake dry and finely chop the parsley.

Put the oil in the pan and heat over a moderate heat. Fry the onion and garlic for about 3 minutes till it is golden, stirring to stop it sticking.

Open the tin of chickpeas and drain. Add to the pan. Open the tin of tomatoes. Pour the juice into the frying-pan. Use the wooden spoon to mash the tomatoes while they are still in the can. Pour the mashed tomatoes into the pan. Add the curry powder and stir round. Bring to the boil, then turn down the heat till it is just boiling (simmering). Put a lid on and cook for 10 minutes. Stir the parsley in and serve.

ADDITIONS & ALTERNATIVES
Serve with rice and pickles.

Try using other curry powders.

TIPS
Prepared garlic is sold in tubes, jars and bottles. Just read the instructions for the suggested equivalent amount. Most keep for 6 weeks in the fridge, but the bottles keep longer.

TOMATO & AUBERGINE CURRY

Serves 4   ⏲ *Preparation 10 min, Cooking 15 min — Easy*

INGREDIENTS
2 medium aubergines, about 500 g (1 lb)
400 g tin tomatoes
2 cm (1 in) piece fresh ginger
1 large onion
1 green chilli
3 tablespoons sunflower oil
1 tablespoon garam masala
1 teaspoon salt
1 teaspoon freshly ground black pepper

EQUIPMENT
Sharp knife
Chopping board
Tin opener
Small bowl
Set of measuring spoons

Frying-pan
Wooden spoon

METHOD

Get everything washed, chopped and ready before starting to cook. Dutch aubergines don't need soaking. Just wash, cut the ends off, and cut into 2 cm (1 inch) cubes.

Open the tin of tomatoes. Pour the juice into the small bowl. Use the wooden spoon to mash the tomatoes while they are still in the can. Pour the mashed tomatoes into the bowl.

Peel the ginger and cut into thin slices. Peel and chop the onion. Chop the end off the chillies, split in half, and scrape out the seeds. Cut the chilli into thin strips.

Put the oil in the frying-pan on a moderate heat. Fry the onion and ginger for about 3 minutes till it is golden, stirring to stop it sticking. Add the aubergine and fry for about 3 minutes, then add the tomatoes, chillies, garam masala, salt and black pepper to taste. Cook gently for 10 minutes until the vegetables are tender.

ADDITIONS & ALTERNATIVES

Serve with rice or noodles.

TIPS

FRESH CHILLI — A WARNING! When you chop up the chillies be careful and avoid getting juice on your hands. If you touch your eyes, mouth or other sensitive areas, even an hour after chopping them, they will smart and burn. So wash your hands or wear rubber gloves.

Prepared chilli is sold in tubes and jars. Just read the label for the suggested equivalent amount. It keeps for 6 weeks in the fridge.

You can buy prepared ginger in jars and bottles. It will keep for 6 weeks in the fridge or longer, just check on the pack.

Makes a good extra curry with meat curry.

MILD MUSHROOM CURRY

Serves 2   ① *Preparation 10 min, Cooking 15 min — Easy*

INGREDIENTS
250 g (8 oz) button mushrooms
1 large onion
2 cm (1 inch) piece of fresh ginger
3 cloves garlic
4 tablespoons sunflower oil
$\frac{1}{2}$ teaspoon chilli powder
1 teaspoon turmeric
$\frac{1}{2}$ teaspoon salt
$\frac{1}{2}$ cup water

EQUIPMENT
Sharp knife
Chopping board
Garlic crusher
Set of measuring spoons
Saucepan with lid or wok with lid
Wooden spoon or spatula
Set of measuring cups

METHOD
Wipe the mushrooms clean. Discard any nasty ones. Chop the end off the stalks. Peel and chop the onion into thin slices. Peel the ginger and cut into tiny cubes. Peel and crush the garlic into the pan.

Put the oil in the pan and heat over a moderate heat. Fry the onion, ginger and garlic for about 3 minutes till it is golden, stirring to stop it sticking. Add the chilli and turmeric and stir round. Add the mushrooms, salt and water and stir to mix together. Bring to the boil, then turn down the heat till it is just boiling (simmering). Put a lid on and cook for 10 minutes. Check the water level from time to time and top it up if needed.

ADDITIONS & ALTERNATIVES

Serve with rice or other curries.

Try adding 1 teaspoon cumin.

Add 1 teaspoon chilli powder instead of ½ teaspoon and add small carton (142 ml, 5 fl oz) of yoghurt or cream just before serving.

TIPS

Prepared garlic is sold in tubes and jars. Just read the label for the suggested equivalent amount. It keeps for 6 weeks in the fridge.

You can buy prepared chopped ginger root in jars. It will keep for 6 weeks in the fridge.

HOT CHICKPEAS

Serves 4   ① *Preparation 15 min, Cooking 25 min — Easy*

INGREDIENTS

2 × 420 g tins chickpeas
4 cloves garlic
4 tablespoons sunflower oil
2 teaspoons whole cumin seeds
2 tablespoons tomato purée
1 ½ cups water
1 teaspoon salt
2 green chillies
2 tablespoons lemon juice

EQUIPMENT

Food processor or liquidizer (optional)
Tin opener

Set of measuring spoons
Saucepan with lid
Wooden spoon or spatula
Sharp knife
Chopping board
Garlic crusher
Set of measuring cups

METHOD

Open the tins of chickpeas and drain. Peel and slice the garlic.

Put the oil in the pan and heat over a moderate heat. Fry the cumin seed for about 15 seconds, stirring to stop it sticking. Add the garlic and fry for 1 minute. Add the tomato purée and the water and stir round for 1 minute. Add the chickpeas, salt, chillies and lemon juice. Bring to the boil, then turn down the heat till it is just boiling (simmering). Put a lid on and cook for 20 minutes. Check the water level from time to time and top it up if needed.

ADDITIONS & ALTERNATIVES

Serve with other curries or with pitta bread and yoghurt.

TIPS

You do not have to squeeze lemons to get lemon juice, though you can if you like. Lemon juice comes in bottles. One lemon gives about 2 to 3 tablespoons of juice.

INDIAN CRISPY OMELETTE

Serves 2   ① *Preparation 8 min, Cooking 7 min — Easy*

INGREDIENTS
1 small onion
1 green chilli
2 eggs
$\frac{1}{2}$ teaspoon salt
$\frac{1}{2}$ teaspoon pepper
1 tablespoon butter

EQUIPMENT
Sharp knife
Chopping board
Bowl
Set of measuring spoons
Fork
Frying-pan
Wooden spoon or spatula

METHOD
Peel and chop the onion into tiny bits. Chop the end off the chilli, split in half, and scrape out the seeds. Cut the chilli into tiny bits.

Break the eggs into a bowl and pick out any bits of shell. Add the onion, chilli, salt and pepper and mix the eggs up with a fork.

Heat the butter in the pan then pour in the eggs and fry until the underside begins to firm up. Cut the omelette into quarters with the spatula and flip each piece over and cook until golden brown. Lift out the bits on to a plate.

ADDITIONS & ALTERNATIVES
Serve with rice and pickle.

TIPS

With rice this makes a meal for one or a side dish for more than one.

There are full instructions on cooking rice in the 'How to' chapter.

CURRIED EGGS

Serves 4 ① *Preparation 30 min, Cooking 40 min — Easy Think ahead. You can hard-boil the eggs while the sauce is cooking.*

INGREDIENTS

8 large eggs
5 large onions
2 cloves garlic
2 cm (1 inch) piece fresh ginger
$\frac{1}{2}$ cup of sunflower oil
400 g tin tomatoes
2 tablespoons medium curry powder
1 teaspoon salt

EQUIPMENT

Small saucepan
Sharp knife
Chopping board
Bowl
Large saucepan with lid
Wooden spoon or spatula
Tin opener
Set of measuring spoons

174

METHOD

To hard-boil the eggs, put them in a small saucepan nearly full of water. Bring to the boil, and boil for ten minutes. Cool the eggs by putting in cold water. When they are cold, take off the shells.

Meanwhile, peel and chop the onion into small bits. Put in the bowl. Peel the garlic then chop it into tiny pieces. Put it in the bowl. Peel the ginger and cut into tiny cubes.

Put the oil in the saucepan over a moderate heat. Fry the onion, garlic and ginger for about 5 minutes till brown, stirring to stop it sticking.

Open the tin of tomatoes. Pour the juice into the frying-pan. Use the wooden spoon to mash the tomatoes while they are still in the can. Pour the mashed tomatoes into the pan. Continue to cook, stirring as the mixture boils. Add the curry powder and salt and stir round. Bring to the boil, then turn down the heat till it is just boiling (simmering). Put a lid on and cook for 15 minutes. Check the fluid level from time to time and top it up if needed. Add the hard-boiled eggs. Simmer for 5 minutes.

ADDITIONS & ALTERNATIVES

Serve with rice and pickles or naan bread.

TIPS

If you don't have a garlic crusher just squash it with something suitable or chop it up small. Prepared garlic is sold in tubes, jars and bottles. Just read the instructions for the suggested equivalent amount. Most keep for 6 weeks in the fridge, but the bottles keep longer.

You can buy prepared ginger in jars and bottles. It will keep for 6 weeks in the fridge or longer, just check on the pack.

Naan bread is sold in the bread section of many supermarkets.

PRAWNS IN COCONUT

Serves 4   ⏲ *Preparation 20 min, Cooking 20 min — Easy*

INGREDIENTS
500 g (1 lb) medium uncooked shelled prawns
$\frac{1}{2}$ teaspoon turmeric
1 teaspoon vinegar
$\frac{1}{2}$ teaspoon salt
$\frac{1}{2}$ teaspoon pepper
1 medium onion
2 cloves garlic
1 cm ($\frac{1}{2}$ inch) fresh ginger
2 fresh green chillies
3 tablespoons sunflower oil
$\frac{1}{4}$ teaspoon mustard seed
1 teaspoon uncooked rice
2 curry leaves
4 tablespoons desiccated coconut

EQUIPMENT
Sharp knife
Chopping board
Bowl
Wooden spoon or spatula
Set of measuring spoons
Frying-pan

DEFROSTING
Make sure frozen prawns are completely thawed before use. This means leaving them in the fridge for 6 hours or out of the fridge, covered, for 3 hours.

METHOD

Lay the prawns flat, cut down along the back about half-way through the prawn. This lets them open up and curl round when cooked. Put the prawns, turmeric, vinegar, salt and pepper in the bowl and stir round. Leave for 15 minutes.

Meanwhile, peel and chop the onion into small cubes. Peel the garlic then chop it into tiny pieces. Peel the ginger and cut into tiny cubes. Chop the end off the chillies, split in half, and scrape out the seeds. Cut the chilli into tiny bits.

Put the oil in the frying-pan on moderate heat. Fry the mustard seed for 5 seconds. Add the rice and fry for 20 seconds. Add the onion and fry for about 2 minutes. Add the garlic and ginger and fry for another 3 minutes. Add the prawns and juice from the bowl and fry for ten minutes. Stir all the time. If it starts to stick, put a tablespoon or two of water in. Add the curry leaves, chilli and desiccated coconut and stir fry for 5 minutes.

ADDITIONS & ALTERNATIVES

Serve with rice.

TIPS

FRESH CHILLI — A WARNING! When you chop up the chillies be careful and avoid getting juice on your hands. If you touch your eyes, mouth or other sensitive areas, even an hour after chopping them, they will smart and burn. So wash your hands or wear rubber gloves.

Prepared chilli is sold in tubes and jars. Just read the label for the suggested equivalent amount. It keeps for 6 weeks in the fridge.

Prepared garlic is sold in tubes, jars and bottles. Just read the instructions for the suggested equivalent amount. Most keep for 6 weeks in the fridge, but the bottles keep longer.

You can buy prepared ginger in jars and bottles. It will keep for 6 weeks in the fridge or longer, just check on the pack.

PRAWN & MUSHROOM CURRY

Serves 2   ① *Preparation 20 min, Cooking 45 min — Easy*

INGREDIENTS

250 g pack frozen prawns
5 large onions
2 cloves garlic
2 cm (1 inch) piece fresh ginger
100 g ($\frac{1}{4}$ lb) mushrooms, about 10
$\frac{1}{2}$ × 250 g packet butter
400 g tin tomatoes
1 teaspoon salt
2 tablespoons medium curry powder
400 ml tin coconut milk

EQUIPMENT

Sharp knife
Chopping board
Bowl
Garlic crusher
Saucepan with lid or wok with lid
Tin opener
Wooden spoon
Set of measuring spoons

METHOD

You can cook the prawns from frozen.

Peel and chop the onion into small bits. Put in the bowl. Peel the garlic and crush it or chop it into tiny pieces. Put it in the bowl. Peel the ginger and cut into tiny cubes. Wipe the mushrooms clean. Discard any nasty ones. Chop the end off the stalks.

Put the butter in the saucepan over a moderate heat. Fry the

178

onion, garlic and ginger for about 5 minutes till brown, stirring to stop it sticking.

Open the tin of tomatoes. Pour the juice into the pan. Use the wooden spoon to mash the tomatoes while they are still in the can. Pour the mashed tomatoes into the pan. Continue to cook, stirring as the mixture boils. Add the salt and the curry powder and stir round. Add the prawns and mushrooms and stir over a medium heat for 15 minutes.

Open the tin of coconut milk and add to the mixture. Bring to the boil, then turn down the heat till it is just boiling (simmering). Put a lid on and cook for 10 minutes.

ADDITIONS & ALTERNATIVES

Try using white fish fillets (cod, hake, hoki or halibut) cut into strips 2 cm by 4 cm (1 inch by 2 inch).

You can cook the fish from frozen.

TIPS

Prepared garlic is sold in tubes and jars. Just read the label for the suggested equivalent amount. It keeps for 6 weeks in the fridge.

You can buy prepared chopped ginger root in jars. It will keep for 6 weeks in the fridge.

MADRAS FISH CURRY

Serves 4　　　① *Preparation 15 min, Cooking 25 min — Easy*

INGREDIENTS
600 g ($1\frac{1}{4}$ lb) pack white fish fillets (cod, hake, hoki or halibut)
1 large onion
2 cloves garlic
400 g tin tomatoes
2 tablespoons sunflower oil
2 tablespoons Madras curry powder
1 tablespoon lemon juice
1 teaspoon salt
2 tablespoons single cream

EQUIPMENT
Sharp knife
Chopping board
Tin opener
Saucepan
Wooden spoon or spatula
Set of measuring spoons

METHOD
You can cook the fish from frozen. Cut the fish into 4 cm (2 inch) chunks. Peel and chop the onion finely. Peel the garlic, then chop it into tiny pieces. Open the tin of tomatoes. Pour the juice away. Use the wooden spoon to mash the tomatoes while they are still in the can.

Put the oil in the pan on a moderate heat. Fry the onion and garlic for about 2 minutes then add the curry powder and cook for another 3 minutes. Pour the mashed tomatoes, lemon juice and salt into the pan. Continue to cook, stirring as the mixture boils. Turn the heat down low. Add the fish and cook for 12 minutes till done.

ADDITIONS & ALTERNATIVES

Serve with rice and pickles.

You can use cooked prawns instead. Just add near the end and warm through and don't let them boil.

Use yoghurt instead of cream.

TIPS

Prepared garlic is sold in tubes, jars and bottles. Just read the instructions for the suggested equivalent amount. Most keep for 6 weeks in the fridge, but the bottles keep longer.

You do not have to squeeze lemons to get lemon juice, though you can if you like. Lemon juice comes in bottles. One lemon gives about 2 to 3 tablespoons of juice.

CHILLI GARLIC PRAWNS

Serves 4 ① *Preparation 20 min, Cooking 10 min — Easy*

INGREDIENTS

500 g pack large uncooked shelled prawns
1 large onion
3 cloves garlic
1 green pepper
2 tablespoons cornflour
2 tablespoons water
1 tablespoon chilli sauce
2 teaspoons oyster sauce
1 tablespoon tomato ketchup
1 chicken stock cube
1 teaspoon soy sauce
1 teaspoon sesame oil
2 teaspoons sugar

$^1\!/_2$ teaspoon salt
$^1\!/_2$ teaspoon pepper
5 tablespoons sunflower oil

EQUIPMENT
Sharp knife
Chopping board
Cup
Frying-pan
Bowl
Set of measuring spoons
Wooden spoon or spatula
Slotted spoon
Plate

DEFROSTING
Make sure frozen prawns are completely thawed before use. This means leaving them in the fridge for 6 hours or out of the fridge, covered, for 3 hours.

METHOD
Get everything washed, chopped and ready before starting to cook. Peel and chop the onion into 1 cm ($^1\!/_2$ inch) cubes. Peel the garlic then chop it into tiny pieces. Chop the end off the green pepper and cut out the core and seeds. Cut the pepper into 1 cm ($^1\!/_2$ inch) squares.

Mix 1 tablespoon of the cornflour and the water together in the cup till smooth. Add the water slowly or it will go lumpy. Add the chilli sauce, oyster sauce and ketchup and mix.

Put the garlic, chicken stock cube, soy sauce, sesame oil, 1 tablespoon of the cornflour, sugar, salt and pepper in the bowl and mix round. Add the prawns and stir to get covered. Leave for 15 minutes.

Put 3 tablespoons of oil in the frying-pan on a moderate heat. Fry the prawns for about 5 minutes, stirring to stop them sticking.

Lift out with the slotted spoon and put on a plate. Add the rest of the oil to the pan and cook the onion for 3 minutes. Add the green pepper and the prawns and stir round. Add the cornflour and chilli mixture from the cup and stir round for 5 minutes.

ADDITIONS & ALTERNATIVES
Serve with rice and pickles.

TIPS
Prepared garlic is sold in tubes, jars and bottles. Just read the instructions for the suggested equivalent amount. Most keep for 6 weeks in the fridge, but the bottles keep longer.

Try using white fish fillets (cod, hake, hoki or halibut) cut into 2 cm (1 inch) chunks. Thaw it out before cooking.

MILD FISH CURRY

Serves 4   ⏱ *Preparation 20 min, Cooking 25 min* — *Easy*

INGREDIENTS
600 g pack white fish fillets (cod, hake, hoki or halibut)
2 small onions
3 cloves garlic
2 cm (1 inch) fresh ginger
½ teaspoon chilli powder
2 tablespoons garam masala
1 teaspoon turmeric
2 tablespoons vinegar
2 tablespoons sesame oil
1 teaspoon whole cumin seed
400 ml tin coconut milk
1 teaspoon salt

EQUIPMENT
Sharp knife
Chopping board
Set of measuring spoons
Cup
Saucepan or wok
Wooden spoon or spatula
Set of measuring cups

METHOD
You can cook the fish from frozen. Cut the fish into 2 cm (1 inch) chunks. Peel and chop the onion into thin slices. Peel the garlic then chop it into tiny pieces. Peel the ginger and cut into tiny cubes. Mix the chilli powder, garam masala, turmeric and vinegar in the cup to make a paste.

Put the oil in the pan on a moderate heat. Fry the onion, garlic, ginger and cumin seed for about 3 minutes, stirring to stop it sticking. Add the spice paste and cook for 5 minutes. Add the coconut milk and salt and stir round. Add the fish. Bring to the boil, then turn down the heat till it is just boiling (simmering). Cook for 15 minutes until the fish is tender. Stir gently from time to time. Check the fluid level occasionally and top it up if it gets really dry.

ADDITIONS & ALTERNATIVES
Serve with rice and pickles.

Try serving with Universal Salsa (p. 333).

TIPS
Prepared garlic is sold in tubes, jars and bottles. Just read the instructions for the suggested equivalent amount. Most keep for 6 weeks in the fridge, but the bottles keep longer.

You can buy prepared ginger in jars and bottles. It will keep for 6 weeks in the fridge or longer, just check on the pack.

CHICKEN & CASHEW CURRY

Serves 4   ⏱ *Preparation 20 min, Cooking 1 hr — Easy*

INGREDIENTS
8 to 12 chicken thighs
2 medium onions
2 cm (1 inch) ginger
2 cloves garlic
400 g tin tomatoes
100 g raw cashew nuts
3 tablespoons sunflower oil
1 teaspoon chilli powder
3 tablespoons medium curry powder
1 teaspoon salt
Small carton (142 ml, 5 fl oz) natural yoghurt

EQUIPMENT
Sharp knife
Chopping board
Tin opener
Bowl
Wooden spoon or spatula
Plastic bag
Set of measuring spoons
Saucepan with lid

DEFROSTING
Make sure frozen chicken is completely thawed before use. This means leaving it in the fridge overnight, or out of the fridge, covered, for 6 hours.

METHOD
Peel and chop the onion up small. Peel the ginger and cut into tiny cubes. Peel the garlic, then chop it into tiny pieces.

185

Open the tin of tomatoes. Pour the juice into the bowl and keep. You can use it if the curry starts to get dry while cooking. Use the wooden spoon to mash the tomatoes while they are still in the can.

Put the cashew nuts in the plastic bag and crush into tiny bits with something suitable.

Put the oil in the pan on a moderate heat. Fry the onion, ginger and garlic for about 3 minutes till it is golden, stirring to stop it sticking. Add the chilli, curry powder and salt and stir. Pour the mashed tomatoes into the pan. Continue to cook, stirring as the mixture boils. Add the chicken, stirring well to coat chicken with the curry mixture. Gently bring to the boil, then turn down the heat till it is just boiling (simmering). Put a lid on and cook for 45 minutes. Check the fluid level from time to time and top it up with the tomato juice if needed. Add the yoghurt and cashews. Stir and cook for 5 minutes.

ADDITIONS & ALTERNATIVES

Serve with rice and pickles.

You can use chicken drumsticks or small breasts instead.

TIPS

Prepared garlic is sold in tubes, jars and bottles. Just read the instructions for the suggested equivalent amount. Most keep for 6 weeks in the fridge, but the bottles keep longer.

You can buy prepared ginger in jars and bottles. It will keep for 6 weeks in the fridge or longer, just check on the pack.

DRY CHICKEN CURRY

Serves 4   ⏲ *Preparation 15 min, Cooking 50 min — Moderate*

INGREDIENTS

8 or 12 chicken thighs
2 large onions
2 cloves garlic
4 tablespoons sunflower oil
2 tablespoons medium curry powder
1 tablespoon of tomato purée
1 teaspoon salt
1 tablespoon lemon juice
1 tablespoon desiccated coconut

EQUIPMENT

Sharp knife
Chopping board
Saucepan with lid or wok with lid
Wooden spoon or spatula
Set of measuring spoons

DEFROSTING

Make sure frozen chicken is completely thawed before use. This means leaving it in the fridge overnight, or out of the fridge, covered, for 6 hours.

METHOD

Peel and chop the onion into thin slices. Peel the garlic, then chop it into tiny pieces.

Put the oil in the frying-pan and heat over a moderate heat. Fry the onion and garlic for about 2 minutes, stirring to stop it sticking. Add the curry powder, tomato purée and stir round for 2 minutes. Add the chicken. Stir round to coat the chicken. Put a lid on the pan and cook over a low heat for 45 minutes. Keep checking and stirring otherwise it may stick. If it gets too dry add a couple of tablespoons of water. You may have to do this a few times, but remember it is meant to be a dry curry. Add the salt, lemon juice and desiccated coconut. Stir round.

ADDITIONS & ALTERNATIVES

Serve with wet curries, rice or salad.

Use other chicken pieces.

TIPS

Tomato purée comes in tubes. It keeps for 4 weeks in the fridge.

Prepared garlic is sold in tubes and jars. Just read the label for the suggested equivalent amount. It keeps for 6 weeks in the fridge.

You can buy prepared chopped ginger root in jars. It will keep for 6 weeks in the fridge.

You do not have to squeeze lemons to get lemon juice, though you can if you like. Lemon juice comes in bottles. One lemon gives about 2 to 3 tablespoons of juice.

BUTTER CHICKEN CURRY

Serves 4   ⏲ *Preparation 15 min, Cooking 45 min — Easy*

INGREDIENTS

12 skinless chicken thighs
6 large onions
3 cloves garlic
4 cm (2 inch) piece fresh ginger
250 g pack butter
400 g tin tomatoes
1 teaspoon salt
1 teaspoon chilli powder
2 teaspoons garam masala
1 teaspoon turmeric
3 cups water

EQUIPMENT

Sharp knife
Chopping board
Bowl
Large saucepan with lid or wok with lid
Wooden spoon or spatula
Tin opener
Set of measuring spoons
Set of measuring cups

DEFROSTING

Make sure frozen chicken is completely thawed before use. This means leaving it in the fridge overnight, or out of the fridge, covered, for 6 hours.

METHOD

Skin the thighs. Peel and chop the onion into small bits. Put in the bowl. Peel the garlic, then chop it into tiny pieces. Put it in the bowl. Peel the ginger and cut into tiny cubes.

Put the butter in the pan over a moderate heat. Fry the onion, garlic and ginger for about 5 minutes till brown, stirring to stop it sticking.

Open the tin of tomatoes. Pour the juice into the pan. Use the wooden spoon to mash the tomatoes while they are still in the can. Pour the mashed tomatoes into the pan.

Continue to cook, stirring as the mixture boils. Add the salt, chilli powder, garam masala and turmeric and stir round. Add the chicken pieces and stir over a medium heat for 15 minutes. Add the water. Bring to the boil, then turn down the heat till it is just boiling (simmering). Put a lid on and cook for 20 minutes. Check the water level from time to time and top it up if needed.

ADDITIONS & ALTERNATIVES
Serve with rice and pickles or naan.

TIPS
Prepared garlic is sold in tubes and jars. Just read the label for the suggested equivalent amount. It keeps for 6 weeks in the fridge.

You can buy prepared chopped ginger root in jars. It will keep for 6 weeks in the fridge.

Naan bread is sold in the bread section of many supermarkets.

TENDER CURRIED CHICKEN

Serves 4 ① *Preparation 20 min, Cooking 1 hr — Easy*
Think ahead. This needs to stand in the fridge for an hour
before cooking.

INGREDIENTS
8 to 12 chicken thighs (1 kg or 2 lb)
1 teaspoon chilli powder
1 teaspoon turmeric
2 teaspoons ground cumin seeds
1 teaspoon mustard
2 tablespoons white wine vinegar
1 large onion
3 tablespoons sunflower oil
2 cloves garlic
$1\frac{1}{2}$ cups water
1 teaspoon salt

EQUIPMENT
Sharp knife
Chopping board
Set of measuring spoons
Bowl
Garlic crusher
Saucepan with lid
Slotted spoon
Set of measuring cups
Wooden spoon

DEFROSTING
Make sure frozen chicken is completely thawed before use. This
means leaving it in the fridge overnight, or out of the fridge,
covered, for 6 hours.

METHOD

Make three or four cuts 1 cm ($\frac{1}{2}$ in) deep into the chicken through the skin. Put the chilli powder, turmeric, cumin, mustard and vinegar in a bowl and stir round. Add the chicken, stir and put in the fridge for an hour.

Peel and slice the onion. Put the oil in the pan on a moderate heat. Peel and crush the garlic into the pan. Fry the onion and garlic for about 6 minutes till it is brown, stirring to stop it sticking. Lift out with a slotted spoon.

Fry the chicken pieces four at a time until browned. Add the onion, water and salt and bring to the boil, then turn down the heat till it is just boiling (simmering). Put a lid on and cook for 45 minutes, until it is completely tender.

ADDITIONS & ALTERNATIVES

Serve with rice

TIPS

If you don't have a garlic crusher just squash it with something suitable or chop it up small. Prepared garlic is sold in tubes, jars and bottles. Just read the instructions for the suggested equivalent amount. Most keep for 6 weeks in the fridge.

MILD LAMB CURRY

Serves 4   ⏱ *Preparation 15 min, Cooking 1 hr — Easy*

INGREDIENTS
750 g (1½ lb) lamb
5 large onions
2 cloves garlic
4 cm (2 inch) piece fresh ginger
2 red chillies
½ × 250 g pack of butter
400 g tin tomatoes
1 teaspoon salt
2 tablespoons garam masala
1 teaspoon turmeric
Small carton (142 ml, 5 fl oz) yoghurt
2 cups of water

EQUIPMENT
Sharp knife
Chopping board
Bowl
Large saucepan with lid
Wooden spoon or spatula
Tin opener
Set of measuring spoons
Set of measuring cups

METHOD
Cut the lamb into 1 cm (½ inch) cubes. Peel and chop the onion into small bits. Put in the bowl. Peel the garlic, then chop it into tiny pieces. Put it in the bowl. Peel the ginger and cut into tiny cubes. Chop the end off the chillies, split in half, and scrape out the seeds. Cut the chilli into thin strips, then into tiny bits.

193

Put the butter in the saucepan over a moderate heat. Fry the onion, garlic and ginger for about 5 minutes till brown, stirring to stop it sticking.

Open the tin of tomatoes. Pour the juice into the frying-pan. Use the wooden spoon to mash the tomatoes while they are still in the can. Pour the mashed tomatoes into the pan. Continue to cook, stirring as the mixture boils. Add the salt, chilli, garam masala and turmeric and stir round. Add the chicken pieces and stir over a medium heat for 15 minutes. Add the water. Bring to the boil, then turn down the heat till it is just boiling (simmering). Put a lid on and cook for 10 minutes. Stir in the yoghurt and put the lid on and cook for 10 minutes.

ADDITIONS & ALTERNATIVES
Serve with rice and pickles.

TIPS
FRESH CHILLI — A WARNING! When you chop up the chillies be careful and avoid getting juice on your hands. If you touch your eyes, mouth or other sensitive areas, even an hour after chopping them, they will smart and burn. So wash your hands or wear rubber gloves.

Prepared chilli is sold in tubes and jars. Just read the label for the suggested equivalent amount. It keeps for 6 weeks in the fridge.

Prepared garlic is sold in tubes and jars. Just read the label for the suggested equivalent amount. It keeps for 6 weeks in the fridge.

You can buy prepared chopped ginger root in jars. It will keep for 6 weeks in the fridge.

LAMB & AUBERGINE CURRY

Serves 4 ⏲ *Preparation 30 min, Cooking 45 min — Easy*

INGREDIENTS

2 aubergines about 500 g (1 lb)
500 g (1 lb) boneless lean lamb
2 medium onions
2 cloves garlic
2 cm (1 in) piece fresh root ginger
$\frac{1}{4}$ cup sunflower oil
2 tablespoons black poppy seeds
2 teaspoons ground coriander
2 teaspoons ground cumin
1 teaspoon black pepper
1 teaspoon powdered turmeric
5 cm (2 in) stick cinnamon
3 whole cloves
3 curry leaves
2 × 400 ml tins coconut milk

EQUIPMENT

Sharp knife
Chopping board
Food processor or liquidizer (optional)
Set of measuring cups
Large saucepan or wok
Set of measuring spoons
Wooden spoon
Garlic crusher

METHOD

Dutch aubergines don't need soaking. Just wash the aubergines, cut the ends off, and cut the aubergines and the lamb into 1 cm ($\frac{1}{2}$ inch) pieces.

You can use a food processor or liquidizer to prepare the onion, garlic and ginger, or just chop it up small. Peel the garlic, then chop it into tiny pieces. Peel the ginger and cut into tiny cubes. Peel and chop the onion.

Put the oil in the frying-pan on a moderate heat. Fry the onion, garlic and ginger for about 3 minutes till it is golden, stirring to stop it sticking. Add the poppy seeds, ground coriander, cumin, black pepper and turmeric and cook for 2 minutes more. Add the lamb and stir round and cook until evenly coloured, about 3 minutes. Add the cinnamon, cloves and curry leaves. Add the coconut milk and aubergine. Bring to the boil, then turn down the heat till it is just boiling (simmering). Cook for 30 minutes.

ADDITIONS & ALTERNATIVES

Serve with rice or noodles.

TIPS

There are full instructions on cooking rice and noodles in the 'How to' chapter.

KEEMA CURRY

Serves 4   ① *Preparation 20 min, Cooking 1 hr 30 min — Easy*

INGREDIENTS
5 large onions
2 cloves garlic
2 cm (1 inch) piece fresh ginger
1 cup water
1 stock cube
750 g (1 $\frac{1}{2}$ lb) minced beef or lamb
1 teaspoon salt
1 teaspoon chilli powder
$\frac{1}{2}$ × 250 g pack butter
400 g tin tomatoes
2 teaspoons garam masala
1 teaspoon turmeric
Small carton (142 ml, 5 fl oz) yoghurt

EQUIPMENT
Sharp knife
Chopping board
Bowl
Large saucepan with lid
Wooden spoon or spatula
Tin opener
Set of measuring spoons
Set of measuring cups

METHOD
Peel and chop the onion into small bits. Put in the bowl. Peel the garlic, then chop it into tiny pieces. Put it in the bowl. Peel the ginger and cut into tiny cubes. Dissolve the stock cube in the water.

Put the mince, onions, garlic, ginger, salt and chilli in a pan and cook slowly for 30 minutes, stirring to stop it sticking. Add the butter and cook for 15 minutes.

Open the tin of tomatoes. Pour the juice into the frying-pan. Use the wooden spoon to mash the tomatoes while they are still in the can. Pour the mashed tomatoes into the pan. Continue to cook, stirring as the mixture boils. Add the garam masala and turmeric and stir round. Add the water and stock cube mixture. Bring to the boil, then turn down the heat till it is just boiling (simmering). Put a lid on and cook for 15 minutes. Stir in the yoghurt for the last five minutes.

ADDITIONS & ALTERNATIVES
Serve with rice and pickles.

Try minced turkey.

TIPS
Prepared garlic is sold in tubes and jars. Just read the label for the suggested equivalent amount. It keeps for 6 weeks in the fridge.

You can buy prepared chopped ginger root in jars. It will keep for 6 weeks in the fridge.

BASIC BEEF CURRY

Serves 4   ⊕ *Preparation 15 min, Cooking 1 hr 30 min — Easy*

INGREDIENTS
750 g ($1\frac{1}{2}$ lb) stewing beef
5 large onions
2 cloves garlic
4 cm (2 inch) piece fresh ginger
1 teaspoon salt
$\frac{1}{2}$ × 250 g pack of butter
400 g tin tomatoes
1 teaspoon chilli powder
2 tablespoons garam masala
1 teaspoon turmeric
2 cups of water

EQUIPMENT
Sharp knife
Chopping board
Bowl
Large saucepan with lid or wok with lid
Wooden spoon or spatula
Tin opener
Set of measuring spoons
Set of measuring cups

METHOD
Cut beef into 1 cm ($\frac{1}{2}$ inch) pieces. Peel and chop the onions into small bits. Put in the bowl. Peel the garlic, then chop it into tiny pieces. Put it in the bowl. Peel the ginger and cut into tiny cubes.

Melt the butter in the pan over a low heat. Put the beef, onions, garlic, ginger and salt in the pan and cook slowly for 45 minutes, stirring frequently to stop it sticking.

199

Open the tin of tomatoes. Pour the juice into the pan. Use the wooden spoon to mash the tomatoes while they are still in the can. Pour the mashed tomatoes into the pan. Continue to cook, stirring as the mixture boils. Add the chilli powder, garam masala and turmeric and stir round. Add the water. Bring to the boil, then turn down the heat till it is just boiling (simmering). Put a lid on and cook for 30 minutes. Check the water level from time to time and top it up if needed.

ADDITIONS & ALTERNATIVES
Serve with rice and pickles and naan bread.

TIPS
Prepared garlic is sold in tubes and jars. Just read the label for the suggested equivalent amount. It keeps for 6 weeks in the fridge.

You can buy prepared chopped ginger root in jars. It will keep for 6 weeks in the fridge.

Naan bread is sold in the bread section of many supermarkets.

SAFFRON SHRIKAND

Serves 2 ⏲ *Preparation 10 min — Easy*
Think ahead. The yoghurt needs to drain for two or three hours and then stand in the fridge to cool.

INGREDIENTS
Large (500 g) carton plain Greek-style yoghurt
$\frac{1}{4}$ teaspoon saffron
2 teaspoons warm milk
1 tablespoon shelled, unsalted pistachio nuts
$\frac{1}{4}$ cup caster sugar
$\frac{1}{4}$ teaspoon cardamom seeds

EQUIPMENT
Sieve
Bowl
Kitchen towel
Cup
Set of measuring cups
Set of measuring spoons
Sharp knife
Chopping board
Wooden spoon or spatula
2 small bowls or plates
Pestle and mortar or tablespoon and plate

METHOD
This is the best Indian dessert and quite addictive.

Put the sieve over the bowl. Line the sieve with kitchen towel. Put the yoghurt in the lined sieve. Put another couple of bits of kitchen towel on top and leave for 2 to 3 hours. Meanwhile, put the saffron and the warm milk in the cup and leave for 1 hour.

Cut the pistachio nuts into tiny slivers. Crush the cardamom seeds. You could use a pestle and mortar, but the back of a spoon on a plate works well, though some of the seeds might skid off the sides. Replace them.

Throw away the watery stuff in the bowl that has drained from the yoghurt. Put the strained yoghurt in the bowl. (The kitchen paper just peels off). Add the saffron milk and sugar. Mix round until absolutely smooth. Add the cardamom and stir. Put the mixture into two bowls then put the pistachio on top and keep in the fridge until you are ready to serve.

NORTH EUROPEAN

BEER SOUP

Serves 4   ① *Preparation 10 min, Cooking 5 min — Easy*

INGREDIENTS
2 large tins light ale
2 eggs
Medium carton (284 ml, 10 fl oz) sour cream
1 tablespoon butter
1 tablespoon sugar
1 teaspoon salt

EQUIPMENT
Egg separator
2 cups
Bowl
Set of measuring spoons
Fork
Saucepan
Wooden spoon or spatula

METHOD

Open the tins of beer. Do not weaken — no drinking! Break the eggs one at a time into a cup and pick out any bits of shell. Hold the egg separator over a cup. Put the eggs one at a time into the egg separator and let the white fall away into the cup beneath. Put the yolks into the bowl. Add the sour cream, butter, sugar and salt and mix together with the fork. Slowly pour in the beer and stir. Pour into a saucepan on a low heat and gently bring up to the point where it is just boiling, stirring round. Serve at once. If you boil it all the alcohol evaporates.

ADDITIONS & ALTERNATIVES

Serve with croûtons (page 243) or toast.

You can separate the yolks by cracking the egg in half and then juggling the egg from one eggshell half to the other but this takes practice. The downside is that the yolk can get popped on the shell, and of course your fingers tend to get covered with egg white. Another method is to break the egg into a cup and then to lift the yolks out with a tablespoon.

You can use German or French lager.

This is a real recipe and not just something we put in to pander to blokes.

LEMON BARLEY SOUP

Serves 4 to 6 ⏱ *Preparation 5 min, Cooking 1 hr 40 min — Easy*

INGREDIENTS
5 cups cold water
$\frac{1}{4}$ cup pearl barley
$\frac{1}{2}$ cup green lentils
1 beef stock cube
1 cup boiling water
4 onions
1 tablespoon tomato purée
3 tablespoons lemon juice
$\frac{1}{2}$ teaspoon paprika pepper
$\frac{1}{4}$ teaspoon cayenne pepper
$\frac{1}{2}$ teaspoon salt
1 teaspoon freshly ground black pepper

EQUIPMENT
Set of measuring cups
Large saucepan with lid
Cup
Sharp knife
Chopping board
Set of measuring spoons
Wooden spoon

METHOD
Put 1 cup of water and the barley in a large saucepan. Bring to the boil, then turn down the heat till it is just boiling (simmering). Put a lid on and cook for 20 minutes, until the barley is just cooked and the water has been absorbed.

Meanwhile, rinse the lentils and check for any small stones.

Dissolve the stock cube in 1 cup of boiling water. Peel and thinly slice the onions.

Add the lentils, dissolved stock cube, 4 cups of cold water, onions and tomato purée to the pan. Bring to the boil, then turn down the heat till it is just boiling (simmering). Put a lid on and cook for 1 hour. Add the lemon juice, paprika, cayenne pepper, salt and pepper and simmer with the lid off for 20 minutes.

ADDITIONS & ALTERNATIVES

Serve with fresh bread.

TIPS

You can buy ready-made stock in cartons from most supermarkets. You can also buy Swiss vegetable bouillon powder (vegetable stock), if you are worried about the stuff that goes into stock cubes.

Tomato purée comes in tubes. It keeps for 4 weeks in the fridge.

You do not have to squeeze lemons to get lemon juice, though you can if you like. Lemon juice comes in bottles. One lemon gives about 2 to 3 tablespoons of juice.

CHERRY SOUP

Serves 4   ① *Preparation 10 min, Cooking 15 min — Easy*

INGREDIENTS
400 g tin pitted morello cherries
3 tablespoons sugar
1 ½ cups water
½ cup red wine
½ teaspoon cinnamon
4 tablespoons sour cream
2 tablespoons lemon juice

EQUIPMENT
Tin opener
Saucepan
Set of measuring spoons
Set of measuring cups
Sieve
Bowl
Wooden spoon

METHOD
Open the tin of cherries and drain. Put in the pan with the sugar and water. Bring to the boil, then turn down the heat till it is just boiling (simmering). Cook for 5 minutes, stirring from time to time. Put the sieve over the bowl. Pour the cherries in and use the back of the spoon to push them through the mesh. Put the contents of the bowl back in the pan. Add the wine, cinnamon, sour cream and lemon juice and simmer gently for one minute, stirring all the time.

ADDITIONS & ALTERNATIVES
Serve as a weird starter or dessert with Amareti biscuits.

TIPS

You do not have to squeeze lemons to get lemon juice, though you can if you like. Lemon juice comes in bottles. One lemon gives about 2 to 3 tablespoons of juice.

RUSSIAN FRUIT PILAU RICE

Serves 4   ⊕ *Preparation 5 min, Cooking 25 min — Easy*

INGREDIENTS

$^1_2$ cup currants
2 cups hot water
$^1_4$ cup ready-to-eat stoned apricots
4 Californian ready-to-eat stoned prunes
$^1_4$ cup blanched almonds
$^1_4$ cup butter
1 tablespoon honey
1 cup long grain rice
2 cups cold water

EQUIPMENT

Set of measuring cups
Bowl
Sieve or colander
Sharp knife
Chopping board
Saucepan with lid
Wooden spoon or spatula
Set of measuring spoons
Fork

METHOD

Put the currants in the bowl. Cover with the hot water and leave to soak for 20 minutes. Drain the currants in a sieve.

Chop the apricots and prunes. Chop the almonds. Melt the butter in the pan over a medium heat. Add the apricots, prunes and currants and stir round. Turn the heat to low and cook for 3 minutes. Add the honey and rice. Stir once, then add the cold water. Bring to the boil, then turn down the heat till it is just boiling (simmering). Put the lid on the pan.

Read the packet to get the correct cooking time for the rice. Cook for the correct time until the fluid is absorbed (10–15 minutes for long grain or Basmati rice). Do not stir! After the cooking time, take it off the heat and let it stand for a couple of minutes. Fluff it up with a fork to separate the grains and serve.

ADDITIONS & ALTERNATIVES

Serve with salad.

If you use dried apricots or prunes instead of ready-to-eat, soak them for 20 minutes with the currants, increasing the hot water and removing the stones before chopping.

CHICORY & ORANGE SALAD

Serves 4   ① *Preparation 10 min — Easy*

INGREDIENTS
2 heads of chicory (endive)
1 orange
1 apple
2 tablespoons mayonnaise

EQUIPMENT
Sharp knife
Chopping board
Grater or zester
Apple corer
Bowl
Wooden spoon or spatula

METHOD
Remove the outer leaves of the chicory, cut off the end. Wash, dry and slice the remainder. Use the zester or grater to get the rind off half the orange. Peel the rest of the rind and the white pith off the orange. Cut the orange into thin slices. Peel and core the apple and cut in fine slices. Put the chicory, orange and apple in the bowl with the mayonnaise and stir round.

ADDITIONS & ALTERNATIVES
Serve as a salad with cold meat or chicken.

Substitute 1 tablespoon of sour cream for the some of the mayonnaise.

Use banana instead of the apple.

TIPS
Chicory looks like a white and green pointed smooth spearhead.

CHEESE & FENNEL SALAD

Serves 4 as starter ⓘ *Preparation 15 min — Easy*

INGREDIENTS
1 lettuce
250 g (8 oz) ripe Camembert
$\frac{1}{2}$ cup mayonnaise
1 teaspoon Worcestershire sauce
2 tablespoons tomato ketchup
1 tablespoon brandy
2 tablespoons single cream
$\frac{1}{2}$ teaspoon salt
$\frac{1}{2}$ teaspoon black pepper
2 Braeburn or other red eating apples
1 tablespoon lemon juice
1 fennel bulb
50 g packet of chopped walnuts

EQUIPMENT
Sharp knife
Chopping board
Set of measuring cups
Set of measuring spoons
Bowl
Spoon
Apple corer
4 serving bowls or plates

METHOD
Wash and dry the lettuce. Cut the cheese into 1 cm ($\frac{1}{2}$ inch) cubes.

Mix the mayonnaise, Worcestershire sauce, ketchup, brandy, cream, salt and pepper in the bowl to make the dressing.

Arrange some lettuce leaves in the bottom of four bowls.

Wash the apples, take the core out and slice the apple. Dribble a bit of lemon juice on the apple to stop it going brown. Clean the fennel bulb and chop it into small dice. Divide the fennel and apple slices between the bowls, add the cheese and walnuts and pour some dressing on.

TIPS

Do this at the last minute or the apples and fennel will go brown.

Use Brie instead of Camembert.

EGG & CHEESE BAKE

Serves 4   ① *Preparation 10 min, Cooking 20 min — Easy*

INGREDIENTS

8 eggs

$\frac{1}{2}$ teaspoon salt

Small carton (142 ml, 5 fl oz) single cream

1 bunch fresh chives

150 g (6 oz) Emmental cheese

1 tablespoon butter

EQUIPMENT

Bowl

Set of measuring spoons

Fork

Sharp knife

Chopping board

Ovenproof dish

METHOD

Break the eggs into a bowl and pick out any bits of shell. Add the salt and cream and mix the eggs up with a fork.

Wash, shake dry and finely chop the chives. Cut the cheese into thin slices.

Rub the butter on the ovenproof dish. Line the dish with the cheese slices. Pour in the egg mixture and cook in the oven for 20 minutes at 220°C, 425°F, Gas mark 7 until golden.

ADDITIONS & ALTERNATIVES

Serve with salad.

Use Gouda, Gruyère or Edam instead of Emmental.

TIPS

Some supermarkets sell packs of sliced Gruyère and Emmental or Gouda cheeses.

SALMON & MUSTARD

Serves 4   ⓘ *Preparation 10 min, Cooking 12 min — Easy*

INGREDIENTS

1 kg (2 lb) salmon fillet
1 lemon
50 g pack fresh dill
1 teaspoon honey
2 tablespoons French mustard
$\frac{1}{2}$ teaspoon salt
$\frac{1}{2}$ teaspoon freshly ground black pepper
2 tablespoons sunflower oil

EQUIPMENT

Grater or zester
Juicer
Sharp knife
Chopping board
Set of measuring spoons

Aluminium foil
Grill pan

METHOD
Wash and dry the salmon fillet. Use the zester or grater to take the skin off half the lemon. Use the juicer to get the juice from half the lemon. Slice the other half to serve with the cooked salmon.

Wash, shake dry and finely chop the dill. Mix the dill, honey, mustard, lemon rind and juice, salt and pepper with 1 tablespoon of the oil in a small bowl.

Put a piece of aluminium foil on the grill pan and brush it with 1 tablespoon of the oil. Put the salmon on skin-side down. Spread the honey and mustard mixture over the salmon. Cook for 12 minutes under a high temperature grill.

ADDITIONS & ALTERNATIVES
Serve with new potatoes, green vegetable or salad.

This barbecues very well.

FISH & POTATO PIE

Serves 4   ① *Preparation 20 min, Cooking 50 min — Easy*

INGREDIENTS
600 g pack white fish fillets (cod, hake, hoki or halibut)
8 large potatoes
2 teaspoons salt
2 eggs
¾ cup milk
1 teaspoon pepper
1 tablespoon butter
3 cups breadcrumbs

EQUIPMENT
Sharp knife
Chopping board
Vegetable peeler
Saucepan
Sieve or colander
Set of measuring spoons
Bowl
Set of measuring cups
Fork
Grater
Ovenproof dish

METHOD
You can cook the fish from frozen. Take the skin off and cut the fish into 1 cm (½ inch) slices.

Peel the potatoes, cutting away any nasty bits, and cutting out any eyes. Cut into quarters. Put in a saucepan with 1 teaspoon of the salt and enough water to cover them and boil for 20 minutes. Drain in the sieve and cut into slices.

Meanwhile, break the eggs into a bowl and pick out any bits of shell. Add the milk, salt and pepper and mix up with a fork.

Wipe the butter on the inside of the ovenproof dish. Put alternate layers of potato and fish into the dish, ending with a layer of potatoes. Pour the egg and milk mixture over the fish and potatoes. Cover with breadcrumbs and dot with butter. Cook in the oven at 180°C, 350°F, Gas mark 4 for 30 minutes.

ADDITIONS & ALTERNATIVES
Serve with green vegetables, carrots or salad.

TIPS
You can buy packets of breadcrumbs, some of which have been flavoured or pre-cooked, or you can make them yourself. There are full instructions on making breadcrumbs in the 'How to' chapter.

RUSSIAN CHICKEN SALAD

Serves 4   ① *Preparation 20 min, Cooking 30 min* — *Easy*

INGREDIENTS
2 large or 4 small cooked chicken breasts
or other cooked boneless chicken leftovers
12 small new potatoes
1 cup frozen peas
4 eggs
2 large gherkins
2 tablespoons capers
$\frac{1}{2}$ cup mayonnaise
Small carton (142 ml, 5 fl oz) sour cream
2 teaspoons Worcestershire sauce
$\frac{1}{2}$ teaspoon salt
$\frac{1}{2}$ teaspoon freshly ground black pepper
100 g (4 oz) pitted black olives

EQUIPMENT
Ovenproof dish (if cooking the chicken)
2 or 3 saucepans
Sharp knife
Chopping board
Bowl
Fork
Set of measuring cups
Set of measuring spoons
Small bowl
Wooden spoon

DEFROSTING & COOKING THE CHICKEN
If you need to cook the chicken, make sure frozen chicken is
completely thawed before use. This means leaving it in the fridge

215

overnight, or out of the fridge, for 6 hours. Then just brush with oil and cook in an ovenproof dish in the oven for 30 minutes at 200°C, 400°F, Gas mark 6.

METHOD

You can cook the different bits in turn if you don't have enough pans.

Scrub the potatoes, cutting away any nasty bits, and cutting out any eyes. Put in a saucepan with enough salted water to cover them and boil for 20 minutes. Drain and slice thinly and put in the bowl.

Boil the peas in enough salted water to cover for 5 minutes then drain. Put in the bowl.

To hard-boil the eggs, put it in a small saucepan nearly full of water. Bring to the boil, and boil for ten minutes. Cool the eggs by putting them in cold water. When the eggs are cold, take off the shell. Chop two of the eggs up really small and put in the bowl. It is easier to chop the white separately then lightly mash the yolk with the fork.

Meanwhile, chop the gherkins into small cubes and add to the bowl.

Slice the chicken into 1 cm ($\frac{1}{2}$ inch) cubes and add to the bowl with the capers.

Mix the mayonnaise, sour cream, Worcestershire sauce, salt and pepper in the small bowl. Add all this to the chicken mixture and stir round. Cut the olives in half. Chop the other two eggs into quarters. Arrange on top of the rest and then scatter the black olives on top.

ADDITIONS & ALTERNATIVES

Add some chopped fresh dill to the mayonnaise.

Serve with green salad and French bread or garlic bread or as a starter for 6 to 8 people.

TIPS

If the saucepan for the potatoes is big enough you could boil the eggs with them; they won't overcook.

Potatoes are cooked when a fork will go into them without pushing hard. If you push too hard they will fall apart.

CHICKEN, POTATO & BEAN SALAD

Serves 4   ◑ *Preparation 15 min, Cooking 30 min — Easy*
Think ahead. You need to cook and cool the chicken,
eggs, potatoes and beans.

INGREDIENTS
2 cooked chicken breasts
2 eggs
125 g pack frozen green beans
3 large potatoes
1 teaspoon salt
Small bunch parsley
1 lettuce
4 large tomatoes
50 g tin anchovy fillets
1 cup pitted green olives
1 cup vinaigrette dressing

EQUIPMENT
Ovenproof dish
Saucepan
Saucepan with lid
Sharp knife
Chopping board
Set of measuring cups
Set of measuring spoons
Tin opener

DEFROSTING & COOKING THE CHICKEN

If you need to cook the chicken, make sure frozen chicken is completely thawed before use. This means leaving it in the fridge overnight, or out of the fridge, covered, for 6 hours. Then just brush with oil and cook in an ovenproof dish in the oven for 30 minutes at 200°C, 400°F, Gas mark 6.

METHOD

Cut the chicken into 1 cm ($\frac{1}{2}$ inch) cubes.

To hard-boil the eggs, put them in a small saucepan nearly full of water. Bring to the boil, and boil for ten minutes. Cool by putting them in cold water. When they are cold, take off the shell. Cut them into quarters.

Cook the beans according to the instructions on the pack, in boiling water, probably for about 10 minutes.

Peel the potatoes, cutting away any nasty bits, and cutting out any eyes. Chop the potatoes into quarters. Cook for about 20 to 25 minutes in boiling water with 1 teaspoon of salt. Cool and slice.

While everything is cooking, get the rest ready. Wash, shake dry and finely chop the parsley. Wash and shake dry the lettuce. Slice the tomatoes. Open the tin of anchovies.

Assemble the salad in a bowl with the lettuce on the bottom, with tomato and potato slices on top. Next, put the chicken and beans on, followed by the olives, eggs, anchovies, parsley and lastly the vinaigrette.

ADDITIONS & ALTERNATIVES

Serve with French bread or garlic bread.

TIPS

There are full instructions on cooking potatoes in the 'How to' chapter.

There's a recipe for Vinaigrette on page 244. You can buy ready-made vinaigrette.

CHICKEN WITH TOMATOES & BRANDY

Serves 4 ℗ *Preparation 5 min, Cooking 1 hr 15 min — Easy*

INGREDIENTS
4 chicken quarters
1 teaspoon salt
1 teaspoon pepper
$\frac{1}{2}$ cup sunflower oil
2 cloves garlic
1 cup dry white wine
1 teaspoon oregano
1 bay leaf
1 teaspoon sugar
400 g tin tomatoes
2 tablespoons brandy

EQUIPMENT
Set of measuring spoons
Set of measuring cups
Large saucepan with lid
Garlic crusher
Sharp knife
Chopping board
Tin opener
Wooden spoon

DEFROSTING
Make sure frozen chicken is completely thawed before use. This means leaving it in the fridge overnight, or out of the fridge, covered, for 6 hours.

METHOD

Rub the chicken pieces with the salt and pepper. Heat the oil in a very large pan and gently fry the chicken until brown on both sides. Put the lid on and leave the chicken to cook over a low heat for about 1 hour.

Peel and crush the garlic or chop it up very small and put it into the pan. Add the wine, oregano, bay leaf and sugar.

Open the tin of tomatoes. Pour the juice into the pan. Use the wooden spoon to mash the tomatoes while they are still in the can. Pour the mashed tomatoes into the pan.

Continue to cook, stirring as the mixture boils. Turn down the heat till it is just boiling (simmering). Cook for 30 minutes. Add the brandy and stir just before serving.

ADDITIONS & ALTERNATIVES

Serve with rice, new potatoes, green vegetable or salad.

TIPS

Prepared garlic is sold in tubes and jars. Just read the label for the suggested equivalent amount. It keeps for 6 weeks in the fridge.

There are full instructions on cooking rice in the 'How to' chapter.

If you have a wok with a lid you can use it to cook this.

TURKEY & APRICOT CASSEROLE

Serves 4   ⏲ *Preparation 15 min, Cooking 45 min — Easy*

INGREDIENTS
750 g (1 ½ lb) boneless turkey chunks
½ × 250 g pack ready-to-eat stoned dried apricots
3 onions
2 cloves garlic
2 tablespoons sunflower oil
1 tablespoon flour
½ cup white wine
1 teaspoon wine vinegar
2 tablespoons sugar
¼ teaspoon cayenne pepper
1 tablespoon freeze dried or dried parsley
1 tablespoon freeze dried or dried tarragon
2 bay leaves

EQUIPMENT
Sharp knife
Chopping board
Garlic crusher
Set of measuring spoons
Frying-pan
Wooden spoon or spatula
Slotted spoon
Casserole with lid.
Set of measuring cups

DEFROSTING
Make sure frozen turkey is completely thawed before use. This means leaving it in the fridge overnight, or out of the fridge, covered, for 6 hours.

METHOD

Cut the apricots in half. Peel and thinly slice the onion. Peel and crush the garlic.

Put the oil in the frying-pan and heat over a moderate heat. Fry the turkey, stirring round till it is sealed. Lift out with the slotted spoon and put in the casserole.

Fry the onion and garlic for about 3 minutes till it is golden, stirring to stop it sticking. Add the flour for the last minute. Add the apricots, wine, vinegar, sugar, cayenne, parsley, tarragon and bay leaves. Stir round for 5 minutes. Pour on top of the turkey pieces. Put the lid on the casserole and cook in the oven for 30 minutes at 180°C, 350°F, Gas mark 4.

ADDITIONS & ALTERNATIVES

Serve with new potatoes, green vegetable or rice.

Try adding a couple of tablespoons of sour cream or smatana to this.

Try using prunes instead of apricots.

TIPS

If you don't have a garlic crusher just squash it with something suitable or chop it up small. Prepared garlic is sold in tubes, jars and bottles. Just read the instructions for the suggested equivalent amount. Most keep for 6 weeks in the fridge, but the bottles keep longer.

There are full instructions on cooking rice in the 'How to' chapter.

SAUSAGE & APPLE SALAD

Serves 4   ⏲ *Preparation 10 min — Easy*

INGREDIENTS
250 g (8 oz) German ham sausage
1 iceberg lettuce
2 dessert apples
6 tablespoons vinaigrette dressing

EQUIPMENT
Sharp knife
Chopping board
Apple corer
Set of measuring spoons
Bowl

METHOD
Cut the sausage into slices or cubes. Wash and dry the lettuce. Tear the lettuce into pieces. Wash the apples, take the core out and slice the apples. Mix the apple, lettuce and sausage in a bowl and pour the vinaigrette over the top. Stir round.

ADDITIONS & ALTERNATIVES
Serve with new potatoes, green vegetable or salad.

Use frankfurters or garlic sausage instead of the German ham sausage.

There is a recipe for Vinaigrette on page 244. You can buy ready-made vinaigrette.

SMOKED BACON & PLUMS

Serves 4 　　　 ⏲ *Preparation 10 min, Cooking 1 hr 6 min — Easy*

INGREDIENTS
1 large onion
1 kg (2 lb) plums
500 g (1 lb) smoked streaky bacon
1 tablespoon butter
$\frac{1}{2}$ cup water
2 tablespoons lemon juice
2 tablespoons white wine
1 tablespoon sugar

EQUIPMENT
Sharp knife
Chopping board
Frying-pan
Set of measuring spoons
Ovenproof dish
Wooden spoon
Set of measuring cups
Bowl
Spoon
Lemon juicer

METHOD
Peel and chop the onion into thin slices. Cut the plums in half and throw away the stones.

Put the bacon in the frying-pan over a moderate heat and fry for 3 minutes. Add the onion and fry for another 3 minutes.

Rub the butter over the inside of the ovenproof dish. Put alternate layers of the bacon and onion mixture and the plums in the dish.

Mix the water, lemon juice, wine and sugar in a bowl and pour over the mixture in the dish.

Cook in the oven for 60 minutes at 200°C, 400°F, Gas mark 6.

ADDITIONS & ALTERNATIVES
Serve with potatoes and green vegetable or salad.

TIPS
Use ready-to-eat prunes instead of the fresh plums.

GERMAN CHEESE & HAM BAKE

Serves 4 ① *Preparation 20 min, Cooking 25 min — Easy*

INGREDIENTS
3 eggs
2 cups milk
$\frac{1}{2}$ teaspoon salt
$\frac{1}{2}$ teaspoon pepper
$\frac{1}{2}$ teaspoon grated nutmeg
6 slices smoked ham
8 slices white bread
8 large slices Emmental cheese

EQUIPMENT
Bowl
Set of measuring cups
Set of measuring spoons
Fork
Sharp knife
Chopping board
Ovenproof dish

METHOD

Break the eggs into a bowl and pick out any bits of shell. Add the milk, salt, pepper and nutmeg and mix up with a fork. Cut the ham into tiny cubes.

Lay the bread and cheese in alternate overlapping slices in the ovenproof dish. Spread the ham on top. Pour the egg mixture over the top. Cook in the oven at 200°C, 400°F, Gas mark 6 for 25 minutes.

ADDITIONS & ALTERNATIVES

Serve with salad.

Use a packet of ready-sliced cheese: you can pick from Gouda, Cheddar or Gruyère and Emmental

RUSSIAN LAMB & TOMATO STEW

Serves 4   ① *Preparation 20 min, Cooking 1 hr 10 min — Easy*

INGREDIENTS

750 g (1½ lb) lamb fillet
3 large potatoes
2 medium onions
30 g packet parsley
15 g packet fresh basil leaves
30 g packet fresh coriander
2 tablespoons olive oil
2 × 400 g tins tomatoes
½ teaspoon salt
1 teaspoon freshly ground black pepper
4 cloves garlic

EQUIPMENT

Sharp knife
Chopping board
Set of measuring spoons
Large saucepan with lid
Wooden spoon or spatula
Tin opener
Garlic crusher

METHOD

Cut the lamb into 2 cm (1 inch) cubes. Peel the potatoes, cutting away any nasty bits, and cutting out any eyes. Chop the potatoes into about eight cubes each. Peel and cut the onions into thin slices. Wash, shake dry and finely chop the parsley, basil and coriander.

Put the oil in the pan and heat over a moderate heat. Add the lamb and stir round for 10 minutes till it goes brown. Add the onion and fry for about 3 minutes, stirring to stop it sticking.

Open the tins of tomatoes. Pour the juice into the frying-pan. Use the wooden spoon or spatula to mash the tomatoes while they are still in the can. Pour the mashed tomatoes into the pan.

Continue to cook, stirring as the mixture boils. Add the potatoes, salt and pepper. Stir round. Bring to the boil, then turn down the heat till it is just boiling (simmering). Put a lid on and cook for 45 minutes. Check the water level from time to time and top it up if needed.

Turn the heat up and add the parsley, basil and coriander. Peel and crush the garlic into the pan. Stir as it boils for 10 minutes. Leave to stand for a couple of minutes before serving.

ADDITIONS & ALTERNATIVES

Serve with new potatoes, green vegetable or rice or couscous (page 296).

Try using chicken instead of the lamb.

TIPS

If you don't have a garlic crusher just squash it with something suitable or chop it up small. Prepared garlic is sold in tubes, jars and bottles. Just read the instructions for the suggested equivalent amount. Most keep for 6 weeks in the fridge, but the bottles keep longer.

You can buy little pots of growing herbs. You can cut off what you need as you need it.

You can buy basil and other herbs in jars, either freeze dried or in oil are best. Some supermarkets sell tubs of frozen fresh herbs as well as dried.

There are full instructions on cooking rice in the 'How to' chapter.

UKRAINIAN LAMB CHOPS

Serves 4   ① *Preparation 10 min, Cooking 50 min — Easy*

INGREDIENTS
4 lamb chops
1 large onion
2 cups boiling water
1 stock cube
1 tablespoon sunflower oil
$\frac{1}{2}$ × 250 g pack ready-to-eat stoned Californian prunes
1 teaspoon tomato purée
1 tablespoon vinegar
2 teaspoons sugar
$\frac{1}{4}$ teaspoon ground cinnamon or mixed spice
1 teaspoon salt
$\frac{1}{2}$ teaspoon black pepper
1 teaspoon cornflour

EQUIPMENT
Sharp knife
Chopping board
Set of measuring cups
Bowl
Wooden spoon or spatula
Saucepan with lid
Set of measuring spoons
Cup

DEFROSTING
Make sure frozen lamb is completely thawed before use. This means leaving the chops in the fridge overnight, or out of the fridge, covered, for 2 to 3 hours.

METHOD
Peel and finely chop the onion. Put the boiling water in the bowl. Crumble the stock cube into the water and stir till dissolved.

Put the oil in the saucepan on a moderate heat. Fry the lamb for about 3 minutes each side till brown, stirring to stop it sticking. Add the water and stock cube to the saucepan. Bring to the boil, then turn down the heat till it is just boiling (simmering). Put a lid on and cook for 10 minutes. Add the prunes, tomato purée, vinegar, sugar, cinnamon, salt and pepper. Put the lid back on and simmer for 30 minutes.

Lift out the chops and prunes and keep warm. Mix the cornflour and 2 tablespoons of cold water together in the cup till smooth. Add the water slowly or it will go lumpy. Stir into the sauce and cook for a couple of minutes till it thickens.

Pour the sauce over the chops and prunes and serve.

ADDITIONS & ALTERNATIVES
Serve with couscous (page 296).

TIPS

Tomato purée comes in tubes. It keeps for 4 weeks in the fridge.

You can use dried prunes but they need to be soaked in water overnight.

LAMB & POTATO STEW

Serves 6   ① *Preparation 10 min, Cooking 2 hrs 30 min — Easy*

INGREDIENTS
1.5 kg (3 lb) stewing lamb
12 small potatoes
3 medium carrots
3 leeks
3 small onions
2 sticks celery
1 meat stock cube
4 cups water
1 teaspoon salt
1 teaspoon pepper
1 bouquet garni (looks like a herb tea bag)

EQUIPMENT
Sharp knife
Chopping board
Vegetable peeler
Set of measuring cups
Small bowl
Bowl
Set of measuring spoons
Spoon
Casserole with lid

METHOD

Cut the lamb into 2 cm ($\frac{1}{2}$ inch) cubes. Peel the potatoes, cutting away any nasty bits, and cutting out any eyes. Peel and chop the carrots into slices, cutting off both ends.

Clean the leeks. First take off the outer leaves, cut the roots off and trim the top. Split the leeks in half lengthways. Hold the leeks under running water and wash any grit out. Shake them dry. Cut into 1 cm ($\frac{1}{2}$ inch) slices.

Peel and chop the onion into quarters. Chop the ends of the celery. Chop the celery into thin slices.

Dissolve the stock cube in the water in the small bowl. Put the lamb in the bowl with the salt and pepper and stir round to coat it.

Put layers of lamb, carrots and leeks in the casserole putting the bouquet garni in between the middle layers. Add enough water and stock cube to cover the meat. Cook in the oven for $1\frac{1}{2}$ hours at 200°C, 400°F, Gas mark 6. Add the potatoes, onion and celery. Put the lid on and cook for 45 minutes.

ADDITIONS & ALTERNATIVES

Use 12 small shallots instead of the onions, and cook them whole.

TIPS

You can buy ready-made stock in cartons from most super-markets. You can also buy Swiss vegetable bouillon powder (vegetable stock), if you are worried about the stuff that goes into stock cubes.

Bouquet garni has a mixture of herbs in it, so you can substitute a teaspoon of mixed Mediterranean herbs. It means you get little specks of herb in the dish, but so what, some people like that.

ꓭEEF STROGANOFF

Serves 4   ① *Preparation 10 min, Cooking 20 min — Easy*

INGREDIENTS

750 g (1 $\frac{1}{2}$ lb) rump steak
3 tablespoons plain flour
$\frac{1}{2}$ teaspoon salt
$\frac{1}{2}$ teaspoon pepper
2 large onions
3 tablespoons sunflower oil
2 tablespoons butter
2 tablespoons English mustard
$\frac{1}{2}$ cup water
Small carton (142 ml, 5 fl oz) sour cream

EQUIPMENT

Sharp knife
Chopping board
Set of measuring spoons
Plastic bag
Frying-pan
Wooden spoon or spatula
Set of measuring cups

METHOD

Cut the steak into thin strips about 4 cm (2 inch) long. Put the flour in the plastic bag with a little salt and pepper. Put a few pieces of steak in the bag and holding the top tightly closed, shake them up. They will get coated in flour. Pick them out. Repeat till all the steak is coated.

Peel and thinly slice the onion.

Put the oil and butter in the frying-pan and heat over a low heat. Gently fry the onion for about 3 minutes till it goes clear but not brown, stirring to stop it sticking. Turn up the heat, add the beef and fry for about 10 minutes. Add the mustard and water and stir round as it comes to the boil. Cook gently for about 10 minutes, stirring. Add the sour cream and warm through.

ADDITIONS & ALTERNATIVES

Serve with mashed potato or chips and salad.

Use crême fraiche instead of sour cream.

Use beef stock instead of the water or add a stock cube.

Use Dijon mustard instead of the English mustard.

You can use fillet steak for this, but cut the frying time to about 5 minutes.

Add 200 g (8 oz) button mushrooms, wiped and cut into thin slices. Cook them for 5 minutes with the onions before you add the steak.

Add 1 tablespoon tomato purée when you add the mustard.

Russians would choose to serve this with sautéed potatoes. Seventies restaurants would choose rice.

TIPS

Tomato purée comes in tubes. It keeps for 4 weeks in the fridge.

ROAST BEEF WITH BEER

Serves 8 ⏲ *Preparation 10 min, Cooking 1 hr 30 min — Easy*

INGREDIENTS
1½ kg (3 lb) beef for roasting
1 teaspoon salt
1 teaspoon pepper
2 tablespoons sunflower oil
1 pint German beer
3 medium onions
2 green peppers
2 leeks
2 carrots
500 g (1 lb) button mushrooms

EQUIPMENT
Set of measuring spoons
Roasting tin
Sharp knife
Chopping board

METHOD
Rub the meat with salt and pepper. Heat the oil in the roasting tin and brown the meat on both sides. Pour the beer over the beef and put the roasting tin in the oven for 30 minutes at 180°C, 350°F, Gas mark 4. Meanwhile, prepare the vegetables.

Peel and chop the onions. Chop the end off the green peppers and cut out the cores and seeds. Cut the peppers into rings. Clean the leeks. First take off the outer leaves, cut the roots off and trim the top. Split the leeks in half lengthways. Hold the leeks under running water and wash any grit out. Shake them dry. Cut into 1 cm (½ inch) slices. Peel and chop the carrots, cutting off both ends.

Wipe the mushrooms clean. Discard any nasty ones. Chop the ends off the stalks.

Add the onion, peppers, leek, carrots and mushrooms to the meat and beer and cook for 1 hour more.

ADDITIONS & ALTERNATIVES
Serve with new potatoes or rice.

GERMAN BAKED APPLE & CHEESE

Serves 4   ⏲ *Preparation 10 min, Cooking 20 min — Easy*

INGREDIENTS
200 g (7 oz) Brie
4 medium-sized Granny Smith apples
3 eggs
3 tablespoons single cream
2 tablespoons milk
$\frac{1}{2}$ teaspoon salt
$\frac{1}{2}$ teaspoon pepper
$\frac{1}{2}$ teaspoon grated nutmeg
$\frac{1}{2}$ cup white wine

EQUIPMENT
Sharp knife
Chopping board
Apple corer
Bowl
Set of measuring spoons
Fork
Spoon
Ovenproof dish

METHOD

Cut the cheese into 1 cm (½ inch) cubes. Cut the top off each apple. Do not throw away. Use the corer to dig out the core and seeds, then scoop out as much of the apple as you can without cutting through the skin. Cut the apple flesh into cubes. Put the apple and Brie in the apple cases.

Break the eggs into a bowl and pick out any bits of shell. Add the cream, milk, salt, pepper and nutmeg, and mix the eggs up with a fork. Spoon the mixture into the apples. Put the tops back on. Put the apples into an ovenproof dish. Pour the wine over the apples. Cook in the oven at 180°C, 350°F, Gas mark 4 for 25 minutes.

SWEET PASTA & ALMONDS

Serves 4   ⓘ *Preparation 2 min, Cooking about 15 min — Easy*

INGREDIENTS

100 g (4 oz) dried smallish pasta shapes or broken-up spaghetti
4 cups water
1 teaspoon salt
¼ × 250 g packet butter
3 tablespoons clear honey
50 g pack flaked almonds

EQUIPMENT

Saucepan
Bowl
Sharp knife
Sieve or colander
Chopping board
Set of measuring cups

Set of measuring spoons
Wooden spoon or spatula

METHOD

Check the packet for the correct cooking time for the pasta. Put the water and salt into a large saucepan. Bring to the boil. Add the pasta and cook for the time indicated. Drain the pasta in the sieve. Put back in the pan with the butter and stir round to coat the pasta and stop it sticking together.

Heat the honey and almonds in the other pan. When it is hot pour it over the pasta and stir in. Heat together, in the saucepan, gently for 5 minutes.

ADDITIONS & ALTERNATIVES

Add $\frac{1}{4}$ teaspoon ground cardamom to the honey.
Try maple syrup, or even golden syrup, instead of the honey.
Try different nuts, whole, chopped or flaked.
Add sultanas to the nuts and honey.

TIPS

It is best to use pasta tubes or shapes. If using something long like spaghetti or tagliatelle then break it up into short bits before cooking.

FRENCH

FRENCH ONION SOUP

Serves 4   ① *Preparation 15 min, Cooking 30 min — Easy*

INGREDIENTS
2 beef stock cubes
5 cups water
3 large onions
1 tablespoon olive oil
2 tablespoons butter
2 teaspoons sugar
$\frac{1}{2}$ teaspoon salt
$\frac{1}{2}$ teaspoon black pepper

EQUIPMENT
Bowl
Set of measuring cups
Sharp knife
Chopping board
Set of measuring spoons
Wooden spoon
Saucepan with lid

METHOD

Dissolve the stock cube in the water in the bowl. Peel and chop the onion into $\frac{1}{2}$ cm ($\frac{1}{4}$ inch) slices.

Put the oil and butter in the saucepan and heat over a low heat. Add the onions and stir. Put the lid on and cook over low heat for 10 minutes until soft. Add the sugar, turn the heat up to moderate and stir for 1 minute. Add the water and stock cube, salt and pepper. Bring to the boil, then turn down the heat till it is just boiling (simmering). Put a lid on and cook for 25 minutes.

ADDITIONS & ALTERNATIVES

Serve with toasted French bread.

Try serving with grated Gruyère, Edam or Gouda cheese.

Try serving a toasted version. First, cut 2 cm (1 inch) thick slices of French bread on the slant. Put in the oven for 30 minutes at 140°C, 275°F, Gas mark 1. Cover these with grated cheese. Put the hot soup in a heatproof bowl, or individual bowls. Float the bread and cheese on top and put under the grill for 3 minutes till the cheese bubbles.

TIPS

You can buy ready-made stock in cartons from most super-markets. You can also buy Swiss vegetable bouillon powder (vegetable stock), if you are worried about the stuff that goes into stock cubes.

FRENCH VEGETABLE SOUP

Serves 4   ① *Preparation 20 min, Cooking 20 min — Easy*

INGREDIENTS
2 medium leeks
1 medium-sized onion
1 medium-sized turnip
2 medium-sized carrots
1 beef stock cube
5 cups water
2 tablespoons butter
1 teaspoon salt
$\frac{1}{2}$ teaspoon black pepper

EQUIPMENT
Sharp knife
Chopping board
Vegetable peeler
Set of measuring cups
Bowl
Saucepan with lid
Set of measuring spoons
Wooden spoon

METHOD
Clean the leeks. First take off the outer leaves, cut the roots off and trim the top. Split the leeks in half lengthways. Hold the leeks under running water and wash any grit out. Shake them dry. Cut into 1 cm ($\frac{1}{2}$ inch) slices.

Peel and chop the onion. Peel the turnip, cutting away any nasty bits. Chop the turnip into 1 cm ($\frac{1}{2}$ inch) cubes. Peel and chop the carrots, cutting off both ends. Cut into match-sized strips. Dissolve the stock cube in the water in the bowl.

Melt the butter in the saucepan over a low heat. Add the vegetables and cook for 5 minutes, stirring from time to time. Add the water and stock cube, salt and pepper. Bring to the boil, then turn down the heat till it is just boiling (simmering). Put a lid on and cook for 15 minutes.

ADDITIONS & ALTERNATIVES
Serve with garlic bread or croûtons (page 243).

TIPS
You can buy ready-made stock in cartons from most super-markets. You can also buy Swiss vegetable bouillon powder (vegetable stock), if you are worried about the stuff that goes into stock cubes.

THICK VEGETABLE SOUP

Serves 4   ① *Preparation 15 min, Cooking 30 min — Easy*

INGREDIENTS
2 large leeks
4 medium-sized old potatoes, about 500 g (1 lb)
2 large carrots
1 stick celery
$^1\!/_2$ × 50 g packet parsley
2 tablespoons butter
4 cups water
1 teaspoon salt
3 tablespoons double cream

EQUIPMENT
Sharp knife
Chopping board
Vegetable peeler

Set of measuring spoons
Saucepan with lid
Set of measuring cups
Wooden spoon
Sieve
Bowl

METHOD

Clean the leeks. First take off the outer leaves, cut the roots off and trim the top. Split the leeks in half lengthways. Hold the leeks under running water and wash any grit out. Shake them dry. Cut into 1 cm ($\frac{1}{2}$ inch) slices.

Peel the potatoes, cutting away any nasty bits, and cutting out any eyes. Chop the potatoes into 1 cm ($\frac{1}{2}$ inch) cubes. Peel and chop the carrots, cutting off both ends. Cut into 1 cm ($\frac{1}{2}$ inch) cubes.

Wash the celery, cut off the ends, and cut into 1 cm ($\frac{1}{2}$ inch) slices. Wash, shake dry and finely chop the parsley.

Put the butter in the pan and melt over a low heat. Put the leeks and carrots in and stir for about 2 minutes, until they have absorbed the butter. Add the potatoes and celery. Stir round. Add the water and salt. Bring to the boil, then turn down the heat till it is just boiling (simmering). Put a lid on and cook for 30 minutes, until tender.

Put the sieve over the bowl and pour in the soup. Use the back of the spoon to force the cooked vegetables through the sieve. Put it all back in the pan and stir and heat gently. Add the cream and stir in just before serving then sprinkle the parsley on top.

ADDITIONS & ALTERNATIVES

Serve with croûtons on top.

CROÛTONS

Serves 4   ⏱ *Preparation 3 min, Cooking 5 min — Easy*

INGREDIENTS
4 slices white bread
2 tablespoons sunflower oil
$\frac{1}{2}$ teaspoon salt

EQUIPMENT
Sharp knife
Chopping board
Frying-pan
Slotted spoon
Plate

METHOD
Cut the bread into 1 cm ($\frac{1}{2}$ inch) cubes. Put the oil in the frying-pan over a high heat. Put in the bread and fry. When done, lift out with the slotted spoon, put on a plate, and add the salt.

ADDITIONS & ALTERNATIVES
Add to soups or salads. This is, of course just fried bread and so delicious.

GARLIC BREAD

Serves 2   ⏱ *Preparation 5 min, Cooking 5 min — Easy*

INGREDIENTS
1 French loaf
3 tablespoons butter
2 or more cloves garlic

EQUIPMENT
Sharp knife
Chopping board
Garlic crusher
Bowl
Aluminium foil
Fork

METHOD
Cut down through the bread in slices, leaving the slices connected at the bottom. Peel and crush the garlic into the bowl. Add the butter to the garlic and mush together to form a paste. Put a bit of the butter and garlic mixture between each slice. Wrap the bread in aluminium foil and put in the oven at 170°C, 325°F, Gas mark 3 for 10 minutes.

ADDITIONS & ALTERNATIVES
Serve with soups, salads, meat and fish dishes.

TIPS
If you don't have a garlic crusher, just crush it with something suitable or chop it up small.

VINAIGRETTE

① *Preparation 1 min — Easy*

INGREDIENTS
3-5 tablespoons olive oil
1 tablespoon white wine vinegar
Salt and pepper
1 teaspoon mustard (optional)
1 garlic clove (optional)

EQUIPMENT
1 screw-top jar
Garlic crusher
Set of measuring spoons

METHOD
Peel and crush the garlic into the jar.

Put all the other ingredients in the screw-top jar and shake vigorously. The vinaigrette will go opaque and thick. This is an emulsion. It will keep in the fridge for three weeks.

ADDITIONS & ALTERNATIVES
Try mixing half & half ordinary and extra virgin olive oil.

Substitute sunflower oil for the olive oil.

Substitute lemon juice, orange juice or herb vinegar for the wine vinegar.

TIPS
Prepared garlic is sold in tubes, jars and bottles. Just read the instructions for the suggested equivalent amount. Most keep for 6 weeks in the fridge, but the bottles keep longer.

Olive oils vary in taste. Extra Virgin is more fruity and interesting but also more expensive than ordinary olive oil. Different brands of extra virgin even taste different, just like different wines.

Good vinegars to use are white or red wine, sherry or even ones that have had herbs added. Don't use malt vinegar, it is cheap but only good for chip shops, or making pickles.

MUSHROOMS IN WINE

Serves 4 as a starter ① Preparation 5 min, Cooking 10 min — Easy
Think ahead. This needs to cool for 2 hours before serving.

INGREDIENTS
250 g (8 oz) button mushrooms, about 20
1 small onion
$\frac{1}{4}$ cup olive oil
2 tablespoons white wine
1 tablespoon lemon juice
$\frac{1}{4}$ cup water
1 teaspoon tomato purée
1 bay leaf
$\frac{1}{2}$ teaspoon salt
$\frac{1}{4}$ teaspoon ground black pepper

EQUIPMENT
Sharp knife
Chopping board
Set of measuring spoons
Saucepan
Slotted spoon
Bowl

METHOD
Wipe the mushrooms clean. Discard any nasty ones. Chop the end off the stalks.

Peel and chop the onion into tiny cubes. Put the onion in the pan with the oil, white wine, lemon juice, water, tomato purée, bay leaf, salt and pepper. Bring to the boil, then turn down the heat till it is just boiling (simmering). Put a lid on and cook for 5 minutes. Add the mushrooms and simmer for 10 minutes. Lift out with the

246

slotted spoon and put in the bowl. Boil the liquid for 2 minutes and then pour over the top. Allow to cool before serving.

TIPS

You do not have to squeeze lemons to get lemon juice, though you can if you like. Lemon juice comes in bottles. One lemon gives about 2 to 3 tablespoons of juice.

GRATED CARROT SALAD

Serves 4   ⏲ *Preparation 10 min — Easy*

INGREDIENTS

500 g (1 lb) bunch young carrots, about 10 small
3 spring onions
3 tablespoons olive oil
1 tablespoon lemon juice
$\frac{1}{2}$ teaspoon salt

EQUIPMENT

Sharp knife
Chopping board
Vegetable peeler
Grater
Bowl

METHOD

Peel the carrots and shred on a coarse grater.

Clean and prepare the spring onions. Cut the root end off, trim the leaves. Peel off and discard any dried up or slimy leaves. Chop into thin slices.

Mix everything together in the bowl and serve.

ADDITIONS & ALTERNATIVES

Serve with other salads or cold dishes.

Add $\frac{1}{2}$ cup raisins or sultanas.

TIPS

You do not have to squeeze lemons to get lemon juice, though you can if you like. Lemon juice comes in bottles. One lemon gives about 2 to 3 tablespoons of juice.

RICE SALAD

Serves 4   ① *Preparation 20 min — Easy*

INGREDIENTS

1 cooked chicken breast
1 cup rice
1 teaspoon salt
2 cups water
4 tablespoons olive oil
1 tablespoon wine vinegar
1 green pepper
2 tomatoes
10 pitted green olives

EQUIPMENT

Ovenproof dish (if cooking chicken)
Set of measuring cups
Set of measuring spoons
Saucepan with lid
Sharp knife
Chopping board
Salad bowl
Wooden spoon

DEFROSTING & COOKING THE CHICKEN

If you need to cook the chicken, make sure frozen chicken is completely thawed before use. This means leaving it in the fridge overnight, or out of the fridge, for 6 hours. Then, just brush with oil and cook in an ovenproof dish in the oven for 30 minutes at 200°C, 400°F, Gas mark 6.

METHOD

Read the packet to get the correct cooking time for the rice. Put the rice, water and salt in the pan. Bring the water and rice to the boil, stirring once, to stop the rice sticking. Turn down the heat to low. Put the lid on the pan. Cook for the time suggested on the pack (10 to 15 minutes for long grain or Basmati rice). Do not stir! After the cooking time, take it off the heat and let it stand for a couple of minutes. Fluff it up with a fork. Empty into the bowl and stir in the oil and vinegar.

Meanwhile, chop the end off the green peppers and cut out the core and seeds. Cut the pepper into thin slices. Cut the tomatoes into 1 cm ($\frac{1}{2}$ inch) cubes. Chop the chicken into similar cubes. Stir the chicken, pepper, tomato and olives into the rice and serve.

ADDITIONS & ALTERNATIVES

Add $\frac{1}{4}$ cup of raisins.

Use some other left-over chicken instead.

NUT & CHEESE SALAD

Serves 4   ① *Preparation 10 min — Easy*

INGREDIENTS
1 lettuce
1 'designer' lettuce such as frisée or chicory
50 g (2 oz) packet walnuts
100 g (4 oz) Gruyère cheese
Vinaigrette dressing

EQUIPMENT
Sharp knife
Chopping board
Bowl

METHOD
Wash and dry the lettuces. Tear up the lettuce. Chop the chicory or 'designer' lettuce into 2 cm (1 inch) wide pieces. Chop up the walnuts. Cut the cheese into 1 cm (½ inch) cubes.

Make the vinaigrette in the salad bowl. Add the torn lettuce leaves, chopped chicory, nuts and cheese. Stir the salad into the dressing.

ADDITIONS & ALTERNATIVES
Use Edam, Gouda or under-ripe Brie instead of the Gruyère.
Add a peeled, cored, cubed apple.

TIPS
You can revive limp lettuce by immersing it in cold water for about half an hour.

You can buy vinaigrette ready-made, or see recipe on page 244.

Chicory looks like a white and green pointed smooth spear head.

FRENCH LEEKS

Serves 2 to 4   ① *Preparation 10 min, Cooking 30 min — Easy*

INGREDIENTS
4 medium leeks
Small bunch parsley or 1 tablespoon dried parsley
3 tablespoons olive oil
$\frac{1}{2}$ teaspoon salt
$\frac{1}{2}$ teaspoon pepper
2 large ripe tomatoes
1 clove garlic

EQUIPMENT
Sharp knife
Chopping board
Set of measuring spoons
Saucepan with lid
Wooden spoon
Slotted spoon
Plate
Garlic crusher

METHOD
Clean the leeks. First take off the outer leaves, cut the roots off and trim the top. Split the leeks in half lengthways. Hold the leeks under running water and wash any grit out. Shake them dry. Cut in two. Wash, shake dry and finely chop the parsley.

Put the oil in the pan over a low heat. Put in the leeks, salt and pepper. Stir round and arrange leek pieces so they cover the bottom of the pan. Put the lid on and cook over very low heat for 15 minutes, turning once or twice. Lift out with the slotted spoon and put on a plate.

Chop the tomatoes. Peel and crush the garlic into the pan. Add the tomatoes and parsley. Cook for 2 minutes, stirring. Pour over the leeks.

ADDITIONS & ALTERNATIVES

You can eat this on its own, as a vegetable with roast or grilled meat, or cold as a salad or starter with French bread.

Try oregano or mixed Mediterranean herbs instead of the basil.

Try fresh basil if you can get it. It also comes 'fresh' in jars. Look at the label for how to use it.

RATATOUILLE

Serves 4   ① *Preparation 20 min, Cooking 1 hr — Easy*

INGREDIENTS

2 large aubergines
2 large onions
2 red or green sweet peppers
6 tablespoons olive oil
2 cloves garlic
400 g tin tomatoes
$\frac{1}{2}$ teaspoon dried basil
$\frac{1}{2}$ teaspoon salt
$\frac{1}{2}$ teaspoon pepper

EQUIPMENT

Sharp knife
Chopping board
Set of measuring spoons
Saucepan with lid or wok with lid
Garlic crusher
Colander
Wooden spoon

METHOD

Dutch aubergines don't need soaking. Just wash, cut the ends off, and cut into 2 cm (1 inch) cubes. Peel and chop the onion into thick slices. Chop the end off the green peppers and cut out the core and seeds. Cut the peppers into rings.

Put the oil in the frying-pan over a moderate heat. Peel and crush the garlic into the pan. Add the onion and fry for about 3 minutes till it is golden, stirring to stop it sticking. Add the peppers and aubergines, cover, and cook over a very low heat very gently for 30 minutes.

Open the tin of tomatoes. Pour the juice into the pan. Use the wooden spoon to mash the tomatoes while they are still in the can. Pour the mashed tomatoes into the pan. Add the basil, salt and pepper. Cook gently, without the lid, for 20 minutes, until the vegetables are soft, but not too wet and runny.

ADDITIONS & ALTERNATIVES

Serve with French bread or garlic bread or rice, or as an accompaniment to meat dishes.

TIPS

If you are using other aubergines, slice and soak them in water for 20 minutes, drain and pat dry with paper kitchen towel and then chop into cubes.

POTATO, CHEESE & CREAM BAKE

Serves 4   ⓘ *Preparation 15 min, Cooking 1 hr 30 min — Easy*

INGREDIENTS

8 medium waxy potatoes
50 g (2 oz) Gruyère cheese
1 clove garlic
2 tablespoons butter
$\frac{1}{2}$ teaspoon salt
$\frac{1}{2}$ teaspoon pepper
$\frac{1}{2}$ teaspoon grated nutmeg
1 medium carton (284 ml, 10 fl oz) single cream

EQUIPMENT

Vegetable peeler
Sharp knife
Chopping board
Grater
Garlic crusher
Bowl
Ovenproof dish
Set of measuring spoons

METHOD

Peel the potatoes, cutting away any nasty bits, and cutting out any eyes. Chop the potatoes into 1 cm ($\frac{1}{2}$ inch) slices. Grate the cheese.

Peel and crush the garlic into the bowl. Add the butter and mix together. Divide the butter and garlic into three.

Use one lot of garlic butter to spread on the bottom of a shallow ovenproof dish. Put half the potatoes in the dish, and add half the salt, pepper, nutmeg and cheese. Use the next lot of butter to put in bits on top of those potatoes, then add the rest of the potatoes. Add the last of the salt, pepper, nutmeg, cheese and butter, then pour the cream on top. Cook for about $1\frac{1}{2}$ hours at 150°C, 300°F, Gas mark 2 until the potatoes are creamy and the surface golden.

ADDITIONS & ALTERNATIVES

Serve as an accompaniment to grilled meat or fish or casseroles.

Use a cup of water with a beef stock cube dissolved in it instead of the cream.

TIPS

Prepared garlic is sold in tubes and jars. Just read the label for the suggested equivalent amount. It keeps for 6 weeks in the fridge.

You can buy prepared chopped ginger root in jars. It will keep for 6 weeks in the fridge.

FRENCH ANCHOVY TOAST

Serves 2 as snack   ⏱ *Preparation 5 min, Cooking 7 min — Easy*

INGREDIENTS

50 g can anchovy fillets
1 clove garlic
1 tablespoon olive oil
$\frac{1}{4}$ teaspoon wine vinegar
$\frac{1}{2}$ loaf of French bread

EQUIPMENT

Tin opener (most tins of anchovies have ring pulls)
Garlic crusher
Bowl
Fork
Set of measuring spoons
Baking sheet or ovenproof dish

METHOD

Turn the oven on to 220°C, 425°F, Gas mark 7.

Open the tin of anchovies and drain. Peel and crush the garlic into the bowl. Mash up the anchovies and garlic, then add the oil and vinegar.

Cut 4 slices of French bread. Toast on one side. Spread the other side with the paste. Put them on a baking sheet and put in the oven for 5 minutes.

CRISP BAKED FISH

Serves 4   ① *Preparation 15 min, Cooking 25 min — Easy*

INGREDIENTS

1 small onion
100 g (4 oz) mushrooms, about 10
2 tablespoons butter
$\frac{1}{2}$ cup dry white wine
600 g pack frozen small plaice (about 5 fillets)
$\frac{1}{2}$ teaspoon fresh ground black pepper
3 tablespoons breadcrumbs

EQUIPMENT

Sharp knife
Chopping board
Bowl
Set of measuring spoons
Wooden spoon
Spoon
Frying-pan
Grater (if making breadcrumbs)

Ovenproof dish
Set of measuring cups

METHOD

Peel and chop the onion up small. Wipe the mushrooms clean. Discard any nasty ones. Chop the end off the stalks. Chop up small.

Put the 1 tablespoon of butter in the frying-pan and melt over a low heat. Fry the onion for about 3 minutes till it is soft, stirring to stop it sticking. Add the mushrooms and cook for 1 minute. Add the wine, bring to the boil and cook for 1 minute.

Rub the ovenproof dish with the rest of the butter. Put in the fish, grind the pepper over them and a bit of salt if you want, then pour the wine mixture over them. Spread the breadcrumbs over the top. Cook at 220°C, 425°F, Gas mark 7 for 20 minutes until the breadcrumbs are golden.

ADDITIONS & ALTERNATIVES

Serve with new potatoes, green vegetable or salad.

Try using cod, hake or other white fish.

TIPS

You can buy packets of breadcrumbs, some of which have been flavoured or pre-cooked, or you can make them yourself. There are full instructions on making breadcrumbs in the 'How to' chapter.

PLAICE FILLETS IN PRAWN SAUCE

Serves 4   ⏱ *Preparation 15 min, Cooking 10 min — Easy*

INGREDIENTS
600 g (1¼ lb) pack frozen small plaice (about 5 fillets)
2 tablespoons flour
½ teaspoon salt
½ teaspoon black pepper
1 small onion
Small bunch parsley
3 tablespoons lemon juice
4 tablespoons butter
1 tablespoon sunflower oil
½ cup cooked prawns
1 tablespoon capers

EQUIPMENT
Plastic bag
Set of measuring spoons
Sharp knife
Chopping board
Lemon juicer
Frying-pan
Plate
Wooden spatula
Saucepan or small frying-pan

METHOD
You can cook the fish from frozen. Put the flour in the bag with the salt and pepper. Put the fish in the bag, one at a time and shake up to coat in flour.

Peel and chop the onion. Wash, shake dry and finely chop the parsley. Squeeze the juice from the lemon.

Put 2 tablespoons of the butter and the oil in the frying-pan over a moderate heat. Fry the fish, a couple at a time for about 4 minutes each side. Lift out on to a plate to serve.

Meanwhile, melt the other 2 tablespoons of butter in a small frying-pan. Add the onion and cook for 3 minutes till soft, then add prawns, capers, parsley and lemon juice. Warm through and pour over the fish.

ADDITIONS & ALTERNATIVES

Serve with new potatoes, green vegetable or salad.

TIPS

You do not have to squeeze lemons to get lemon juice, though you can if you like. Lemon juice comes in bottles. One lemon gives about 2 to 3 tablespoons of juice.

PROVENÇALE FISH

Serves 4 ① *Preparation 15 min, Cooking 15 min — Easy*

INGREDIENTS

600 g packet cod, haddock or hake fillets
2 tablespoons flour
$\frac{1}{2}$ teaspoon salt
$\frac{1}{2}$ teaspoon black pepper
1 medium-sized onion
1 clove garlic
400 g tin tomatoes
4 tablespoons olive oil
10 pitted black olives

EQUIPMENT

Sharp knife
Chopping board

Set of measuring spoons
Plastic bag
Garlic crusher
Tin opener
Wooden spoon
Frying-pan
Slotted spoon
Plate

METHOD

You can cook the fish from frozen. Cut fish into 4 cm (2 inch) squares. Put the flour in the bag with the salt and pepper. Put the fish in the bag, one at a time and shake up to coat in flour.

Peel and chop the onion into thin slices. Peel and crush the garlic. Open the tin of tomatoes. Pour the juice away. Use the wooden spoon to mash the tomatoes while they are still in the can.

Put 3 tablespoons of the oil in the frying-pan over a moderate heat. Fry the fish for about 7 minutes till it is golden, stirring to stop it sticking. Lift out with the slotted spoon and put on a plate.

Add 1 tablespoonful of the oil to the pan. Fry the onion for 3 minutes till golden. Pour the mashed tomatoes into the pan and add the garlic. Continue to cook, stirring as the mixture boils. Cook for 3 minutes. Add the olives, stir and pour over the fish.

ADDITIONS & ALTERNATIVES

Serve with new potatoes, green vegetable or salad.

PRAWNS & RICE

Serves 4   ① *Preparation 20 min, Cooking 30 min — Easy*

INGREDIENTS
250 g pack frozen prawns
$\frac{1}{2}$ medium onion
1 cup rice
2 cups water
1 teaspoon salt
2 tablespoons butter
2 tablespoons dry white wine
1 tablespoon flour
1 cup milk
2 tablespoons double cream
Salt and pepper

EQUIPMENT
Sharp knife
Chopping board
Set of measuring cups
Set of measuring spoons
Saucepan with lid
Frying-pan
Wooden spoon
Fork
Small saucepan
Whisk

METHOD
You can cook the prawns from frozen. Just run them under cold water to get off any ice from the outside.

Peel and chop the onion finely.

Read the packet to get the correct cooking time for the rice. Put the rice, water and salt in the pan. Bring the water and rice to the boil, stirring once, to stop the rice sticking. Turn down the heat to low. Put the lid on the pan. Cook for the correct time until the fluid is absorbed (10 -15 minutes for long grain or Basmati rice). Do not stir or keep looking! After the cooking time, take it off the heat and let it stand for a couple of minutes. Fluff it up with a fork to separate the grains and serve.

Put 1 tablespoon of butter in the frying-pan over a low heat. Fry the onion for 1 minute then add the prawns. Stir round and then add the wine and stir round again.

Put 1 tablespoon of the butter in the other saucepan and melt; then add the flour, and cook for 2 minutes, stirring all the time. Whisk in the milk and then boil, stirring, for 1 minute. The sauce should go thick but not lumpy. Stir in the cream, prawn mixture, salt and pepper and heat gently without boiling. Pour over the rice.

ADDITIONS & ALTERNATIVES
Serve with green vegetable or salad.

GRILLED CHICKEN WITH MUSTARD

Serves 4   ⏱ *Preparation 10 min, Cooking 30 min — Moderate*

INGREDIENTS
4 chicken quarters
3 spring onions
1 cup breadcrumbs
2 tablespoons butter
2 tablespoons oil
1 teaspoon salt
3 tablespoons French mustard
1 teaspoon Cajun seasoning

EQUIPMENT
Sharp knife
Chopping board
Set of measuring spoons
Saucepan
Grill pan
Fork
Bowl
Wooden spatula

DEFROSTING
Make sure frozen chicken is completely thawed before use. This means leaving it in the fridge overnight, or out of the fridge, covered, for 6 hours.

METHOD
Wash and dry the chicken pieces.

Clean and prepare the spring onions. Cut the root end off, trim the leaves. Peel off and discard any dried up or slimy leaves. Chop into thin slices.

Put the butter and oil in the saucepan and heat till the butter melts. Brush about a half of the oil and butter on the chicken and sprinkle with salt.

Take the rack out of the grill pan. Cook the chicken under the grill for 12 minutes a side.

Meanwhile, mix the mustard, spring onions and Cajun seasoning in the bowl with a fork. Slowly add the rest of the butter and oil. Spread the mixture all over the chicken with the spatula then roll in breadcrumbs. Put the chicken back in the grill pan with the skin side upwards, and grill for 5 minutes, until crisp and golden and the juices run clear when you jab a fork into the thickest part of the meat.

ADDITIONS & ALTERNATIVES

Serve with new potatoes, green vegetable or salad.

Serve, garnished with watercress.

Use paprika pepper or oregano instead of the Cajun seasoning.

You could barbecue this.

TIPS

You can buy packets of breadcrumbs, some of which have been flavoured or pre-cooked, or you can make them yourself. There are full instructions on making breadcrumbs in the 'How to' chapter.

CHICKEN IN RED WINE

Serves 4 ① *Preparation 20 min, Cooking 1 hr 30 min* — *Moderate*

INGREDIENTS

$1\frac{1}{2}$ kg (3 lb) chicken pieces

4 rashers unsmoked streaky bacon

4 small onions

100 g (4 oz) button mushrooms, about 10

1 cup boiling water

1 stock cube

1 tablespoon olive oil

3 tablespoons butter

1 clove garlic

1 bouquet garni (looks like a herb tea bag)

$\frac{1}{2}$ teaspoon salt

$\frac{1}{2}$ teaspoon pepper

2 tablespoons brandy

$\frac{1}{2}$ bottle red wine

EQUIPMENT
Sharp knife
Chopping board
Set of measuring cups
Cup or small bowl
Set of measuring spoons
Big saucepan with lid
Garlic crusher
Wooden spoon or spatula
Casserole with lid

DEFROSTING
Make sure frozen chicken is completely thawed before use. This means leaving it in the fridge overnight, or out of the fridge, covered, for 6 hours.

METHOD
Cut the bacon into quarters. Peel the onion and cut into quarters. Wipe the mushrooms clean. Discard any nasty ones. Chop the end off the stalks. Dissolve the stock cube in the water in a cup or small bowl.

Put the oil and 2 tablespoons of the butter in the large saucepan over a moderate heat. Fry the chicken, bacon and onion for about 10 minutes till it is golden, stirring to stop it sticking.

Peel and crush the garlic into the pan. Add the bouquet garni, salt and pepper, put the lid on and cook over low heat for 10 minutes. Add the brandy, wine and stock and stir round.

Put the lot in a casserole with a lid and cook in the oven for 1 hour at 180°C, 350°F, Gas mark 4 with the lid on. Add the mushrooms and cook for another 15 minutes with the lid off.

ADDITIONS & ALTERNATIVES
Serve with new potatoes, green vegetable or salad. You can also have it with rice.

Use white wine.

Bouquet garni has a mixture of herbs in it, so you can substitute a teaspoon of mixed Mediterranean herbs. It means you get little specks of herb in the dish, but so what.

TIPS
There are full instructions on cooking rice in the 'How to' chapter.

Some casseroles, for instance cast iron ones, are flameproof so you can use them instead of the pan for frying and then put them in the oven.

BAKED HAM, CHEESE & POTATOES

Serves 4   ① *Preparation 15 min, Cooking 1 hr 30 min — Easy*

INGREDIENTS
4–6 medium waxy type potatoes, about 500 g (1 lb)
1 tablespoon of butter
1 gammon steak, about 200 g
$\frac{1}{2}$ cup grated Gruyère cheese
$\frac{1}{2}$ teaspoon ground black pepper
1 cup milk
3 tablespoons double cream

EQUIPMENT
Vegetable peeler
Sharp knife
Chopping board
Ovenproof dish or gratin dish
Grater
Set of measuring cups
Set of measuring spoons
Bowl
Wooden spoon

METHOD

Peel the potatoes, cutting away any nasty bits, and cutting out any eyes. Slice the potato thinly. Rub the ovenproof dish with the butter.

Cut the gammon into small cubes. Grate the Gruyère cheese if you need to. Arrange alternate layers of potatoes, cheese, gammon and pepper, ending with potatoes.

Mix the milk and cream together in the bowl and pour over the potatoes.

Cook for $1\frac{1}{2}$ hours in an oven at 180°C, 350°F, Gas mark 4. The potatoes should be creamy.

ADDITIONS & ALTERNATIVES

Serve with salad.

Try using smoked white fish such as haddock instead of the gammon.

Try Edam or Gouda instead of the Gruyère cheese.

Try leaving out the gammon and milk, increasing the double cream to 1 medium carton (284 ml, 10 fl oz) and then cooking for $1\frac{1}{2}$ hours at 150°C, 300°F, Gas mark 2. They should come out creamy and golden.

TOASTED HAM & CHEESE SANDWICH

Serves 2   ① *Preparation 5 min, Cooking 5 min — Easy*

INGREDIENTS
4 slices white bread
4 slices ham
4 slices Gruyère cheese
Butter to coat bread and fry sandwiches

EQUIPMENT
Sharp knife
Chopping board
Frying-pan

METHOD
Butter the bread on both sides. Put ham, cheese, ham and cheese in layers on a slice of bread. Put another piece of bread on top. Repeat for other sandwich. Press down. Put a tablespoon of butter in the frying-pan and melt. Fry the sandwiches for about 3 minutes a side till golden. Add more butter to the pan if needed.

ADDITIONS & ALTERNATIVES
Serve with a bit of salad. Use other cheeses like Edam, Gouda or Cheddar; some of these cheeses come ready sliced.

CHEAT'S CASSOULET

Serves 4   ⏲ *Preparation 10 min, Cooking 33 min — Easy*

INGREDIENTS

450g (l lb) packet pork sausages with herbs (8 large sausages)
2 × 410 g tin flageolet beans
1 large onion
2 cloves garlic
3 tablespoons sunflower oil
2 tablespoons tomato purée
1 tablespoon thyme
Salt and freshly ground pepper to taste

EQUIPMENT

Sharp knife
Chopping board
Tin opener
Sieve
Set of measuring spoons
Saucepan with lid
Wooden spoon or spatula
Slotted spoon
Plate
Ovenproof dish

METHOD

Cut the sausages into 5 cm (2 inch) pieces. Open the tins of beans. Put in the sieve, rinse and drain. Peel and finely slice the onion. Peel the garlic, then chop it into tiny pieces.

Put the oil in the saucepan on a moderate heat. Add the sausages and fry for 5 minutes to brown. Lift out with the slotted spoon and put on a plate. Add the onion and garlic and fry for about 3 minutes till it is golden, stirring to stop it sticking. Add the beans and stir. Add the tomato purée, thyme, salt and pepper and cook for 10 minutes to warm it through. Add the sausage. Turn the heat to low, put the lid on and cook for 15 minutes or alternately put in the ovenproof dish and cook in the oven for 20 minutes at 180°C, 350°F, Gas mark 4.

ADDITIONS & ALTERNATIVES

Serve with green vegetable or salad.

Try adding half a glass of white wine to the beans and then cook for 5 minutes longer.

Try oregano instead of thyme.

Try adding 2 or 3 chopped rashers of bacon to the sausage at the frying stage.

Try different kinds of beans, such as black-eyed beans or baked beans, or a mixture of them. If you use baked beans then don't rinse or drain them.

TIPS

Tomato purée comes in tubes. It keeps for 4 weeks in the fridge.

PORK IN WINE

Serves 4 ① *Preparation 5 min, Cooking 1 hr 30 min — Easy*

INGREDIENTS

500 g (1 lb) pork fillet
2 medium onions
1 tablespoon sunflower oil
1 tablespoon flour
1 cup white wine
1 bay leaf
½ teaspoon salt
½ teaspoon pepper
400 g tin tomatoes

EQUIPMENT

Sharp knife
Chopping board
Set of measuring spoons
Frying-pan
Wooden spoon or spatula
Slotted spoon
Plate
Set of measuring cups
Tin opener
Casserole with lid

METHOD

Cut the pork into 2 cm (1 inch) cubes. Peel and chop the onions into ½ cm (¼ inch) slices.

Put the oil in the frying-pan over a moderate heat. Fry the pork for about 5 minutes, stirring to stop it sticking. Lift out with the slotted spoon and put on a plate. Fry the onions for 3 minutes, add the flour, stir thoroughly and cook for 1 minute. Add the white

271

wine, bay leaf, salt and pepper. Stir round.

Open the tin of tomatoes. Pour the juice into the frying-pan. Use the wooden spoon to mash the tomatoes while they are still in the can. Pour the mashed tomatoes into the pan. Continue to cook, stirring as the mixture boils.

Pour the mixture into the casserole. Put the lid on and cook for $1\frac{1}{2}$ hours at 140°C, 275°F, Gas mark 1.

ADDITIONS & ALTERNATIVES
Serve with rice and salad.

TIPS
There are full instructions on cooking rice in the 'How to' chapter.

Some casseroles, for instance cast iron ones, are flameproof so you can use them instead of the pan for frying and then put them in the oven.

CRUNCHY ROAST LAMB

Serves 4   ⏲ *Preparation 20 min, Cooking 1 hr — Easy*

INGREDIENTS
1 kg (2 lb) loin of lamb
2 clove garlic (optional)
$\frac{1}{2}$ teaspoon salt
$\frac{1}{2}$ teaspoon ground black pepper
A few bits of fresh parsley or 1 tablespoon of dried parsley
$\frac{1}{2}$ cup breadcrumbs
3 tablespoons butter

EQUIPMENT
Sharp knife
Chopping board
Set of measuring spoons

Roasting tin or ovenproof dish, with a rack if possible
Bowl

DEFROSTING

Make sure frozen lamb is completely thawed before use. This means leaving it in the fridge overnight, or out of the fridge, covered, for 6 hours.

METHOD

Peel the garlic, then chop it into thin slices. Stick the point of the knife into the lamb in a few places. Push the bits of garlic into the cuts. Rub the salt and pepper on to the meat. Put the lamb on the rack in the roasting tin and cook in the oven for 20 minutes at 200°C, 400°F, Gas mark 6.

Wash, shake dry and finely chop the parsley. Mix breadcrumbs, parsley and butter together in the bowl. Press thickly all over top side surface of meat. Put back in the oven for 40 minutes until the meat is cooked and the breadcrumbs have gone brown.

ADDITIONS & ALTERNATIVES

Serve with new potatoes, green vegetable or salad.

Try this with couscous (page 296) and a green salad.

TIPS

You can buy packets of breadcrumbs, some of which have been flavoured or pre-cooked, or you can make them yourself. There are full instructions on making breadcrumbs in the 'How to' chapter.

ROAST LAMB WITH POTATOES

Serves 6 ⏲ *Preparation 20 min, Cooking 1hr 45 min — Easy*

INGREDIENTS
1½ kg (3 lb) leg of lamb
½ teaspoon salt
½ teaspoon pepper
12 medium potatoes, about 1 kg (2 lb)
1 lamb stock cube
1½ cup boiling water
3 medium onions
1 tablespoon butter
1 tablespoon olive oil

EQUIPMENT
Vegetable peeler
Sharp knife
Chopping board
Bowl
Set of measuring cups
Set of measuring spoons
Frying-pan
Wooden spoon
Ovenproof dish or roasting tin

METHOD
Rub lamb with salt and pepper.

Peel the potatoes, cutting away any nasty bits, and cutting out any eyes. Chop the potatoes into thin slices.

Dissolve the stock cube in the water in a bowl. Peel and chop the onion into slices.

Put the butter and oil in the frying-pan and heat over a

moderate heat. Fry the onion for about 3 minutes till it is golden, stirring to stop it sticking.

Put the meat in the middle of the ovenproof dish or roasting tin and arrange layers of sliced onions and potatoes around it, seasoning each layer lightly. Pour the water and stock cube into the dish so that it just covers the potatoes and onion layers. Cook at 180°C, 350°F, Gas mark 4 for 1 ¾ hours.

ADDITIONS & ALTERNATIVES
Serve with green vegetable or salad.

TIPS
You can buy ready-made stock in cartons from most supermarkets. You can also buy Swiss vegetable bouillon powder (vegetable stock), if you are worried about the stuff that goes into stock cubes.

SPRING LAMB STEW

Serves 4 ℗ *Preparation 20 min, Cooking 2 hrs — Easy*

INGREDIENTS
750 g (1½ lb) boneless shoulder of lamb
3 medium-sized potatoes
3 small carrots
4 small onions
1 clove garlic
1 stock cube
1 cup boiling water
2 tablespoons olive oil
1 teaspoon sugar
1 tablespoon flour
1 tablespoon tomato purée
1 bouquet garni (looks like a herb tea bag)
½ teaspoon salt
½ teaspoon pepper
1 cup frozen peas

EQUIPMENT
Sharp knife
Chopping board
Vegetable peeler
Set of measuring cups
Cup or small bowl
Flameproof casserole with lid or frying-pan and casserole
Set of measuring spoons
Wooden spoon or spatula
Garlic crusher

METHOD

Cut meat into 4 cm ($1\frac{1}{2}$ inch) cubes. Peel the potatoes, cutting away any nasty bits, and cutting out any eyes. Chop the potatoes into quarters. Peel and chop the carrots into quarters, cutting off both ends. Peel and chop the onions into quarters. Peel the garlic. Dissolve the stock cube in the water in a cup or small bowl.

If you have a flameproof casserole (say cast iron) you can use this. Otherwise use a frying-pan for the first bit, then transfer it to a casserole for the oven part.

Put the oil in the frying-pan or casserole and heat over a moderate heat. Fry the meat for about 3 minutes till it is browned, stirring to stop it sticking. Add sugar and stir for 1 minute. Add flour and stir for 2 minutes until pale brown, then add the water and stock cube, tomato purée, and bouquet garni. Crush the garlic in the pan. Stir round. Bring to the boil. If you have been using the frying-pan, transfer everything to the casserole with a lid now. Put the lid on and cook at 150°C, 300°F, Gas mark 2 for 1 hour. Add the chopped vegetables, salt and pepper. Put lid back on and cook for another hour. Add peas for the last 5 minutes.

TIPS

You can buy ready-made stock in cartons from most supermarkets. You can also buy Swiss vegetable bouillon powder (vegetable stock), if you are worried about the stuff that goes into stock cubes.

Bouquet garni has a mixture of herbs in it, so you can substitute a teaspoon of mixed Mediterranean herbs. It means you get little specks of herb in the dish, but so what.

Tomato purée comes in tubes. It keeps for 4 weeks in the fridge.

CHOCOLATE MOUSSE

Serves 2 to 4 ① *Preparation 15 min, Melting 10 min* — *Moderate*
Think ahead. This needs to stand in the fridge for
4 hours before serving.

INGREDIENTS
150 g plain chocolate
1 tablespoon butter
2 tablespoons coffee
1 teaspoon rum
3 eggs

EQUIPMENT
Egg separator
Cup
2 bowls
Saucepan
Wooden spoon
Set of measuring cups
Set of measuring spoons
Egg whisk
4 ramekins or serving bowl

METHOD
The secret for this is to make sure the mixture never gets too hot so that the eggs cook. Otherwise you will end up with chocolate scrambled egg. What you do is get a heatproof glass bowl which can sit on top of a saucepan of boiling water. Break up the chocolate and put it in the bowl with the butter and let them melt. Add the coffee and rum and stir in. Take the melted chocolate off the heat.

Break the eggs one at a time into a cup and pick out any bits of shell. Put the egg on to the egg separator on another cup and let the white fall off. Put the yolks into the bowl with the chocolate and gently but thoroughly mix in.

Put the egg whites in the other bowl. Whisk up the egg whites till stiff while the chocolate mixture is cooling down. Add a tablespoon of whisked egg white and stir in. This helps break up the mixture so that the rest of the egg whites go in easily. Fold the egg whites into the chocolate mixture. Put the mixture into ramekins or a serving bowl and chill in the fridge for at least 4 hours.

ADDITIONS & ALTERNATIVES
Serve with a little cream.

Try brandy or whisky instead of rum.

TIPS
A ramekin is a small circular pot roughly 5 cm (2 in) tall, and 8 cm (3 in) across. They are good for making individual desserts in, like chocolate mousse or crème caramel.

You can separate the yolks by cracking the egg in half and then juggling the egg from one eggshell half to the other, but this takes practice. The downside is that the yolk can get popped on the shell, and of course your fingers tend to get covered with egg white. Another method is to break the egg into a cup and then try to lift the yolk out with a tablespoon.

FRENCH APPLE CAKE

Serves 6   ⏱ *Preparation 10 min, Cooking 35 min — Easy*

INGREDIENTS
10 tablespoons plain flour
1 teaspoon baking powder
6 tablespoons sugar
3–4 drops vanilla essence (optional)
1 teaspoon salt
8 tablespoons milk
4 tablespoons sunflower oil
2 large eggs

Fruit topping
4 ripe dessert apples
2 tablespoons lemon juice or juice of 1 lemon
4 tablespoons butter
3 tablespoons sugar

EQUIPMENT
Round pie dish, about 2.5 cm (1 inch) deep by 20 cm (8½ inches)
    diameter (a quiche dish would be ideal)
Bowl
Wooden spoon
Small bowl or cup
Fork
Sharp knife
Apple corer
Chopping board
Frying-pan

METHOD
Preheat the oven to 200°C, 400°F, Gas mark 6. Butter the round
pie dish.

To make the base, put the flour, baking powder and sugar into the bowl and mix them together with a wooden spoon. Hollow out a well in the middle with the spoon and put the salt, vanilla essence, milk and sunflower oil in the middle. Break the eggs into a small bowl or cup and mix them together with a fork. Add the eggs and, stirring slowly, mix the wet ingredients in the middle with the dry ingredients on the edges. Pour the mixture into the buttered pie dish.

Peel, core and slice the apples. Sprinkle with lemon juice. Arrange the apple slices on top of the mixture. The apples may sink but don't let that bother you. Dot some small pieces of the butter over the top of the fruit and sprinkle with the sugar. Bake in the middle of the oven for 35 minutes, when it should be golden and well risen.

ADDITIONS & ALTERNATIVES
Use pears instead of apples.

Serve warm with cream or custard, or, if preferred, cold as a cake.

ITALIAN & MEDITERRANEAN

GREEN FISH SAUCE

Serves 6   ⏱ *Preparation 15 min — Easy*

INGREDIENTS

3 cloves garlic
50 g packet parsley
6 tablespoons olive oil
$\frac{1}{4}$ teaspoon cayenne pepper
$\frac{1}{4}$ teaspoon freshly ground black pepper
$\frac{1}{2}$ teaspoon salt
4 tablespoons lemon juice

EQUIPMENT

Sharp knife
Chopping board
Garlic crusher
Bowl
Spoon
Set of measuring spoons
Set of measuring cups
Wooden spoon or spatula

METHOD

Peel the garlic, then crush into the bowl. Wash, shake dry and finely chop the parsley. Put the parsley in the bowl. Mash the garlic and parsley up with the spoon for about 5 minutes. Add the oil a tablespoon at a time. Add the cayenne pepper, black pepper and salt. Stir round. Add the lemon juice and mix well.

ADDITIONS & ALTERNATIVES
Serve with any sort of cooked fish or prawns. Instant Mediterranean taste.

TIPS
If you don't have a garlic crusher just squash it with something suitable or chop it up small. Prepared garlic is sold in tubes, jars and bottles. Just read the instructions for the suggested equivalent amount. Most keep for 6 weeks in the fridge, but the bottles keep longer.

You do not have to squeeze lemons to get lemon juice, though you can if you like. Lemon juice comes in bottles. One lemon gives about 2 to 3 tablespoons of juice.

ANOTHER ITALIAN GREEN SAUCE

Serves 4   *① Preparation 10 min — Easy*

INGREDIENTS
2 tablespoons capers
30 g pack fresh parsley
3 spring onions
1 clove garlic
4 anchovy fillets (optional)
2 tablespoons lemon juice
3 tablespoons olive oil
Salt and freshly ground pepper to taste

EQUIPMENT
Set of measuring spoons
Sharp knife
Chopping board
Bowl
Wooden spoon or spatula

METHOD
Rinse and drain the capers. Wash, shake dry and finely chop the parsley.

Clean and prepare the spring onions. Cut the root end off, trim the leaves. Peel off and discard any dried up or slimy leaves. Chop into thin slices.

Peel the garlic, then chop it into tiny pieces. Finely chop the anchovies.

Put the capers, parsley, spring onions, garlic and anchovy fillets in the bowl and stir round. Add the lemon juice, oil, salt and pepper.

ADDITIONS & ALTERNATIVES
Serve with meat, chicken or fish.

You can use this as a pasta sauce. Just cook the pasta and stir into the sauce.

TIPS
Anchovy fillet tins generally have ring pulls.

SAILOR'S TOMATO PASTA

Serves 6 ⏱ *Preparation 10 min, Cooking 20 min — Easy*

INGREDIENTS
2 large onions
2 cloves garlic
1 medium red pepper
4 tablespoons of olive oil
2 × 400 g tins plum tomatoes
Salt and freshly ground pepper to taste
1 tablespoon oregano
500 g pack spaghetti
1 teaspoon salt

EQUIPMENT
Sharp knife
Chopping board
Set of measuring spoons
Frying-pan
Wooden spoon or spatula
Tin opener
Large saucepan
Sieve

METHOD
Peel and thinly slice the onion. Peel the garlic then chop it into tiny pieces. Chop the end off the red pepper and cut out the core and seeds. Cut the pepper into small squares.

Put the oil in the frying-pan on a moderate heat. Fry the garlic for about 4 minutes till it is brown, stirring to stop it sticking. Add the onion and cook for 3 minutes.

Open the tins of tomatoes. Pour the juice into the frying-pan. Use the wooden spoon to mash the tomatoes while they are still in the can. Pour the mashed tomatoes into the pan. Add the salt and pepper. Continue to cook, stirring as the mixture boils. Cook for 15 minutes. Add the oregano and the red pepper. Cook 5 minutes longer.

Meanwhile, cook the pasta in a saucepan. Read the packet for the cooking time and instructions for the pasta. Times between 10 and 15 minutes are usual. Cook in at least 1 litre (2 pints) of salted boiling water. Drain the pasta well in the sieve.

Put the pasta in a dish and pour the sauce on top.

TIPS
This is enough sauce for 500 g spaghetti.

There are full instructions on cooking pasta in the 'How to' chapter.

You can use this as a sauce to serve with cooked chicken, or poured over grilled steak or with grilled plain white fish fillets.

TOMATO & MUSHROOM PASTA

Serves 6   ⏱ *Preparation 15 min, Cooking 1 hr — Easy*

INGREDIENTS
500 g (1 lb) button mushrooms, about 40
2 medium onions
2 tablespoons olive oil
2 cloves garlic
2 × 400 g tins tomatoes
Salt and freshly ground pepper to taste
5 tablespoons tomato purée
5 tablespoons water
500 g pack spaghetti
1 teaspoon salt

EQUIPMENT
Sharp knife
Chopping board
Set of measuring spoons
Saucepan with lid or wok or frying-pan with lid
Garlic crusher
Wooden spoon or spatula
Tin opener
Large saucepan

METHOD
Wipe the mushrooms clean. Discard any nasty ones. Chop the end off the stalks.

Peel and thinly slice the onion. Put the oil in the frying-pan on a moderate heat. Peel and crush the garlic into the pan. Add the onion and fry for about 3 minutes, stirring to stop it sticking. Turn the heat down low. Add the mushrooms and stir. Put the lid on and cook gently for 15 minutes, giving the odd shake or stir to stop it sticking. Open the tins of tomatoes. Pour the juice into the pan. Use the wooden spoon to mash the tomatoes while they are still in the can. Pour the mashed tomatoes into the pan. Continue to cook, stirring as the mixture boils, add the salt and pepper and cook for 20 minutes. Add the tomato purée and water and cook for another 20 minutes.

Meanwhile, cook the pasta in a saucepan. If you have a problem with this there are full instructions in the 'How to' chapter. Read the packet for the cooking time and instructions for the pasta. Times between 10 and 15 minutes are usual. Cook in at least 1 litre (2 pints) of salted boiling water. Drain the pasta well in the sieve.

Put the pasta in a dish and pour the sauce on top.

ADDITIONS & ALTERNATIVES
Add $\frac{1}{2}$ a cup of dry white wine and cook for 5 minutes longer.

TIPS

Tomato purée comes in tubes. It keeps for 4 weeks in the fridge.

If you don't have a garlic crusher just squash it with something suitable or chop it up small. Prepared garlic is sold in tubes, jars and bottles. Just read the instructions for the suggested equivalent amount. Most keep for 6 weeks in the fridge, but the bottles keep longer.

BASIC OIL & GARLIC PASTA

Serves 6   ⟳ *Preparation 10 min, Cooking 15 min — Easy*

INGREDIENTS
4 cloves garlic
$\frac{1}{2}$ cup olive oil
500 g packet pasta
1 teaspoon salt
$\frac{1}{4}$ teaspoon cayenne pepper (optional)

EQUIPMENT
Sharp knife
Chopping board
Set of measuring cups
Frying-pan
Wooden spoon or spatula
Large saucepan
Set of measuring spoons
Sieve

METHOD
Peel the garlic, then chop it into tiny pieces. Put the oil in the frying-pan on a moderate heat. Fry the garlic for about 5 minutes till it is brown, stirring to stop it sticking.

Cook the pasta in a saucepan. If you have a problem with this there are full instructions in the 'How to' chapter. Read the packet for the cooking time and instructions for the pasta. Times between 10 and 15 minutes are usual. Cook in at least 1 litre (2 pints) of salted boiling water. Drain the pasta well in the sieve.

Put the pasta in the frying-pan with the oil and garlic and stir until thoroughly coated. Add the pepper and serve.

ADDITIONS & ALTERNATIVES
Serve with salad.

TIPS
There are many different sorts of pasta but spaghetti, spaghettini or linguine (all long thin pastas) are very suitable.

Try chilli powder instead of the cayenne, of even leave out the cayenne.

Prepared garlic is sold in tubes, jars and bottles. Just read the instructions for the suggested equivalent amount. Most keep for 6 weeks in the fridge, but the bottles keep longer.

PARSLEY & GARLIC PASTA

Serves 6   ① *Preparation 10 min, Cooking 15 min — Easy*

INGREDIENTS
100 g pack parsley
4 cloves garlic
$\frac{1}{2}$ cup olive oil
500 g pack pasta
1 teaspoon salt

EQUIPMENT
Sharp knife
Chopping board

Set of measuring cups
Frying-pan
Wooden spoon or spatula
Large saucepan
Set of measuring spoons

METHOD

Wash, shake dry and finely chop the parsley. Peel the garlic, then chop it into tiny pieces.

Put the oil in the frying-pan on a moderate heat. Fry the garlic for about 5 minutes till it is brown, stirring to stop it sticking.

Cook the pasta. If you have a problem with this there are full instructions in the 'How to' chapter. Read the packet for the cooking time and instructions for the pasta. Times between 10 and 15 minutes are usual. Cook in at least 1 litre (2 pints) of salted boiling water. Drain the pasta well.

Put the pasta in the frying-pan with the oil and garlic and stir until thoroughly coated. Add the parsley and serve.

ADDITIONS & ALTERNATIVES

Serve with salad.

TIPS

There are many different sorts of pasta but the long thin sorts: spaghetti, spaghettini or linguine are very suitable.

Prepared garlic is sold in tubes, jars and bottles. Just read the instructions for the suggested equivalent amount. Most keep for 6 weeks in the fridge, but the bottles keep longer.

WALNUT PASTA

Serves 6   ⏱ *Preparation 10 min, Cooking 15 min — Easy*

INGREDIENTS
100 g pack walnuts
4 cloves garlic
$\frac{1}{2}$ cup olive oil
500 g packet pasta
1 teaspoon salt

EQUIPMENT
Sharp knife
Chopping board
Set of measuring cups
Frying-pan
Wooden spoon or spatula
Large saucepan
Sieve or colander
Set of measuring spoons

METHOD
Chop the walnuts into small pieces. Peel the garlic, then chop it into tiny pieces.

Put the oil in the frying-pan on a moderate heat. Fry the garlic for about 5 minutes till it is brown, stirring to stop it sticking.

Cook the pasta in the saucepan. If you have a problem with this there are full instructions in the 'How to' chapter. Read the packet for the cooking time and instructions for the pasta. Times between 10 and 15 minutes are usual. Cook in at least 1 litre (2 pints) of salted boiling water. Drain the pasta well in the sieve.

Put the pasta in the frying-pan with the oil and garlic and stir until thoroughly coated. Serve it up and then sprinkle the top with nuts.

ADDITIONS & ALTERNATIVES

Serve with salad.

Try adding $\frac{1}{4}$ teaspoon cayenne pepper or chilli powder.

This is a traditional winter dish.

TIPS

There are many different sorts of pasta but spaghetti, fidelini or linguine are very suitable.

Prepared garlic is sold in tubes, jars and bottles. Just read the instructions for the suggested equivalent amount. Most keep for 6 weeks in the fridge, but the bottles keep longer.

PEPPER PASTA

Serves 6   ① *Preparation 10 min, Cooking 15 min — Easy*

INGREDIENTS

12 red peppers
4 cloves garlic
$\frac{1}{2}$ cup olive oil
4 red chillies
500 g packet pasta
1 teaspoon salt

EQUIPMENT

Sharp knife
Chopping board
Set of measuring cups
Frying-pan
Wooden spoon or spatula
Large saucepan
Set of measuring spoons
Sieve or colander

METHOD

A dish for the brave. Chop the end off the red peppers and cut out the core and seeds. Cut the pepper into small squares. Peel the garlic then chop it into tiny pieces.

Put the oil in the frying-pan on a moderate heat. Pierce the chillies with a fork. Fry the red peppers, whole chillies and garlic for about 5 minutes till the garlic is brown, stirring to stop it sticking.

Cook the pasta in the saucepan. If you have a problem with this there are full instructions in the 'How to' chapter. Read the packet for the cooking time and instructions for the pasta. Times between 10 and 15 minutes are usual. Cook in at least 1 litre (2 pints) of salted boiling water. Drain the pasta well in the sieve.

Take out the chillies and throw away. Put the pasta in a bowl and pour the pepper mixture over the top.

ADDITIONS & ALTERNATIVES

Serve with salad.

This is a traditional winter dish.

If you want the full hot experience, chop the chillies up before cooking, and leave them in.

TIPS

There are many different sorts of pasta but spaghetti, fidellini or linguine are very suitable.

Prepared garlic is sold in tubes, jars and bottles. Just read the instructions for the suggested equivalent amount. Most keep for 6 weeks in the fridge, but the bottles keep longer.

ITALIAN SPINACH

Serves 4   ① *Preparation 15 min, Cooking 12 min* — *Easy*

INGREDIENTS
1 kg (2 lb) spinach
2 cloves garlic
12 green pitted olives
8 black pitted olives
6 tablespoons olive oil
2 tablespoons raisins
1 tablespoon capers
2 tablespoons pine nuts
50 g tin anchovy fillets

EQUIPMENT
Saucepan with lid
Sharp knife
Chopping board
Set of measuring spoons
Frying-pan
Wooden spoon or spatula

METHOD
Wash the spinach and throw away any slimy leaves. Put the spinach in the saucepan (no need to add any more water). Put the lid on and cook over a moderate heat for 4 minutes. Drain the spinach.

Peel the garlic, then chop it into tiny pieces. Chop the olives into small bits.

Put the oil in the frying-pan on a moderate heat. Add the garlic and cook for 3 minutes, stirring to stop it sticking. Add the olives, raisins, capers, and nuts. Stir well. Open the tin of anchovies and drain. Add anchovies and then fold in the spinach. When it is mixed together, turn the heat up and quickly heat through.

ADDITIONS & ALTERNATIVES

Serve with bread.

Use cauliflower or broccoli instead of the spinach. Just break or cut into florets and cook for about 10 minutes in 5 cm (2 inches) water.

Try other chopped nuts instead of the pine nuts.

TIPS

Anchovy fillet tins generally have ring pulls.

Prepared garlic is sold in tubes, jars and bottles. Just read the instructions for the suggested equivalent amount. Most keep for 6 weeks in the fridge, but the bottles keep longer.

MUSHROOM & PINE NUTS IN BUTTER

Serves 4   ① *Preparation 10 min, Cooking 10 min — Easy*

INGREDIENTS

500 g (1 lb) button mushrooms, about 40
1 large onion
2 tablespoons butter
100 g packet pine nuts
Salt and freshly ground pepper to taste

EQUIPMENT

Sharp knife
Chopping board
Set of measuring spoons
Frying-pan
Wooden spoon or spatula

METHOD

Wipe the mushrooms clean. Discard any nasty ones. Chop the end off the stalks. Slice very thin. Peel and finely chop the onion.

Put the butter in the frying-pan on a moderate heat. Fry the mushrooms for about 2 minutes, stirring to stop them sticking. Add the onion and cook for 5 minutes. Add the nuts. Stir round. Cook for 5 minutes more. Add salt and pepper and serve.

ADDITIONS & ALTERNATIVES

Serve with salad.

Try other chopped nuts such as walnuts or almonds.

Add a finely sliced red pepper, with the seeds taken out. Use a saucepan with a lid. Cook the pepper and an extra tablespoon of butter at the same time as the mushrooms for 5 minutes with the lid on, then continue as above.

Try a small aubergine cut into cubes. Cook like the pepper version but for 10 minutes with the lid on and then 3 minutes with it off.

COUSCOUS

Serves 2   ① *Preparation 2 min, Cooking 10 min — Easy*

INGREDIENTS

1 cup couscous
1 tablespoon olive oil
$1\frac{1}{2}$ cups boiling water
1 tablespoon butter
1 teaspoon salt

EQUIPMENT

Set of measuring cups
Set of measuring spoons

Saucepan with lid
Wooden spoon
Fork

METHOD

Put the couscous, oil, boiling water, butter and salt in the saucepan. Stir it together, put the lid on and leave for 5 minutes.

Fluff up with the fork. If it seems too dry before serving, then add 1 teaspoon of lemon juice or olive oil.

ADDITIONS & ALTERNATIVES

You can serve this when you might use rice, such as with fish, chicken or meat, particularly if they have a sauce with them. We do not recommend it with Chinese or Thai cooking.

Add a couple of tablespoons of raisins, soaked in boiling water for 10 minutes.

Add 2 tablespoons of pine nuts fried for 3 minutes in a tablespoon of sunflower oil.

Add a 15 g pack of coriander. Just wash, shake dry and finely chop it.

MOROCCAN POTATO & LEMON

Serves 4   ① *Preparation 20 min, Cooking 30 min — Easy*

INGREDIENTS
10–12 medium potatoes, about 1 kg (2 lb)
2 medium onions
2 lemons or 5 tablespoons lemon juice
$\frac{1}{2}$ cup olive oil
2 cloves garlic
1 tablespoon ground cumin
1 teaspoon ground coriander
$\frac{1}{4}$ teaspoon cayenne pepper
Salt and freshly ground pepper to taste
1 cup water

EQUIPMENT
Vegetable peeler
Sharp knife
Chopping board
Lemon squeezer
Cup
Set of measuring cups
Saucepan with lid
Garlic crusher
Wooden spoon or spatula
Set of measuring spoons

METHOD
Peel the potatoes, cutting away any nasty bits, and cutting out any eyes. Cut into 1 cm ($\frac{1}{2}$ inch) slices. Peel and finely slice the onions. Squeeze the juice from the lemons into the cup.

Put the oil in the saucepan on a moderate heat. Peel and crush the garlic into the pan. Add the onion and fry for about 3 minutes till it is golden, stirring to stop it sticking. Add the cumin, coriander, cayenne pepper, salt and pepper and stir round for 1 minute. Add the potatoes and stir round for 1 minute. Add the lemon juice and water. Turn the heat down to low. Put the lid on and cook for 25 minutes. Check they are not sticking and add a couple of tablespoons more water if it looks like it needs it.

ADDITIONS & ALTERNATIVES
Serve with yoghurt, bread and salad.

LENTIL ONION RICE BAKE

Serves 2–3 ① *Preparation 5 min, Cooking 1 hr 5 min — Moderate*

INGREDIENTS
$^1_2$ cup whole green lentils (Puy type hold together well)
3 onions
1 cup long grain rice
2 teaspoons cumin
1 teaspoon salt
Small bunch fresh coriander (optional)
1 tablespoon olive oil

EQUIPMENT
Sharp knife
Chopping board
Set of measuring cups
Set of measuring spoons
2 saucepans with lids
Wooden spoon
Frying-pan
Ovenproof dish

METHOD

Check the lentils for any small stones and rinse in the sieve under cold water.

Peel the onions. Cut one in half and put half an onion in a saucepan. Finely slice the rest of the onion. Put the lentils in the saucepan with the half onion in it. Add 2 cups of water and the cumin. Put the lid on and cook for 45 minutes.

Meanwhile, cook the rice in the other saucepan. Read the packet to get the correct cooking time. Put the rice, 2 cups water and 1 teaspoon salt in the pan. Bring the water and rice to the boil, stirring once, to stop the rice sticking. Turn down the heat to low, so it is just boiling (simmering). Put the lid on the pan. Cook for the correct time until the fluid is absorbed (10 to 15 minutes for long grain or Basmati rice). Do not stir! After the cooking time, take it off the heat and let it stand for a couple of minutes.

Put the oil in the frying-pan over a moderate heat. Fry the onion for about 3 minutes till it is golden, stirring to stop it sticking.

Pull the coriander leaves from the stalks and chop them roughly. Put the cooked rice and lentils into an ovenproof dish together with the chopped coriander, and stir together in the dish with the wooden spoon. Pour the fried onions and the olive oil they were cooked in over the rice and lentils. Spread the onions evenly over the rice mixture. Cook for 20 minutes, in the middle of the oven at 170°C, 325°F, Gas mark 3.

ADDITIONS & ALTERNATIVES

This can be served as an accompaniment or as a main dish hot or cold with some salad, or with hummus and pitta.

Try coriander powder instead of cumin.

BAKED AUBERGINE & CHEESE

Serves 4   ⏲ *Preparation 10 min, Cooking 1 hr 30 min — Easy*

INGREDIENTS
1 large or 2 medium aubergines
8 medium tomatoes
4 tablespoons olive oil
Salt and freshly ground pepper to taste
500 g pack sliced Gruyère cheese

EQUIPMENT
Sharp knife
Chopping board
Set of measuring spoons
Ovenproof dish

METHOD
Peel the aubergine. Wash the tomatoes. Cut both into $\frac{1}{2}$ cm ($\frac{1}{4}$ inch) slices. Slice the cheese if not using ready sliced.

Put the oil in the ovenproof dish and swirl round to cover. Add a layer of aubergine. Add a layer of tomatoes, season with a little salt and pepper and put a layer of cheese on top. Put more layers of aubergine, tomatoes and cheese on top till it is all used up. Cook in the oven for 1 $\frac{1}{2}$ hours at 170°C, 325°F, Gas mark 3.

ADDITIONS & ALTERNATIVES
Serve with a green vegetable or salad.

Try other cheeses like Mozzarella or Emmental.

RISOTTO

Serves 6   ① *Preparation 20 min, Cooking 1 hr — Moderate*

INGREDIENTS
2 large onions
100 g (8 oz) mushrooms, about 20 button
5 tablespoons olive oil
12 cloves
8 cups boiling water
$1\frac{1}{2}$ cups rice
3 tablespoons butter
50 g tin anchovy fillets
$\frac{1}{2}$ cup grated Parmesan cheese

EQUIPMENT
Sharp knife
Chopping board
Set of measuring spoons
Frying-pan
Wooden spoon or spatula
Set of measuring cups
Large saucepan
Casserole

METHOD
Peel the onions. Chop one of them finely. Wipe the mushrooms clean. Discard any nasty ones. Chop the end off the stalks. Cut into thin slices.

Put 1 tablespoon of oil in the frying-pan on a moderate heat. Add the whole onion and roll around and fry for about 4 minutes till brown on the outside. Take out of the pan. Carefully stick the cloves into the onion.

Put the water in the saucepan. Put the whole onion into the

boiling water. Gradually add the rice, stirring it round. Cook for 20 minutes till the onion goes mushy. Turn down the heat till the water is just boiling (simmering). Cook for 5 minutes. Drain the rice. Pick out the onion and the cloves.

Meanwhile, put 2 tablespoons of the oil and 2 tablespoons of the butter in the frying-pan on a moderate heat and add the chopped onion. Cook for about 4 minutes. Add the anchovies and the oil from the can. Mash up with the wooden spoon. Add the mushrooms and cook over a low heat for 10 minutes, stirring from time to time.

Rub the inside of the casserole with a bit of butter. Put the rice, the last 2 tablespoons of oil and the anchovy mixture into it. Stir round. Put the cheese on top. Put little bits of butter on top. Put the casserole in the oven and cook for 20 minutes at 180°C, 350°F, Gas mark 4.

ADDITIONS & ALTERNATIVES
Serve with salad.

Try other cheese like Pecorino.

TIPS
Anchovy fillet tins generally have ring pulls.

You can buy ready grated Parmesan in packets or cartons.

MEDITERRANEAN CUCUMBER SALAD

Serves 4 ⓘ *Preparation 10 min — Easy*
Think ahead. This needs to stand in the fridge for
1 hour before serving.

INGREDIENTS

2 large cucumbers
1 clove garlic
$\frac{1}{2}$ cup vinaigrette (page 244)
$\frac{1}{2}$ teaspoon oregano

EQUIPMENT

Vegetable peeler
Sharp knife
Chopping board
Plate
Set of measuring cups
Set of measuring spoons

METHOD

Peel the cucumbers. Cut into thin slices. Put in the fridge on a plate for an hour. Peel the garlic, then chop it into tiny pieces. Arrange the cucumber on a plate. Pour the vinaigrette over the top and then sprinkle with the oregano and garlic.

CANNELLINI BEAN SALAD

Serves 4   ① *Preparation 5 min, Cooking 10 min — Easy*

INGREDIENTS

2 × 420 g tin cannellini beans
220 g (small) tin plum tomatoes
1 clove garlic
3 tablespoons olive oil
1 teaspoon dried sage
$\frac{1}{4}$ teaspoon salt
Freshly ground black pepper
1 tablespoon wine vinegar

EQUIPMENT

Tin opener
Sieve
Kitchen paper towel
Sharp knife
Chopping board
Set of measuring spoons
Saucepan with lid
Wooden spoon or spatula

METHOD

Open the tins of beans and drain in the sieve. Rinse them under cold water. Put on the paper towel to dry.

Open the tin of tomatoes. Pour the juice away. Put the tomatoes in the sieve to drain. Chop the tomatoes into quarters and put back in the sieve.

Peel the garlic, then chop it into tiny pieces.

Put the oil in the saucepan on a moderate heat. Add the garlic and sage and cook, stirring, for 30 seconds. Add the beans, tomatoes, salt and a few grindings of pepper. Put the lid on and bring to the boil, then turn down the heat till it is just boiling (simmering). Cook for 10 minutes. Add the vinegar. Serve.

MEDITERRANEAN POTATO SALAD

Serves 4   ⏱ *Preparation 10 min, Cooking 25 min — Easy*

INGREDIENTS
500 g (1 lb) new potatoes, about 12 small
4 spring onions
5 tablespoons olive oil
2 tablespoons wine vinegar
$\frac{1}{2}$ teaspoon salt
$\frac{1}{2}$ teaspoon pepper
1 teaspoon mixed Mediterranean herbs

EQUIPMENT
Saucepan
Slotted spoon
Plate
Sharp knife
Chopping board
Set of measuring spoons
Bowl
Wooden spoon

METHOD
Scrub the potatoes (do not peel) and boil them in their jackets, in salted water, for 20 minutes till just tender. Lift out with the slotted spoon and put on a plate.

Meanwhile, clean and prepare the spring onions. Cut the root end off, trim the leaves. Peel off and discard any dried up or slimy leaves. Chop into thin slices.

When the potatoes are cool enough to handle, cut into 2 cm (1 inch) slices. Mix the oil, vinegar, spring onion, salt, pepper and herbs together in a bowl. Add the hot potatoes and stir.

TUNA & BEAN SALAD

Serves 4   ⓘ *Preparation 10 min — Easy*

INGREDIENTS
200 g tin tuna in olive oil
420 g tin cannellini beans
3 spring onions
30 g pack fresh parsley
3 tablespoons olive oil
2 teaspoons lemon juice
$\frac{1}{2}$ teaspoon salt
Freshly ground black pepper to taste

EQUIPMENT
Tin opener
Sieve
Sharp knife
Chopping board
Set of measuring spoons
Bowl
Wooden spoon or spatula

METHOD

Open the tin of tuna. Open the tin of beans and drain in the sieve. Rinse the beans under cold water still in the sieve and shake excess water off.

Clean and prepare the spring onions. Cut the root end off, trim the leaves. Peel off and discard any dried up or slimy leaves. Chop into thin slices. Wash, shake dry and finely chop the parsley.

Put the olive oil, lemon juice, salt and pepper in the bowl. Add the beans, spring onions and parsley and stir together with the wooden spoon. Break the tuna into chunks and arrange them on top.

ADDITIONS & ALTERNATIVES

Serve with other antipasto or salad.

Use other tinned beans such as haricot.

GARLIC & ANCHOVY PASTA

Serves 6 ① *Preparation 10 min, Cooking 15 min — Easy*

INGREDIENTS

50 g tin anchovies
4 cloves garlic
$\frac{1}{2}$ cup olive oil
500 g pack pasta

EQUIPMENT

Sharp knife
Chopping board
Set of measuring cups
Frying-pan
Wooden spoon or spatula

Large saucepan
Sieve or colander

METHOD

Open the tin of anchovies and drain. Peel the garlic then chop it into tiny pieces.

Put the oil in the frying-pan on a moderate heat. Fry the garlic for about 3 minutes till it is brown, stirring to stop it sticking. Add the anchovy fillets and mash up till smooth.

Cook the pasta in the saucepan. If you have a problem with this there are full instructions in the 'How to' chapter. Read the packet for the cooking time and instructions for the pasta. Times between 10 and 15 minutes are usual. Cook in at least 1 litre (2 pints) of boiling water. Drain the pasta well in the sieve.

Put the pasta in the frying-pan with the anchovy mixture and stir until thoroughly coated.

ADDITIONS & ALTERNATIVES

Serve with salad.

TIPS

Anchovy fillet tins generally have ring pulls.

Anchovy fillets are very salty. Don't use any salt when you cook the pasta.

There are many different sorts of pasta but spaghetti, spaghettini linguine or fettuccine are very suitable.

Prepared garlic is sold in tubes, jars and bottles. Just read the instructions for the suggested equivalent amount. Most keep for 6 weeks in the fridge, but the bottles keep longer.

ANCHOVY & OLIVE PASTA

Serves 6   ⏱ *Preparation 10 min, Cooking 15 min — Easy*

INGREDIENTS
50 g tin anchovies
12 pitted black olives
12 pitted green olives
4 cloves garlic
$\frac{1}{2}$ cup olive oil
500 g packet pasta

EQUIPMENT
Sharp knife
Chopping board
Set of measuring cups
Frying-pan
Wooden spoon or spatula
Large saucepan
Sieve or colander

METHOD
Open the tin of anchovies and drain. Chop the olives up really small. Peel the garlic, then chop it into tiny pieces.

Put the oil in the frying-pan on a moderate heat. Fry the garlic for about 5 minutes till it is brown, stirring to stop it sticking. Add the anchovy fillets and mash up till smooth. Add the olives.

Cook the pasta in the saucepan. If you have a problem with this there are full instructions in the 'How to' chapter. Read the packet for the cooking time and instructions for the pasta. Times between 10 and 15 minutes are usual. Cook in at least 1 litre (2 pints) of boiling water. Drain the pasta well in the sieve.

Put the pasta in the frying-pan with the anchovies and olives and stir until thoroughly coated.

ADDITIONS & ALTERNATIVES
Serve with salad.

TIPS
Anchovy fillet tins generally have ring pulls.

Anchovy fillets are very salty. Don't use any salt when you cook the pasta. .

There are many different sorts of pasta but spaghetti, spaghettini, fettuccine or linguine (long thin pastas) are very suitable.

Prepared garlic is sold in tubes, jars and bottles. Just read the instructions for the suggested equivalent amount. Most keep for 6 weeks in the fridge, but the bottles keep longer.

ITALIAN PRAWNS

Serves 4   ① *Preparation 15 min, Cooking 35 min — Easy*

INGREDIENTS
500 g pack cooked (pink) prawns
1 large onion
1 clove garlic
1 green pepper
200 g (8 oz) mushrooms, about 20 button
400 g tin plum tomatoes
3 tablespoons olive oil
Salt and freshly ground pepper to taste
$\frac{1}{4}$ cup dry white wine

EQUIPMENT
Sharp knife
Chopping board
Tin opener

311

Set of measuring spoons
Frying-pan
Wooden spoon or spatula
Set of measuring cups

DEFROSTING

Make sure frozen prawns are completely thawed before use. This means leaving them in the fridge for 6 hours, or at room temperature for an hour.

METHOD

Peel and finely chop the onion. Peel the garlic then chop it into tiny pieces. Chop the end off the green pepper and cut out the core and seeds. Cut the pepper into 1 cm ($\frac{1}{2}$ inch) strips. Wipe the mushrooms clean. Discard any nasty ones. Chop the end off the stalks. Cut into thin slices. Open the tin of tomatoes.

Put the oil in the frying-pan on a moderate heat. Fry the onion and garlic for about 4 minutes till the onion is golden, stirring to stop it sticking.

Pour the tomatoes into the pan. Turn the heat to low and cook for 15 minutes. Add the green pepper and cook for 5 minutes. Add the mushrooms and cook for 5 minutes. Turn the heat to moderate, add the salt, pepper and wine, and cook for another 10 minutes, stirring from time to time. Add the prawns and bring to the boil, then take off the heat.

ADDITIONS & ALTERNATIVES

Serve with rice and salad.

TIPS

There are full instructions on cooking rice in the 'How to' chapter.

MEDITERRANEAN TUNA

Serves 4 ℗ *Preparation 15 min, Cooking 30 min — Easy*

INGREDIENTS
700 g (1 ½ lb) fresh tuna
2 small onions
2 cloves garlic
½ lemon or 2 tablespoons lemon juice
2 tablespoons olive oil
400 g tin tomatoes
1 bay leaf
12 pitted black olives
½ teaspoon salt
½ teaspoon pepper

EQUIPMENT
Set of measuring spoons
Sharp knife
Chopping board
Vegetable peeler
Tin opener
Saucepan
Casserole with lid.
Lemon juicer

METHOD
Put the oven on at 180°C, 350°F, Gas mark 4.

Cut the tuna into 4 cm (2 inch) pieces. Peel and slice the onion. Peel the garlic. Squeeze the lemon.

Put the oil in the frying-pan over a moderate heat. Fry the onion for 2 minutes, stirring to stop it sticking. Open the tin of tomatoes. Pour the juice into the frying-pan. Use the wooden spoon to mash the tomatoes while they are still in the can. Pour the mashed tomatoes into the pan. Add the bay leaf. Bring to the boil, then turn down the heat till it is just boiling (simmering). Cook for 10 minutes.

Pour the mixture into a casserole. Add the tuna, olives, whole garlic cloves, salt and pepper. Cook for 25 minutes. Stir in the lemon juice before serving.

ADDITIONS & ALTERNATIVES
Serve with French bread and salad or chips.

TIPS
You do not have to squeeze lemons to get lemon juice, though you can if you like. Lemon juice comes in bottles. One lemon gives about 2 to 3 tablespoons of juice.

OREGANO BAKED FISH

Serves 4   ① *Preparation 10 min, Cooking 20 min — Easy*

INGREDIENTS
600 g pack white fish fillets (cod, hake, hoki or halibut)
1 cup breadcrumbs
2 tablespoons oregano
Salt and freshly ground pepper to taste
½ cup boiling water
1 fish stock cube
½ cup olive oil

EQUIPMENT
Set of measuring cups
Set of measuring spoons
Bowl
Wooden spoon or spatula

Cup
Ovenproof dish

METHOD

You can cook the fish from frozen.

Put the breadcrumbs, oregano, salt and pepper in the bowl and mix. Put the boiling water in the cup. Crumble the stock cube into the water and stir till dissolved.

Put half the oil in the ovenproof dish. Put the fillets in the bottom. Cover with the breadcrumb mixture, then sprinkle the rest of the oil and the stock on top. Put in the oven on at 170°C, 325°F, Gas mark 4 for 20 minutes. Have a look about half-way through. If it looks too dry, add a couple of tablespoons of water.

ADDITIONS & ALTERNATIVES

Serve with new potatoes, green vegetable or salad.

TIPS

You can buy packets of breadcrumbs, some of which have been flavoured or pre-cooked, or you can make them yourself. There are full instructions on making breadcrumbs in the 'How to' chapter.

You can buy ready-made stock in cartons from most supermarkets. You can also buy Swiss vegetable bouillon powder (vegetable stock), if you are worried about the stuff that goes into stock cubes.

CHICKEN & PASTA

Serves 4   ⏱ *Preparation 15 min, Cooking 1 hr — Easy*

INGREDIENTS
4 medium skinless, boneless chicken breasts
3 tablespoons butter
500 g packet pasta, preferably tagliatelle
Small carton (142 ml, 5 fl oz) single cream
$\frac{1}{2}$ cup milk
Salt and freshly ground pepper to taste
$\frac{1}{2}$ cup grated Parmesan cheese
1 tablespoon breadcrumbs

EQUIPMENT
Set of measuring spoons
Frying-pan
Wooden spoon or spatula
Slotted spoon
Plate
Saucepan
Sieve or colander
Ovenproof dish
Set of measuring cups
Bowl
Spoon

DEFROSTING
Make sure frozen chicken is completely thawed before use. This means leaving it in the fridge overnight, or out of the fridge, covered, for 6 hours.

METHOD
Put half the butter in the frying-pan on a low heat. Gently fry the chicken breasts for 30 minutes until almost done, turning

frequently. Lift out with the slotted spoon and put on a plate.

Part cook the pasta for half the time it says on the packet. Cook in at least 1 litre (2 pints) of boiling water in the saucepan. Melt the rest of the butter in the frying-pan on a moderate heat. Drain the pasta in the sieve, and put it in the frying-pan and mix it up while it is still hot. This stops the pasta sticking together in a cold congealed mass.

Put the pasta in the ovenproof dish. Add the cream, milk, salt and pepper and half the cheese. Stir round. Push the chicken into the noodles. Mix the rest of the cheese and the breadcrumbs in a bowl. Spoon on top of the chicken and noodles. Cook in the oven for 30 minutes at 180°C, 350°F, Gas mark 4.

ADDITIONS & ALTERNATIVES
Serve with salad.

Try other cheese like Pecorino.

You could use 8 boneless skinless chicken thighs.

TIPS
Tagliatelle is like a flattened spaghetti, and comes in several colours. You can buy chilled or dried.

You can buy ready grated Parmesan in packets or cartons.

SPANISH CHICKEN & TOMATOES

Serves 4 ⏲ *Preparation 20 min, Cooking 45 min — Easy*

INGREDIENTS
4 chicken quarters
1 teaspoon salt
2 rashers bacon
1 large green pepper
400 g tin tomatoes
200 g (8 oz) mushrooms, about 20
2 tablespoons butter
1 tablespoon oil
$\frac{1}{2}$ cup white wine

EQUIPMENT
Sharp knife
Chopping board
Tin opener
Bowl
Wooden spoon or spatula
Set of measuring spoons
Large saucepan with lid
Set of measuring cups

DEFROSTING
Make sure frozen chicken is completely thawed before use. This means leaving it in the fridge overnight, or out of the fridge, covered, for 6 hours.

METHOD
Sprinkle the chicken with the salt. Chop the bacon into tiny pieces. Chop the end off the green pepper and cut out the core and seeds. Chop the pepper into squares.

Open the tin of tomatoes. Pour the juice into the bowl. Use the wooden spoon to mash the tomatoes while they are still in the can. Pour the mashed tomatoes into the bowl as well.

Wipe the mushrooms clean. Discard any nasty ones. Chop the end off the stalks.

Put the butter and oil in the pan and heat over a low heat. Fry the chicken for about 10 minutes till it is golden, stirring to stop it sticking. Put the bacon in for the last 3 minutes. Add the pepper, tomatoes, mushrooms and wine. Bring to the boil, then turn down the heat till it is just boiling (simmering). Put a lid on and cook for 40 minutes. Check the water level from time to time and top it up if needed.

ADDITIONS & ALTERNATIVES
Serve with couscous (page 296), rice, potatoes or salad.

Use cooked ham instead of bacon.

TIPS
There are full instructions on cooking rice in the 'How to' chapter.

SPICY ITALIAN PORK CHOPS

Serves 4   ① *Preparation 15 min, Cooking 1 hr — Easy*

INGREDIENTS
2 large onions
2 cloves garlic
2 green peppers
2 tablespoons olive oil
8 thin lean pork chops (about 1 kg, 2 lb)
2 × 400 g tins plum tomatoes
2 teaspoons oregano
$\frac{1}{2}$ teaspoon chilli powder
Salt and freshly ground pepper to taste

EQUIPMENT
Sharp knife
Chopping board
Set of measuring spoons
Large saucepan with lid or wok with lid
Wooden spoon or spatula
Slotted spoon
Plate
Tin opener

METHOD
Peel and finely chop the onion and garlic. Chop the end off the green peppers and cut out the core and seeds. Cut the pepper into small squares.

Put the oil in the saucepan or wok on a moderate heat. Fry the onion and garlic for about 4 minutes, stirring. Lift out with the slotted spoon and put on a plate.

Put the chops in the pan and brown for 3 minutes on each side. Add the cooked onions and garlic. Cover with the chopped peppers. Turn the heat down low. Put the lid on and cook for 20 minutes.

Open the tins of tomatoes. Pour the juice into the frying-pan. Use the wooden spoon to mash the tomatoes while they are still in the can. Pour the mashed tomatoes into the pan. Continue to cook, stirring as the mixture boils. Cook slowly for 15 minutes. Add the oregano, chilli, salt and pepper. Stir round and cook for 10 minutes longer, slowly.

ADDITIONS & ALTERNATIVES
Serve with potatoes and a green vegetable or pasta, couscous (page 296), or rice and salad.

You can leave out the chilli powder.

Add about 10 button mushrooms, wiped and cut in half at the same time as the peppers.

TIPS

Prepared garlic is sold in tubes, jars and bottles. Just read the instructions for the suggested equivalent amount. Most keep for 6 weeks in the fridge, but the bottles keep longer.

SPANISH BACON & EGGS

Serves 4   ① *Preparation 20 min, Cooking 25 min — Easy*

INGREDIENTS

4 medium eggs
2 green peppers
1 medium onion
1 clove garlic
3 tablespoons olive oil
400 g tin tomatoes
$\frac{1}{2}$ teaspoon salt
8 rashers bacon

EQUIPMENT

Bowl
Fork
Sharp knife
Chopping board
Garlic crusher
Set of measuring spoons
Frying-pan
Tin opener
Wooden spoon
Grill or second frying-pan

METHOD

All the time you are cooking this you want to have the heat down quite low, so it all cooks gently.

Break the eggs into a bowl and pick out any bits of shell. Mix the eggs up with a fork.

Chop the end off the green peppers and cut out the core and seeds. Cut the pepper into strips. Peel and chop the onion. Peel and crush the garlic.

Put the oil in the frying-pan and heat over a low heat. Fry the peppers, onion and garlic gently for 15 minutes, stirring to stop it sticking.

Open the tin of tomatoes. Pour the juice away. Use the wooden spoon to mash the tomatoes while they are still in the can. Pour the mashed tomatoes into the pan. Bring to the boil, then turn down the heat till it is just boiling (simmering). Add the salt and cook for about 5 minutes, till the tomatoes are just pulp and the mixture is not too wet. Keep stirring.

Meanwhile, grill or fry the bacon in another pan. Add the eggs to the vegetables and keep stirring over a gentle heat until eggs are lightly scrambled. Serve at once in a shallow dish, with bacon rashers on top.

ADDITIONS & ALTERNATIVES

Serve with fresh crusty bread and salad.

SPANISH BACON & LENTILS

Serves 6 ⏱ *Preparation 20 min, Cooking 2 hrs — Easy*

INGREDIENTS
750 g (1½ lb) joint collar bacon or similar piece of boiling bacon
3 medium onions
2 medium carrots
1 stick celery or 2 teaspoons celery salt
1 tablespoon olive oil
1 bouquet garni (looks like a herb tea bag)
1 teaspoon ground black pepper
500 g pack brown lentils

EQUIPMENT
Large saucepan with lid
Sharp knife
Chopping board
Vegetable peeler
Set of measuring spoons
Wooden spoon or spatula
Slotted spoon

METHOD
Put the bacon in the pan, cover with water and bring to the boil. Drain, rinse in cold water and leave to dry.

Peel and chop the onion into quarters. Peel and chop the carrots, cutting off both ends, then cut into slices. Wash the celery, chop the ends off, then cut in half.

Put the oil in the pan over a moderate heat. Fry the bacon and onions for about 3 minutes, stirring to stop them sticking. Add the carrots, celery or celery salt, bouquet garni, pepper and lentils. Cover with cold water. Bring to the boil, then turn down the heat till it is just boiling (simmering). Put a tight lid on and cook for 2 hours. Check the water level from time to time and top it up if needed.

Lift out the bacon. Lift out the lentils and vegetables with a slotted spoon and put on a plate. Cut the bacon into slices and arrange on top.

ADDITIONS & ALTERNATIVES
Serve with French bread and salad.

TIPS
Bouquet garni has a mixture of herbs in it, so you can substitute a teaspoon of mixed Mediterranean herbs. It means you get little specks of herb in the dish, but so what.

NEAPOLITAN LAMB STEW

Serves 4   ① *Preparation 20 min, Cooking 1 hr — Easy*

INGREDIENTS
1 kg (2 lb) lean lamb steak
2 small onions
1 clove garlic
2 medium carrots
4 tablespoons olive oil
250 g tin tomato juice
1 cup frozen peas
$\frac{1}{4}$ teaspoon celery seeds (optional)
Salt and freshly ground pepper to taste
$\frac{1}{2}$ cup dry sherry

EQUIPMENT
Sharp knife
Chopping board
Vegetable peeler

Set of measuring spoons
Saucepan with lid
Wooden spoon or spatula
Tin opener
Set of measuring cups

METHOD

Cut the lamb into 2 cm (1 inch) chunks.

Peel and finely chop the onion and garlic. Peel and finely chop the carrots, cutting off both ends.

Put the oil in the saucepan on a moderate heat. Fry the garlic for about 3 minutes, stirring to stop it sticking. Add the meat and brown on all sides for 3 minutes. Lower the heat, add the onion and cook for 5 minutes. Open the tin of tomato juice and add to the pan. Put the lid on and cook for 25 minutes.

Add carrots, peas, celery seeds, salt and pepper. Bring to the boil and cook for 15 minutes. Take off the heat, add the sherry and put the lid on. Leave for 5 minutes and serve.

ADDITIONS & ALTERNATIVES

Serve with couscous (page 296), new potatoes and green vegetable or pasta and salad.

TIPS

Prepared garlic is sold in tubes, jars and bottles. Just read the instructions for the suggested equivalent amount. Most keep for 6 weeks in the fridge, but the bottles keep longer.

There are full instructions on cooking pasta in the 'How to' chapter.

MEDITERRANEAN LAMB HOT POT

Serves 4   ① *Preparation 25 min, Cooking 1 hr — Easy*

INGREDIENTS

12 medium potatoes, about 1 kg (2 lb)
2 large onions
1 meat stock cube
1 cup boiling water
2 tablespoons olive oil
4 thick lamb chops
$\frac{1}{2}$ teaspoon salt
$\frac{1}{2}$ teaspoon pepper
1 bouquet garni (looks like a herb tea bag)

EQUIPMENT

Vegetable peeler
Sharp knife
Chopping board
Set of measuring cups
Bowl or cup
Set of measuring spoons
Frying-pan
Slotted spoon
Plate
Wooden spoon
Casserole or ovenproof dish
Aluminium foil to cover dish if no lid

METHOD

Put the oven on at 180°C, 350°F, Gas mark 4.

Peel the potatoes, cutting away any nasty bits, and cutting out any eyes. Chop the potatoes into thin slices. Peel and thinly slice the onions. Dissolve the stock cube in the water in a bowl or cup.

Put 1 tablespoon of oil in the frying-pan over a moderate heat. Fry the chops until lightly browned. Lift out with the slotted spoon and put on a plate. Fry half the onion and potatoes for about 3 minutes till they start to turn golden, stirring to stop them sticking. Put them in the bottom of the casserole. Put the lamb chops on top with the salt, pepper and bouquet garni.

Put 1 tablespoon of oil in the frying-pan on a moderate heat and fry rest of onions and potato. Put them on top of the lamb. Pour in the water and stock cube. Cover with a lid or foil and cook in the oven for about 40 minutes. Remove bouquet garni before serving.

TIPS

Bouquet garni has a mixture of herbs in it, so you can substitute a teaspoon of mixed Mediterranean herbs. It means you get little specks of herb in the dish, but so what.

You can buy ready-made stock in cartons from most supermarkets. You can also buy Swiss vegetable bouillon powder (vegetable stock), if you are worried about the stuff that goes into stock cubes.

OVEN BAKED BEEF

Serves 6   ⏱ *Preparation 20 min, Cooking 1 hr 15 min — Easy*

INGREDIENTS

1½ kg (3 lb) small new potatoes
½ cup boiling water
1 beef stock cube
Medium (250 g) tin tomato purée
1 tablespoon rosemary, fresh if possible
½ cup olive oil
2 cloves garlic
1½ kg (3 lb) braising steak, in one piece if possible
Salt and freshly ground pepper to taste

EQUIPMENT

Flameproof casserole
or frying-pan and casserole
Sharp knife
Chopping board
Set of measuring cups
Bowl
Fork or spoon
Tin opener
Wooden spoon or spatula
Set of measuring spoons
Garlic crusher

METHOD

Some casseroles, for instance cast iron ones but not normally
Pyrex or earthenware ones, are flameproof so you can use them
instead of the pan for frying and then put them in the oven as well.
If you have one of these use it now. If not, you will have to start

things off in a frying-pan and then put them in a casserole for the oven.

Scrub the potatoes, cutting away any nasty bits, and cutting out any eyes. Put the boiling water in the bowl. Crumble the stock cube into the water and stir with the fork till dissolved. Open the tin of tomato purée and add to stock. Crumble or chop the rosemary and add to the stock. Stir with the fork.

Put the oil in the flameproof casserole or frying-pan on a moderate heat. Peel and crush the garlic into the pan. Cook for 4 minutes. Add the meat and cook for 10 minutes for each side. If using a frying-pan, transfer the meat to the casserole. Add the stock and tomato mixture and salt and pepper to taste. Cook in the oven for 25 minutes at 180°C, 350°F, Gas mark 4. Put the potatoes in with the beef and cook for another 25 minutes.

ADDITIONS & ALTERNATIVES
Serve with green vegetable or salad.

Use other cheap cuts of beef like chuck steak.

TIPS
Tomato purée comes in tubes. It keeps for 4 weeks in the fridge.

If you don't have a garlic crusher just squash it with something suitable or chop it up small. Prepared garlic is sold in tubes, jars and bottles. Just read the instructions for the suggested equivalent amount. Most keep for 6 weeks in the fridge, but the bottles keep longer.

PASTA PUDDING

Serves 8   ⏲ *Preparation 15 min, Cooking 20 min — Easy*

INGREDIENTS

4 eggs
2 pints (1 litre) milk
2 cups sugar
1 teaspoon vanilla extract
500 g packet pasta, preferably tagliolini
2 sticks cinnamon
$\frac{1}{2}$ teaspoon grated nutmeg

EQUIPMENT

Bowl
Set of measuring cups
Fork
Saucepan with lid
Sieve or colander
Ovenproof dish
Set of measuring spoons

METHOD

Break the eggs into a bowl and pick out any bits of shell. Add the milk, sugar and vanilla and mix up with a fork.

Part cook the pasta for half the time it says on the packet. Cook in at least 1 litre (2 pints) of boiling water in the saucepan. Drain the pasta in a sieve. Put it in the ovenproof dish.

Press the cinnamon sticks into the pasta. Pour the milk mixture over the pasta and sprinkle the grated nutmeg on top. Cook in the oven for 20 minutes at 170°C, 325°F, Gas mark 3. Let it cool and cut into sections, or it eat it straight from the oven.

TIPS

Nutmeg is best ground fresh. Just rub against a grater. You can buy it ready ground.

AMERICAN & MEXICAN

PUMPKIN SOUP

Serves 4 to 6   ⓘ *Preparation 15 min, Cooking 25 min — Easy*

INGREDIENTS
500 g (1 lb) piece pumpkin
1 small onion
2 cups boiling water
1 chicken stock cube
2 tablespoons butter
1 pint milk
1 teaspoon lemon juice
$\frac{1}{2}$ teaspoon sugar
$\frac{1}{4}$ teaspoon ground cloves
2 drops Tabasco sauce
1 teaspoon salt
Small carton (142 ml, 5 fl oz) double cream

EQUIPMENT
Sharp knife
Chopping board
Large saucepan with lid
Slotted spoon
Sieve

Set of measuring cups
Bowl
Set of measuring spoons
Wooden spoon

METHOD

Peel the skin off the pumpkin and scrape out the seeds. Cut the pumpkin into 2 cm (1 inch) cubes and put in the saucepan with enough water to cover well. Bring to the boil, then turn down the heat till it is just boiling (simmering). Put a lid on and cook for 5 minutes. Lift out with the slotted spoon, drain in the sieve and leave to one side. Pour the cooking water away and rinse and dry the pan.

Meanwhile, peel and thinly slice the onion. Put the boiling water in the bowl. Crumble the stock cube into the water and stir till dissolved.

Put the butter in the pan on a moderate heat. Fry the onion for about 3 minutes till it is golden, stirring to stop it sticking. Add the pumpkin, chicken stock, milk, lemon juice, sugar, cloves, Tabasco and salt. Stir round. Bring to the boil, then turn down the heat till it is just boiling (simmering). Put a lid on and cook for 15 minutes, stirring from time to time.

Take the pan off the heat and either mash the pumpkin with the spoon or put the sieve over the bowl and push the soup through the sieve with the back of a spoon. Put it back in the pan. Bring to the boil, stirring, take off the heat and stir in the cream. Serve.

ADDITIONS & ALTERNATIVES

You may be able to find tinned pumpkin although we couldn't. We've been told that it exists.

This is good with croûtons (page 243) on top.

You can serve this soup chilled in the summer.

TIPS

You can buy ready-made stock in cartons from most super-markets. You can also buy Swiss vegetable bouillon powder (vegetable stock), if you are worried about the stuff that goes into stock cubes.

UNIVERSAL SALSA

Serves 4   ⏱ *Preparation 10 min — Easy*

INGREDIENTS

50 g pack coriander
1 small (bird's eye) red chilli
2 limes
1 lemon
1 teaspoon salt
1 teaspoon sugar

EQUIPMENT

Sharp knife
Chopping board
Juicer
Bowl
Spoon
Set of measuring spoons

METHOD

Wash, shake dry and finely chop the coriander, stalks as well as leaves. Chop the end off the chilli, split in half, and scrape out the seeds. Cut the chilli into tiny bits. Squeeze the juice out of the limes and lemon. Put the juice, coriander, chilli, salt and sugar in the bowl and stir round. Leave for 10 minutes so the flavours mix.

ADDITIONS & ALTERNATIVES

This is the sauce that demonstrates the common themes in food that run round the world. You can use this with Indian or Indonesian, Chinese or Mexican food. It also makes a great sauce to accompany fish or even cold chicken.

TIPS

You can buy coriander in street markets or corner shops. It is the one with the roots still on and is cheaper than the prepared and ready to use packets.

FRESH CHILLI — A WARNING! When you chop up the chillies be careful and avoid getting juice on your hands. If you touch your eyes, mouth or other sensitive areas, even an hour after chopping them, they will smart and burn. So wash your hands or wear rubber gloves.

Prepared chilli is sold in tubes and jars. Just read the label for the suggested equivalent amount. It keeps for 6 weeks in the fridge.

You do not have to squeeze lemons to get lemon juice, though you can if you like. Lemon and lime juice comes in bottles. One lemon gives about 2 to 3 tablespoons of juice.

FRESH RED SALSA

Serves 4   ⏲ *Preparation 10 min — Easy*

INGREDIENTS

3 spring onions
50 g pack coriander leaves
2 green chillies
4 medium tomatoes
2 tablespoons lemon juice
$\frac{1}{4}$ teaspoon salt
$\frac{1}{4}$ teaspoon black pepper

EQUIPMENT

Sharp knife
Chopping board
Set of measuring spoons
Bowl
Spoon

METHOD

Clean and prepare the spring onions. Cut the root end off, trim the leaves. Peel off and discard any dried up or slimy leaves. Chop into thin slices.

Wash, shake dry and finely chop the coriander. Chop the end off the chillies, split in half, and scrape out the seeds. Cut the chillies into tiny bits. Chop the tomatoes into $\frac{1}{2}$ cm ($\frac{1}{4}$ inch) cubes. Put the tomatoes, onion, coriander, chillies, lemon juice, salt and pepper in a bowl and stir round. Leave for 30 minutes so the flavours mix.

ADDITIONS & ALTERNATIVES

Serve with any Mexican dish. It has a fresh hot taste.

TIPS

FRESH CHILLI — A WARNING! When you chop up the chillies
be careful and avoid getting juice on your hands. If you touch your
eyes, mouth or other sensitive areas, even an hour after chopping
them, they will smart and burn. So wash your hands or wear
rubber gloves.

Prepared chilli is sold in tubes and jars. Just read the label for
the suggested equivalent amount. It keeps for 6 weeks in the
fridge.

You do not have to squeeze lemons to get lemon juice, though
you can if you like. Lemon juice comes in bottles. One lemon gives
about 2 to 3 tablespoons of juice.

GUACAMOLE SPECIAL

Serves 4   ① *Preparation 10 min — Easy*

INGREDIENTS

2 medium ripe avocados
2 tablespoons lime juice or juice of small lime
3 spring onions
15 g pack coriander
2 large ripe tomatoes
$\frac{1}{2}$ to 1 teaspoon chilli powder or 1 or 2 fresh shredded chillies with
    the seeds removed
Salt and freshly ground pepper to taste

EQUIPMENT

Sharp knife
Chopping board
Bowl

Set of measuring spoons
Wooden spoon or spatula

METHOD

Ripe avocados mash easily. Cut the avocados in half, peel and remove the stone. Mash the avocado in the bowl with a fork, adding the lime juice.

Clean and prepare the spring onions. Cut the root end off, trim the leaves. Peel off and discard any dried up or slimy leaves. Chop into thin slices.

Wash, shake dry and finely chop the coriander. Chop the tomatoes into tiny cubes. Add the spring onion, coriander, tomato, chilli powder, salt and pepper to the avocado and mix well.

ADDITIONS & ALTERNATIVES

Serve with tortilla chips or as an accompaniment to other dishes. A spoonful goes well with barbecued chicken.

There is a basic recipe for guacamole in our last book *Cooking for Blokes*, but you can't really do Mexican food without a recipe for it.

Use lemon juice instead of the lime.

TIPS

Don't let it stand too long as it goes brown. If you put the stone from one of the avocados into the mixture it may stop it going brown so quickly.

FRESH CHILLI — A WARNING! When you chop up the chillies be careful and avoid getting juice on your hands. If you touch your eyes, mouth or other sensitive areas, even an hour after chopping them, they will smart and burn. So wash your hands or wear rubber gloves.

Prepared chilli is sold in tubes and jars. Just read the label for the suggested equivalent amount. It keeps for 6 weeks in the fridge.

MUSHROOMS IN SOUR CREAM

Serves 4 to 6   ⏱ *Preparation 10 min, Cooking 15 min — Easy*

INGREDIENTS
500 g (1 lb) button mushrooms, about 40
2 medium onions
30 g packet fresh parsley
$\frac{1}{4}$ × 250 g pack butter
Large carton (568 ml, 20 fl oz) sour cream
1 teaspoon lemon juice
1 teaspoon salt
$\frac{1}{4}$ teaspoon fresh ground black pepper

EQUIPMENT
Sharp knife
Chopping board
Large saucepan with lid
Wooden spoon or spatula
Set of measuring spoons

METHOD
Wipe the mushrooms clean. Discard any nasty ones. Chop the end off the stalks. Peel and thinly slice the onion. Wash, shake dry and finely chop the parsley.

Put the butter in the pan and heat over a moderate heat. Fry the onion for about 4 minutes, stirring to stop it sticking. Add the mushrooms and put the lid on for another 7 minutes, shaking the pan from time to time. Add the sour cream, lemon juice, salt and pepper. Turn the heat down low and gradually bring the cream to the point where it is about to boil, stirring. Don't let it boil. Take off the heat and stir in the parsley.

ADDITIONS & ALTERNATIVES
Serve with toast as a first course or as a vegetable.

THREE BEAN SALAD

Serves 8   ① *Preparation 10 min — Easy*
Think ahead. This needs to stand for 1 hour before eating.

INGREDIENTS

420 g tin red kidney beans
420 g tin cannellini or borlotti beans
420 g tin chickpeas
8 spring onions
1 clove garlic
50 g pack parsley
1 small green pepper
1 teaspoon salt
$\frac{1}{2}$ teaspoon freshly ground black pepper
3 tablespoons wine vinegar
8 tablespoons olive oil

EQUIPMENT

Tin opener
Sieve
Sharp knife
Chopping board
Set of measuring spoons
Bowl
Wooden spoon or spatula

METHOD

Open the tins of beans and chickpeas. Put them in the sieve and rinse thoroughly under the cold tap. Leave them to drain.

Clean and prepare the spring onions. Cut the root end off, trim the leaves. Peel off and discard any dried up or slimy leaves. Chop into thin slices. Peel the garlic, then chop it into tiny pieces. Wash, shake dry and finely chop the parsley. Chop the end off the green peppers and cut out the core and seeds. Cut the pepper into 1 cm ($\frac{1}{2}$ inch) squares.

Put the chickpeas, beans, spring onions, garlic, parsley and green pepper in a large bowl. Add the salt, pepper and the wine vinegar and stir round. Add the olive oil and mix again. Leave for an hour before serving.

ADDITIONS & ALTERNATIVES
Use other sorts of cooked tinned beans.

TIPS
This is the approved accompaniment to chilli con carne. Great for parties. A good excuse to drink beer.

EASY FRIED BEANS

Serves 4   ⏱ *Preparation 5 min, Cooking 10 min — Easy*

INGREDIENTS
1 medium onion
2 green chillies
2 tablespoons sunflower oil
2 cloves garlic
2 × 400 g cans red kidney beans
1 teaspoon sugar
1 teaspoon salt

EQUIPMENT
Sharp knife
Chopping board
Frying-pan
Set of measuring spoons
Garlic crusher
Wooden spoon or spatula

METHOD

Peel and finely chop the onion. Chop the end off the chillies, split in half, and scrape out the seeds. Cut the chilli into tiny bits.

Put the oil in the frying-pan on a moderate heat. Peel and crush the garlic into the pan. Fry the onion and garlic for about 3 minutes till it is golden, stirring to stop it sticking.

Open the tins of beans and add them with their liquid to the pan. Turn the heat down low. Add the sugar and salt. Cook for about 7 minutes till the beans are like porridge, stirring from time to time.

ADDITIONS & ALTERNATIVES

Serve with corn chips or with tortillas and salad or as an accompaniment to other dishes.

These beans form the basis of the richer and more filling refried beans, which are the next recipe.

Substitute a tin of baked beans for one of tins of the kidney beans.

TIPS

FRESH CHILLI — A WARNING! When you chop up the chillies be careful and avoid getting juice on your hands. If you touch your eyes, mouth or other sensitive areas, even an hour after chopping them, they will smart and burn. So wash your hands or wear rubber gloves. Prepared chilli is sold in tubes and jars. Just read the label for the suggested equivalent amount. It keeps for 6 weeks in the fridge.

If you don't have a garlic crusher just squash it with something suitable or chop it up small. Prepared garlic is sold in tubes, jars and bottles. Just read the instructions for the suggested equivalent amount. Most keep for 6 weeks in the fridge, but the bottles keep longer.

REFRIED BEANS

Serves 4   ⏱ *Preparation 5 min, Cooking 6 min — Easy*

INGREDIENTS
1 medium onion
2 tablespoons sunflower oil
1 quantity Easy Fried Beans (p. 340) left for 24 hours in the fridge
3 tablespoons grated Cheddar cheese
$\frac{1}{2}$ teaspoon salt

EQUIPMENT
Sharp knife
Chopping board
Set of measuring spoons
Wooden spoon or spatula
Frying-pan

METHOD
Peel and finely chop the onion. Put the oil in the frying-pan over a moderate heat. Fry the onion for about 1 minute, stirring to stop it sticking. Add the beans and mash about. If they are really dry add a couple of tablespoons of water. Add the cheese and salt. Turn the heat down low. Cook and mash for about 5 minutes till the beans are smooth.

ADDITIONS & ALTERNATIVES
Serve with tortillas or salad or as an accompaniment to enchiladas.

Try using other cheeses such as Lancashire, Cheshire, Leicester or even feta.

Add 2 or 3 rashers smoked bacon, chopped up very small and fried for 5 minutes before the onion and continue with the recipe.

Try a 50 g (2 oz) piece of chorizo from the deli counter, chopped up small and fried for 5 minutes before the onion and continue with the recipe.

REFRIED BEAN SANDWICH

Serves 4   ① *Preparation 5 min, Cooking 15 min — Easy*

INGREDIENTS
1 French loaf
2 tablespoons butter
Refried Beans (page 342)
50 g (2 oz) grated cheddar cheese
Salt and freshly ground pepper to taste
Fresh Red Salsa (page 335) or Universal Salsa (page 333)

EQUIPMENT
Grater
Sharp knife
Chopping board
Set of measuring spoons
Ovenproof dish or baking tray

METHOD
Cut the French bread into 4 equal lengths. Cut each in half lengthways. Remove the soft bread from the middle. Butter inside each crust. Divide the refried beans between the 8 pieces of bread. Grate the cheese if not using ready grated. Put the cheese, salt and pepper on top. Put in the ovenproof dish. Cook in the oven for 15 minutes at 180°C, 350°F, Gas mark 4. Serve with the salsa.

ADDITIONS & ALTERNATIVES
Try using other cheeses such as Lancashire, Cheshire, Leicester, Edam, or Gouda.
 Add a slice or two of avocado or tomato to each sandwich.

You can use bought chilli salsa. Pace is a particular favourite. It isn't too sweet and comes in various hotnesses.

Thinly slice a small onion and put between the refried beans and the cheese.

Put a few sliced jalapeño chillies on top before serving.

You can buy refried beans in tins.

EASY ENCHILADA SAUCE

Serves 4   ⓘ *Preparation 5 min, Cooking 25 min — Easy*

INGREDIENTS
1 large onion
2 fresh chillies
2 tablespoons sunflower oil
2 cloves garlic
2 x 400 g tins tomatoes
$\frac{1}{4}$ teaspoon fresh ground pepper

EQUIPMENT
Sharp knife
Chopping board
Set of measuring cups
Set of measuring spoons
Bowl
Wooden spoon or spatula
Spoon
Tin opener
Frying-pan

METHOD
Peel and chop the onion. Pierce the chillies a couple of times with a fork.

Put the oil in the frying-pan over a moderate heat. Peel and crush the garlic into the pan. Add the onion and whole chillies and fry for about 3 minutes, stirring to stop it sticking.

Open the tins of tomatoes. Pour the juice into the frying-pan. Use the wooden spoon to mash the tomatoes while they are still in the can. Pour the mashed tomatoes into the pan. Continue to cook, stirring as the mixture boils. Turn down the heat till it is just boiling (simmering). Cook for 20 minutes. Throw the chillies away.

ADDITIONS & ALTERNATIVES

Use this instead of bought tomato sauce for enchiladas and in some of the following recipes.

TIPS

If you don't have a garlic crusher just squash it with something suitable or chop it up small. Prepared garlic is sold in tubes, jars and bottles. Just read the instructions for the suggested equivalent amount. Most keep for 6 weeks in the fridge, but the bottles keep longer.

TORTILLA CHIPS IN TOMATO

Serves 4   ① *Preparation 5 min, Cooking 20 to 25 min — Easy*

INGREDIENTS

Half quantity Easy Enchilada Sauce (page 344)
4 spring onions
15 g packet coriander
$\frac{1}{2}$ × 250 g packet grated mozzarella
Small carton (142 ml, 5 fl oz) sour cream
Salt and freshly ground pepper to taste
500 g packet tortilla chips

EQUIPMENT
Grater
Sharp knife
Chopping board
Bowl
Wooden spoon or spatula

METHOD
Make the tomato sauce according to the previous recipe, using only half of the ingredients.

Clean and prepare the spring onions. Cut the root end off, trim the leaves. Peel off and discard any dried up or slimy leaves. Chop into thin slices. Wash the coriander and shake dry.

Mix the spring onions, coriander, mozzarella, sour cream, salt and pepper in the bowl.

Put the tortilla chips in a flat serving bowl. Pour the hot enchilada sauce over the tortillas and stir round. Put the mozzarella mixture on top and serve.

ADDITIONS & ALTERNATIVES
Serve as a light meal or at a party.

Use bought enchilada sauce instead of the Easy Enchilada Sauce.

Use Cheddar cheese instead of mozzarella.

BAKED TORTILLA CHIPS & CHEESE

Serves 8   ① *Preparation 2 min, Cooking 10 min — Easy*

INGREDIENTS
500 g bag tortilla chips
250 g packet grated Cheddar cheese
$\frac{1}{2}$ × 250 g packet grated mozzarella cheese
4 tablespoons chopped bottled jalapeno chillies

EQUIPMENT
Grater
Ovenproof dish or baking tray

METHOD
Put the tortilla chips in the dish. Grate the cheese if not using ready grated. Spread the cheeses over the tortilla chips and top off with the chillies. Cook in the oven at 200°C, 400°F, Gas mark 6 for 10 minutes, until the cheese melts.

ADDITIONS & ALTERNATIVES
Try using other cheeses like Lancashire, Cheshire or even feta instead of the cheddar.

This is a good quick party recipe.

QUICK ENCHILADAS

Serves 4   ⏲ *Preparation 10 min, Cooking 30 min — Moderate*

INGREDIENTS
1 Iceberg lettuce
250 g (8 oz) Lancashire cheese
1 medium onion
1 pack 12 small wheat tortillas
1 quantity Easy Enchilada Sauce (page 344)

EQUIPMENT
Sharp knife
Chopping board
Grater
Bowl
Ovenproof dish
Aluminium foil

METHOD
Wash, dry and finely slice the lettuce. Grate the cheese into the bowl. Peel and finely chop the onion. Add to the bowl and stir round. Divide up the cheese mixture between the tortillas. Roll each tortilla up and put it in an ovenproof dish. Cover the dish with aluminium foil. Cook in the oven for 20 minutes at 180°C, 350°F, Gas mark 4.

Meanwhile, make the tomato sauce. Pour the sauce over the tortillas and serve with the lettuce.

ADDITIONS & ALTERNATIVES
Try using other cheeses such as Cheshire or even feta.

Use bought enchilada sauce instead of cooking the Easy Enchilada Sauce.

Add a few slices of sliced chorizo, chopped and fried for 5

minutes to the cheese and onion. You can even do the same with chopped, fried smoked bacon.

You can fry 200 g (7 oz) lean mince till it is browned and cooked through. Lift it out with a slotted spoon and add to the Easy Enchilada Sauce before pouring over the enchiladas.

Serve with chopped spring onions, sour cream, guacamole (page 336) and Fresh Red Salsa (page 335) or Universal Salsa (page 333).

FRIED CHEESE TORTILLAS

Serves 3　　　　　　① *Preparation 5 min Cooking 20 min — Easy*

INGREDIENTS
1 medium onion
2 medium tomatoes
200 g jar sliced jalapeño chillies
250 g packet grated Cheddar cheese
6 wheat flour tortillas
3 tablespoons sunflower oil

EQUIPMENT
Kitchen paper towel
Ovenproof dish
Sharp knife
Chopping board
Bowl
Wooden spoon or spatula
Frying-pan

METHOD
Put some kitchen paper towel in the bottom of the ovenproof dish. This will soak up some of the spare oil.

Peel and finely chop the onion. Cut the tomatoes into small cubes. Drain the chillies and put in the bowl with the onions, tomatoes and cheese and mix together. Spread the mixture over one half of each tortilla. Fold the tortillas to cover the cheese.

Put 1 tablespoon of oil in the frying-pan and heat over a moderate heat. Fry two tortillas for about 3 minutes until the cheese starts to melt. Turn them over with the spatula. Cook on the other side for 2 minutes. Lift them out and put them in the ovenproof dish. Put in the oven to keep warm at 140°C, 275°F, Gas mark 1. Repeat for the other tortillas.

ADDITIONS & ALTERNATIVES
Try using other cheeses such as Cheddar, Lancashire, Cheshire, Leicester, Edam, Gouda, mozzarella or even feta.

Serve with chopped spring onions, salad, sour cream, guacamole (page 336) and Fresh Red Salsa (page 335) or Universal Salsa (page 333).

TIPS
Save money; grate your own cheese.

CAESAR SALAD

Serves 4 to 6　　　⏱ *Preparation 15 min, Cooking 5 min — Easy*

INGREDIENTS
2 medium-sized cos lettuce
2 cloves garlic
50 g tin anchovy fillets
Small loaf bread
6 tablespoons sunflower oil
2 eggs
8 tablespoons olive oil
4 tablespoons lemon juice
1 teaspoon salt
250 g pack grated Parmesan cheese
$\frac{1}{2}$ teaspoon freshly ground black pepper

EQUIPMENT
Kitchen paper towel
Sharp knife
Chopping board
Set of measuring spoons
Frying-pan
Wooden spatula
Slotted spoon
Plate
Large salad bowl
Saucepan
Mixing bowl
2 large spoons or salad servers

METHOD

Break the leaves off the lettuce. Throw away any slimy ones. Wash in cold water and shake dry. Wrap in kitchen paper towel and put in the fridge.

Peel the garlic, then chop it into tiny pieces. Open the tin of anchovies and drain. Cut the crust off the loaf of bread and cut the bread into 2 cm (1 inch) cubes.

Put the sunflower oil in the frying-pan on a high heat. Add the bread and fry till brown on all sides. Add the garlic, stir round and take off the heat. Lift out with the slotted spoon and put on kitchen towel on the plate. Break the lettuce leaves into serving sized pieces and put them in the bottom of a large salad bowl.

Half fill the saucepan with water, add the eggs and boil for 1 minute. Take out with the slotted spoon and put to one side. Put the olive oil, lemon juice, salt and pepper in the mixing bowl. Mix round and then break in the eggs which should be quite runny. Mash and mix round. Add to the lettuce and toss with two large spoons. Add the cheese and the anchovies and mix again. Top off with the fried bread croûtons.

ADDITIONS & ALTERNATIVES

You can grate your own cheese or even better use a clean vegetable peeler to make thin curls.

TIPS

Prepared garlic is sold in tubes, jars and bottles. Just read the instructions for the suggested equivalent amount. Most keep for 6 weeks in the fridge, but the bottles keep longer.

CHICKEN ENCHILADAS

Serves 4   ⊕ *Preparation 10 min, Cooking 25 min* — *Easy*

INGREDIENTS

2 large or 4 small cooked chicken breasts
1 small onion
1 packet 12 small wheat tortillas
$\frac{1}{2}$ × 250 g pack grated cheddar cheese
$\frac{1}{2}$ × 250 g pack grated Gouda cheese
Small carton (142 ml, 5 fl oz) sour cream
1 quantity Easy Enchilada Sauce (page 344)

EQUIPMENT

Sharp knife
Chopping board
Ovenproof dish with lid or cooking foil
Set of measuring cups
Set of measuring spoons

DEFROSTING & COOKING THE CHICKEN

If you need to cook the chicken, make sure frozen chicken is completely thawed before use. This means leaving it in the fridge overnight, or out of the fridge, for 6 hours. Then just brush with oil and cook in an ovenproof dish in the oven for 30 minutes at 200°C, 400°F, Gas mark 6.

METHOD

Cut the chicken into chunks. Peel and chop the onion. Divide up the chicken and onion between the tortillas. Roll them up and put in the ovenproof dish. Cover the dish with the lid or aluminium foil. Put in the oven and cook at 180°C, 350°F, Gas mark 4 for 15 minutes. Meanwhile, make the tomato sauce. Take the lid or foil off the tortillas. Pour the tomato sauce over the tortillas. Put the cream and then the cheese on the top. Put the dish back in the oven at 200°C, 400°F, Gas mark 6 for 5 minutes, uncovered, till it is brown on top.

ADDITIONS & ALTERNATIVES

Serve with salad, chopped spring onions, and Fresh Red Salsa (page 335) or Universal Salsa (page 333).

Try using other cheeses such as Lancashire, Cheshire, Leicester, Edam, mozzarella or even feta.

Use bought enchilada sauce instead of cooking the Easy Enchilada Sauce.

Add some drained chopped jalapeño chillies to the chicken.

Try using left-over turkey.

Use corn tortillas instead of the wheat ones. Just follow the instructions but they are more difficult because they need to be fried for a couple of seconds to soften them up and they will not roll if you let them cool.

Try taco shells (unrolled) just as they come filled and then covered with Easy Enchilada Sauce etc.

TORTILLAS WITH CRISPY CHICKEN

Serves 4   ① *Preparation 10 min, Cooking 20 min* — *Easy*

INGREDIENTS
750 g cooked chicken leftovers or 4 cooked chicken breasts
2 medium onions
2 fresh chillies or 1 teaspoon chilli powder
3 medium tomatoes
1 crisp lettuce
3 tablespoons sunflower oil
Pinch salt
$\frac{1}{2}$ teaspoon black pepper
1 pack 8 wheat tortillas
Universal Salsa (page 333)
$\frac{1}{2}$ × 250 g pack grated cheddar cheese

EQUIPMENT
Ovenproof dish (if cooking chicken)
Sharp knife
Chopping board
Set of measuring spoons
Frying-pan
Grater (if grating cheese)

DEFROSTING & COOKING THE CHICKEN
If you need to cook the chicken, make sure frozen chicken is completely thawed before use. This means leaving it in the fridge overnight, or out of the fridge, for 6 hours. Then just brush with oil and cook in an ovenproof dish in the oven for 30 minutes at 200°C, 400°F, Gas mark 6.

METHOD
Grate the cheese if not using ready grated. Shred the chicken either by cutting up very small or using two forks to pull it apart

355

into little stringy bits. Peel and chop the onions. Chop the end off the chillies, split in half, and scrape out the seeds. Cut the chilli into thin strips, then into tiny bits. Chop the tomato up small. Wash, dry and slice the lettuce.

Put the oil in the frying-pan over a moderate heat. Fry the onion for about 3 minutes till it is golden, stirring to stop it sticking. Add the chicken, chilli, salt and pepper. Cook for 10 to 15 minutes, stirring, until the meat is very well heated through and has reached the degree of crispness that you want. (In Mexico this is very crisp). Put the meat mixture into a bowl.

Warm the tortillas (as directed on the packet), and serve the tortillas with the meat and the salsa. Each person makes up their own tortillas. In a line up the middle of the tortilla you put in lettuce, meat mixture, tomatoes, salsa and grated cheese. Roll or fold up the tortillas and eat.

ADDITIONS & ALTERNATIVES

Serve with sour cream or guacamole (page 336).

Try Fresh Red Salsa (page 335) instead of Universal Salsa.

You can use bought chilli salsa. Pace is a particular favourite. It isn't too sweet and comes in various hotnesses.

Use other meat such as beef instead of the chicken. About 750 g (1½ lb) should do. Leftover Christmas turkey is really good for this recipe.

Grate your own cheese.

GEORGIA CHICKEN WITH CREAM GRAVY

Serves 4   ⏲ *Preparation 15 min, Cooking 25 min — Easy*

INGREDIENTS
1 kg (2 lb) chicken pieces
$\frac{3}{4}$ cup flour
1 teaspoon salt
1 teaspoon freshly ground pepper
2 teaspoons paprika
1 cup groundnut oil
*2 tablespoons flour
*$\frac{1}{2}$ teaspoon salt
*$\frac{1}{2}$ teaspoon freshly ground pepper
$\frac{1}{2}$ cup water
Small carton (142 ml, 5 fl oz) single cream

Ingredients marked with * are not a repetition but are for the gravy.

EQUIPMENT
Plastic bag
Set of measuring cups
Set of measuring spoons
Frying-pan
Wooden spoon or spatula
Slotted spoon
Ovenproof dish
Cup
Whisk or fork

DEFROSTING

Make sure frozen chicken is completely thawed before use. This means leaving it in the fridge overnight, or out of the fridge, covered, for 6 hours.

METHOD

Put the flour in the plastic bag with the salt, pepper and paprika. Put a couple of pieces of chicken in the bag and holding the top tight closed shake them up. They will get coated in flour. Pick them out. Repeat till all the chicken is coated.

Put the oil in the frying-pan. The oil needs to be $\frac{1}{2}$ cm ($\frac{1}{4}$ inch) deep, so top it up if you need to. Put on a high heat. Add some chicken pieces, skin side down. Cook them for about 8 minutes a side. When one side is done and golden, turn it over. When they are done the juice runs clear if you stick a knife in them. Lift out with the slotted spoon and put on the ovenproof dish. Keep warm in the oven at 140°C, 275°F, Gas mark 1 while you make the gravy.

Let the oil cool down a bit then pour it off into something heatproof, like an empty cup. Take 2 tablespoons of the oil in the cup and put it back into the pan and add the flour, salt and pepper (for the gravy) and stir until the fat and flour are well combined. Put back on a moderate heat and stir for about 30 seconds. Add the water and about half the cream. Use a whisk or the back of a fork to combine everything so you get a smooth thick gravy. Add the rest of the cream and stir round to thin it down a bit.

Serve the chicken and gravy together.

ADDITIONS & ALTERNATIVES

Serve with new potatoes, green vegetable or salad.

Use chicken stock instead of water in the gravy.

CHORIZO SCRAMBLED EGGS

Serves 4   ⏲ *Preparation 5 min, Cooking 10 min — Easy*

INGREDIENTS
200 g (8 oz) sliced chorizo (Spanish slicing sausage)
1 medium onion
$\frac{1}{2}$ to 1 teaspoon chilli powder or 1 to 2 fresh chillies
4 medium tomatoes
6 eggs
Salt and freshly ground pepper to taste
2 tablespoons sunflower oil

EQUIPMENT
Sharp knife
Chopping board
Bowl
Fork
Measuring spoons
Slotted spoon
Frying-pan
Wooden spoon or spatula
Plate

METHOD
If the chorizo is in a piece, slice it very finely. Peel and finely chop the onion. Chop the end off the chillies, split in half, and scrape out the seeds. Cut the chilli into tiny bits. Cut the tomatoes into 1 cm ($\frac{1}{2}$ inch) cubes.

Break the eggs into a bowl and pick out any bits of shell. Add the chillies, salt and pepper and mix the eggs up with a fork.

Put the oil in the frying-pan over a moderate heat. Fry the chorizo for about 3 minutes, stirring to stop it sticking. Lift out with the slotted spoon and put on a plate.

Put the onions and tomato in the pan and cook for 3 minutes, stirring. Add the chorizo and egg mixture and cook for about 3 minutes till the eggs are done. Take the eggs from the pan just before they are done as much as you would like. They will continue to cook on the plate.

ADDITIONS & ALTERNATIVES
Use other spicy sausage like salami or French garlic sausage instead of the chorizo.

TIPS
FRESH CHILLI — A WARNING! When you chop up the chillies be careful and avoid getting juice on your hands. If you touch your eyes, mouth or other sensitive areas, even an hour after chopping them, they will smart and burn. So wash your hands or wear rubber gloves.

Prepared chilli is sold in tubes and jars. Just read the label for the suggested equivalent amount. It keeps for 6 weeks in the fridge.

HOT CHORIZO & CHEESE

Serves 4   ① *Preparation 5 min, Cooking 20 min — Easy*

INGREDIENTS
200 g (8 oz) sliced chorizo (Spanish sausage)
1 medium onion
$\frac{1}{2}$ to 1 teaspoon chilli powder or 1 to 2 fresh chillies
1 tablespoon sunflowers oil
250 g pack grated Cheddar cheese
250 g pack grated mozzarella cheese

EQUIPMENT
Sharp knife
Chopping board
Set of measuring spoons
Frying-pan
Wooden spoon or spatula
Slotted spoon
Ovenproof dish

METHOD
If the chorizo is in a piece, slice it very finely. Peel and thinly slice the onion. If using fresh chillies, chop the end off, split in half, and scrape out the seeds. Cut the chilli into thin strips.

Put the oil in the frying-pan on a moderate heat. Add the chorizo and fry for about 5 minutes till really crispy. Quite a lot of oil will come out. Add the onion and chillies and fry for about 3 minutes till the onion is golden, stirring to stop it sticking. Lift out with the slotted spoon and put into the ovenproof dish. Put the cheese on the chorizo mixture and put in the oven for 10 minutes at 190°C, 375°F, Gas mark 5. The cheese should be brown and bubbling.

ADDITIONS & ALTERNATIVES
Serve with refried beans or salad and Fresh Red Salsa (page 335) or Universal Salsa (page 333).

Grate your own cheese.

TIPS
FRESH CHILLI — A WARNING! When you chop up the chillies be careful and avoid getting juice on your hands. If you touch your eyes, mouth or other sensitive areas, even an hour after chopping them, they will smart and burn. So wash your hands or wear rubber gloves.

Prepared chilli is sold in tubes and jars. Just read the label for the suggested equivalent amount. It keeps for 6 weeks in the fridge.

BARBECUED SPARE RIBS

Serves 4 ① Preparation 10 min, Cooking 1 hr 15 min — Moderate

INGREDIENTS
2 kg (4 lb) spare ribs
Small (140 g) tin tomato purée
4 tablespoons wine vinegar
$\frac{1}{2}$ cup boiling water
1 beef stock cube
2 medium onions
1 clove garlic
4 tablespoons vegetable oil
$\frac{1}{2}$ cup Worcestershire sauce
4 tablespoons clear honey
1 teaspoon mustard
1 teaspoon dried oregano
1 teaspoon salt

EQUIPMENT
Tin opener
Cup
Fork
Set of measuring cups
Bowl
Sharp knife
Chopping board
Set of measuring spoons
Frying-pan

Wooden spoon or spatula
Wire rack from your grill pan
Ovenproof dish or roasting dish
Spoon

METHOD

Buy plain spare ribs and look for ones that have at least some meat on them.

Make the barbecue sauce first. Open the tin of tomato purée. Put it in the cup with the vinegar and mix together with the fork.

Put the boiling water in the bowl. Crumble the stock cube into the water and stir till dissolved. Peel and finely chop the onion. Peel the garlic then chop it into tiny pieces.

Put the oil in the frying-pan on a high heat. Fry the onion and garlic for about 3 minutes till golden, stirring to stop it sticking. Add the tomato purée mixture to the pan and stir round. Add the beef stock, Worcestershire sauce, honey, mustard, oregano and salt. Mix together. Bring to the boil, then turn down the heat till it is just boiling (simmering). Cook for 10 minutes.

Put the oven on at 200°C, 400°F, Gas mark 6. Put the spare ribs on the rack in the ovenproof dish. Coat the ribs with the barbecue sauce by spooning it over them. Put them in the oven for about 1 hour. Put more barbecue sauce on every 10 minutes or so. They should end up brown and crisp. Serve hot.

ADDITIONS & ALTERNATIVES

Serve with salad or some rice.

TIPS

You can get ribs in a piece as well as ready cut into individual ones. You can then cook them in a piece and cut them up before serving. They tend to be even more succulent when cooked in one piece.

Tomato purée also comes in tubes. It keeps for 4 weeks in the fridge.

Prepared garlic is sold in tubes, jars and bottles. Just read the instructions for the suggested equivalent amount. Most keep for 6 weeks in the fridge, but the bottles keep longer.

There are full instructions on cooking rice in the 'How to' chapter.

JAMBALAYA

Serves 4 to 6 ① *Preparation 15 min, Cooking 35 min* — *Moderate*

INGREDIENTS
500 g pack medium prawns
4 rashers streaky bacon
250 g ($\frac{1}{2}$ lb) cooked smoked ham
2 medium onions
1 clove garlic
2 medium green peppers
2 × 400 g tin plum tomatoes
1 $\frac{1}{2}$ cups boiling water
1 chicken stock cube
1 tablespoon sunflower oil
1 cup uncooked rice
$\frac{1}{2}$ teaspoon oregano
1 teaspoon salt
$\frac{1}{4}$ teaspoon fresh ground black pepper

EQUIPMENT
Sharp knife
Chopping board
Tin opener
Wooden spoon or spatula
Bowl
Set of measuring cups

Large flameproof casserole with lid
Slotted spoon
Kitchen paper towel
Plate
Set of measuring spoons

METHOD

You do need a casserole that can be heated on the top of the cooker for this dish. Cast iron is ideal.

Put the oven on at 180°C, 350°F, Gas mark 4.

Cut the bacon and the smoked ham into 2 cm (1 inch) pieces. Peel and finely chop the onion. Peel the garlic, then chop it into tiny pieces. Chop the end off the green peppers and cut out the core and seeds. Cut the peppers into 2 cm (1 inch) strips.

Open the tins of tomatoes. Pour the juice away. Use the wooden spoon to mash the tomatoes while they are still in the can.

Put the boiling water in the bowl. Crumble the stock cube into the water and stir till dissolved.

Put the oil in the casserole and heat over a moderate heat. Fry the bacon for about 3 minutes till it is brown, stirring to stop it sticking. Lift out with the slotted spoon and put on kitchen paper towel on the plate. Put the onion in the pan and fry for 5 minutes, stirring from time to time. Add the green peppers and stir for 3 minutes. Add the rice and stir round for a minute or so. Add the garlic, tomatoes, bacon, oregano, salt and pepper, stirring thoroughly. Add the chicken stock and bring to a boil. Add the ham and stir again. Put the lid on the casserole and put it in the oven for 10 minutes. Add the prawns, pushing them down into the rice. Cook with the lid on for another 10 minutes. If the rice looks dry at any time add a tablespoon or so of water.

TIPS

You can buy ready-made stock in cartons from most supermarkets. You can also buy Swiss vegetable bouillon powder (vegetable stock), if you are worried about the stuff that goes into stock cubes.

CHILLI CON CARNE

Serves 8   ① *Preparation 20 min, Cooking 1 hr 30 min — Easy*

INGREDIENTS
$1\frac{1}{2}$ kg (3 lb) braising beef
4 large onions
4 cloves garlic
1 medium red pepper
3 cups boiling water
1 beef stock cube
140 g tin tomato purée
420 g tin red kidney beans
6 tablespoons groundnut oil
$1\frac{1}{2}$ tablespoons chilli powder
1 teaspoon oregano
1 teaspoon ground cumin
1 teaspoon salt
Freshly ground black pepper

EQUIPMENT
Sharp knife
Chopping board
Set of measuring cups
Bowl
Spoon
Tin opener
Set of measuring spoons
Large flameproof casserole with lid

Wooden spoon or spatula
Slotted spoon
Plate

METHOD

You either need a casserole that can be heated on the top of the cooker for this dish or a very big solid saucepan. Cast iron is ideal.

Cut the beef into 2 cm (1 inch) cubes. Peel and chop the onion into 1 cm (½ inch) cubes. Peel the garlic, then chop it into tiny pieces. Chop the end off the red pepper and cut out the core and seeds. Cut the pepper into 1 cm (½ inch) squares.

Put the boiling water in the bowl. Crumble the stock cube into the water and stir till dissolved. Open the tin of tomato purée. Open the tin of red kidney beans and drain.

Put 4 tablespoons of the oil in the casserole on a moderate heat. Add the meat and cook for 3 minutes, stirring, until the meat is lightly browned. Lift out with the slotted spoon and put on a plate.

Put the rest of the oil in the casserole and cook the onion, garlic and red pepper for 3 minutes, stirring to stop it sticking. Add the chilli powder, oregano, cumin and mix. Add the tomato purée and beef stock and mix together. Put the meat back in the casserole. Add the salt and a few grinds of black pepper. Bring to the boil, stirring a couple of times, then turn down the heat till it is just boiling (simmering). Put a lid on and cook for about 1 hour. Check the fluid level from time to time and top it up if needed, also give it the odd stir.

Add the beans and cook for another 15 minutes. This may end up rather greasy. If it does, skim the fat off the top before serving.

ADDITIONS & ALTERNATIVES

Serve with salad and beer. If you serve with Three Bean Salad (p. 339) then leave out the beans from the chilli.

You can serve taco shells or wheat tortillas, guacamole, shredded lettuce, chopped tomato and cheese.

Try using lean mince instead of the beef. Break up the mince while frying. It is better as this chunky version.

This is a fairly mild version. It can stand to have twice as much chilli powder if that is to your taste.

TIPS

You can cook this the day before you need it and keep in the fridge overnight and reheat. It is even better the next day.

Tomato purée comes in tubes. It keeps for 4 weeks in the fridge.

You can buy ready-made stock in cartons from most supermarkets. You can also buy Swiss vegetable bouillon powder (vegetable stock), if you are worried about the stuff that goes into stock cubes.

PUMPKIN PIE

Serves 4 to 6　　　① *Preparation 15 min, Cooking 50 min — Easy*

INGREDIENTS
450 g pack ready-rolled shortcrust pastry
500 g (1 lb) piece pumpkin,
3 eggs
Small carton (142 ml, 5 fl oz) double cream
$\frac{1}{2}$ cup milk
$\frac{3}{4}$ cup dark brown sugar
1 teaspoon cinnamon
$\frac{1}{2}$ teaspoon ground cloves
$\frac{1}{2}$ teaspoon ground ginger
2 tablespoons Calvados

EQUIPMENT
Sharp knife
Chopping board
Saucepan with lid
Slotted spoon
Sieve
Fork
Pie dish
Bowl
Measuring cups
Measuring spoons

DEFROSTING
Thaw frozen pastry according to the instructions on the packet. Four hours in the fridge seems typical.

METHOD
Peel the skin off the pumpkin and scrape out the seeds. Cut the pumpkin into 2 cm (1 inch) cubes and put in the saucepan with enough water to cover well. Bring to the boil, then turn down the heat till it is just boiling (simmering). Put a lid on and cook for 5 minutes. Lift out with the slotted spoon, drain in the sieve and then put it back in the cooled down, empty pan. Mash up with the fork and leave to one side.

Meanwhile, unroll the pastry. Grease the pie dish and then put the pastry in it. Pastry is fairly flexible so you can push it into place. If it tears, patch it with a spare bit, moistening with a bit of water to make sure it sticks. Pastry shrinks when it cooks, so trim it 1 cm (½ inch) above the top of the rim.

Break the eggs into a bowl and pick out any bits of shell. Mix the eggs up with a fork. Add the cream, milk, sugar, cinnamon, cloves, ginger and Calvados. Mix in thoroughly. Stir in the mashed pumpkin. Pour the filling into the pie case. Cook for 45 minutes at 180°C, 350°F, Gas mark 4 till the pie is set.

ADDITIONS & ALTERNATIVES

Serve with ice cream or cream.

Use a block of prepared pastry and roll it yourself. Full instructions are in the 'How to' chapter.

You may be able to find tinned pumpkin.

FLORIDA LIME PIE

Serves 4 to 6 ⊕ Preparation 15 min, Cooking 50 min — Moderate

INGREDIENTS

450 g pack ready-rolled shortcrust pastry
5 eggs
400 g tin sweetened condensed milk
$\frac{1}{2}$ cup fresh lime or lemon juice
Large carton (568 ml, 20 fl oz) double cream

EQUIPMENT

Pie dish or perforated pie dish
Greaseproof paper, if using ordinary pie dish
Cheap dried beans, if using ordinary pie dish.
Egg separator or cup and spoon
Cup
2 bowls
Egg whisk
Tin opener
Set of measuring cups
Plastic spatula
Spoon

METHOD

Preheat the oven to 200°C, 400°F, Gas mark 6. Make sure the pastry is thawed. Check the packet for times, but generally about 4 hours in the fridge.

Lightly grease the dish. Unroll the pastry and place in the dish. Pastry is fairly flexible so you can push it into place. If it tears patch it with a spare bit, moistening with water to make sure it sticks. Prick the bottom of the pastry with a fork at least 5 times to let steam out. Cut a piece of greaseproof paper to fit and press gently on to the pastry. Fill the bottom with a layer of cheap dried beans, for instance butter beans. Cook the pastry case for 10 to 15 minutes until the top edges go golden. Take the pastry case out of the oven. Wait for it to cool, then take out the beans and greaseproof paper.

Break the eggs one at a time into a cup and pick out any bits of shell. Hold the separator over another cup and put the egg on to the egg separator and let the white fall off. Put the yolks into the bowl. You will need to keep 3 egg whites to whip up. Whisk the yolks for 3 minutes until they are thick. Open the tin of condensed milk and slowly add it followed by the lime juice.

Wash and dry the whisk (if you get yolk in the whites they will not whisk up properly). In another bowl, whisk the egg whites until they are white and light and make soft peaks when you lift the whisk out. If you whisk them too long they will go too stiff. Fold them gently into the egg yolk mixture with the spatula. Put the mixture in the pie shell. Cook at 170°C, 325°F, Gas mark 3 for 20 minutes, or until the filling is firm.

Let the pie cool down to room temperature or put in the fridge for an hour to achieve perfection.

Serve the pie with the whipped cream.

ADDITIONS & ALTERNATIVES

It is possible to buy a tin with a perforated base (a bit like Aertex). If you have one of these you can skip the instructions for pricking the base of the pastry case and the part cooking of the pastry case.

Just add the mixture to the pastry shell and proceed.

Try single cream or ice cream instead of the double cream.

You can buy ready-made pastry and roll it out yourself.

You can separate the yolks by cracking the egg in half and then juggling the egg from one eggshell half to the other. The downside is that the yolk can get popped on the shell, and of course your fingers tend to get covered with egg white. Another method is to break the egg into a cup and then pour it into the tablespoon.

4 limes or 3 lemons produce about $\frac{1}{2}$ cup juice.

PECAN PIE

Serves 4   ① *Preparation 15 min, Cooking 50 min — Easy*

INGREDIENTS
450 g pack ready-rolled shortcrust pastry
4 eggs
1 $\frac{1}{2}$ cups golden syrup
2 tablespoons melted butter
1 teaspoon vanilla
200 g pack pecan nuts

EQUIPMENT
Pie dish or perforated pie dish
Greaseproof paper, if using ordinary pie dish
Dried beans for baking, if using ordinary pie dish
Bowl
Egg whisk
Set of measuring cups
Set of measuring spoons
Saucepan

METHOD

Preheat the oven to 200°C, 400°F, Gas mark 6.

Unroll the pastry. Grease the dish and then put the pastry in the dish. Pastry is fairly flexible so you can push it into place. If it tears patch it with a spare bit, moistening with a bit of water to make sure it sticks. Pastry shrinks when it cooks so trim it 1 cm (½ inch) above the top of the rim. Prick the bottom of the pastry with a fork at least 5 times to let steam out. Cut a piece of greaseproof paper to fit and press gently on to the pastry. Fill the bottom with a layer of cheap dried beans, for instance butter beans. Part cook the pastry case in the oven for 8 minutes. Take the pastry case out of the oven. Wait for it to cool, then take out the beans and greaseproof paper.

Break the eggs into a bowl and pick out any bits of shell. Mix the eggs up with the whisk. Slowly add the syrup and continue to whisk. Put the butter in the saucepan and melt over a low heat. Whisk into the eggs, then add the vanilla. Add the pecan nuts and stir round. Pour the mixture into the pie case. Put in the oven and cook for 35 to 40 minutes until the filling is firm.

ADDITIONS & ALTERNATIVES

It is possible to buy a tin with a perforated base (a bit like Aertex). If you have one of these you can skip the instructions for pricking the base of the pastry case and the part cooking of the pastry case. Just add the mixture to the pastry shell and proceed.

Serve with ice cream.

Substitute maple syrup for half of the golden syrup.

You can buy ready-made pastry and roll it out yourself.

INDEX

COOKING FOR BLOKES

Duncan Anderson & Marian Walls

Hungry?
Can't find the menu from the takeaway up the road?
Can't face beans on toast again?
Trying to convince someone that men aren't completely
hopeless in the kitchen?
Don't panic!

Cooking For Blokes tells you all you need to know – from
what knife to buy, which pots you need in your cupboard,
what spoons you need in your drawers, to what to put in
the spice rack . . .

From the simplest of 'half-eleven on a Friday night, drunk,
absolutely starving' snacks (cheese on toast) to dishes that
might even impress Mum (Trout & Almonds) the simple,
short recipes in *Cooking For Blokes* take you through the
process step-by-step.

From beginner to cordon bleu chef (well, nearly), it's all
there: Indian, Chinese & Far Eastern, Italian, Tex-Mex,
Vegetarian, Salads, Party Food, Drink (from lager to
punch, and even something called water) . . .

FAST CAKES

Mary Berry

The recipes in *Fast Cakes* are *really* fast! Most of them can be prepared in less than ten minutes and baked in under an hour. These are *not* instant cakes but proper cakes of all kinds – from old nursery favourites such as Fruit Cake, Gingerbread and the reassuringly named Can't-Go-Wrong Chocolate Cake to the more adventurous but equally speedy delights of Praline Meringue, Iced Queen Cakes and Mocha Gateau.

This tempting selection includes delicious chapters on tray bakes, no-bake cakes, tea breads, scones and biscuits as well as an invaluable introduction, a sensible emergency section, useful hints and straightforward children's recipes. Altogether this is the complete book for busy bakers.

Other bestselling titles available by mail:

TIME WARNER
BOOKS